MESSAGE FROM THE UNDER SECRETARY OF THE NAVY

I enthusiastically recommend Mary Walton's book to everyone in the Navy and Marine Corps--officers, enlisted personnel, and civilians alike. Ms. Walton has expertly captured the stories of six organizations that have embarked on a journey of applying Deming's principles to a variety of businesses and processes. Of particular interest is Chapter 5, which focuses on the Department of the Navy and its bold plan to implement total quality throughout its commands.

To lead future efforts, H. Lawrence Garrett III, Secretary of the Navy, formed an Executive Steering Group (ESG), composed of the Department's top 26 military and civilian leaders, a group I now chair. Our shore commands have already shown significant improvements over the past few years, and we have learned much from these successes. Now we are beginning to apply these same principles and methods to our operational commands.

In acknowledgement of the unique role of *leadership* in military operational commands and Deming's emphasis on leadership responsibilities, the ESG recently adopted the term Total Quality Leadership (TQL) to describe what the Department of the Navy will be practicing in the years ahead.

Leadership is the cornerstone of TQL. And, through the ESG, we have the vehicle by which to bring about a transformation to a quality-focused organization. The ESG has developed a strategic plan to guide day-to-day decisions. Under this broad plan, our work systems and our culture are changing to meet the challenge of becoming a smaller, leaner, more efficient Department. Through TQL we are shaping a Navy and Marine Corps that can meet the demands of this decade of change and those of the coming century.

J. Daniel Howard
Under Secretary of the Navy

ALSO BY MARY WALTON

The Deming Management Method

DEMING MANAGEMENT AT WORK

Mary Walton

A PERIGEE BOOK

Perigee Books
are published by
The Putnam Publishing Group
200 Madison Avenue
New York, NY 10016

First Perigee Edition 1991

Library of Congress Cataloging-in-Publication Data

Walton, Mary, date.
Deming management at work / Mary Walton.—1st Perigee ed.
          p.   cm.
Includes index.
1. Deming, W. Edwards (William Edwards), date—Contributions
in management.   2. Management—Case studies.   I. Title.
        HD38.D439W34   1991   91-9978   CIP
          658—dc20

Cover design by Mike Stromberg

ISBN 0-399-13753-X (hardcover)
    5   6   7   8   9   10

Printed in the United States of America
This book is printed on acid-free paper.

ACKNOWLEDGMENTS

In this book appear many names of people who were working day in and day out on quality and gave both generously and patiently of their time and expertise. There were others, however, who played an invaluable but less visible role, opening doors for my inquiries, scheduling tours and interviews, providing research materials, checking facts. To them I owe tremendous gratitude, for it was they who made this book possible. Frank Voehl, vice president of QualTec, FPL Group's training subsidiary, was a hero, overseeing all of the above services and more at Florida Power & Light. At Hospital Corporation of America, Tom Gillem took care of similar chores and was a source of continual insights, encouragement and good cheer. Mark McLaughlin took time from his considerable duties as manager of human resources at Bridgestone's Tennessee operations to help; training coordinator Mattie Pratt patiently squired me around for three days. Laurie Broedling swept away layers of government bureaucracy to part the waters at the U.S. Navy. Her colleague Linda Doherty supplied suggestions and helpful materials.

Brian Joiner kindly allowed me to sit through one of his excellent executive seminars on "statistical thinking." The people at GOAL, particularly Bob King, as always were there when I needed them. So too were my friends at the Philadelphia Area Council for Excellence, particularly Maureen Glassman and Nancy Brout. Dr. Deming's secretary, Cecelia Kilian, graciously lent assistance. I am grateful to *The Philadelphia Inquirer* for allowing me the time to do this book, and to my editor there, Charles Layton, who didn't forget me.

This person who persuaded me to do this book was Putnam editor Lindley Boeghold, who left soon afterward. I forgive her. Thanks to Gene Brissie and Rena Wolner for picking up the reins. I am especially grateful to my agent Alice Martell, who was there when it counted.

The contribution of W. Edwards Deming is beyond thanks. In reading my manuscript, he provided encouragement, suggestions and accuracy. His "profound knowledge" has changed my life in both professional and personal ways.

CONTENTS

FOREWORD

The economic position of the U.S. has been on the decline for three decades. The main cause of this decline is the prevailing system of management—management by fact, ranking people, plants, teams, divisions, companies, suppliers, with reward and punishment. We have been led astray by faith in adversarial competition.

Management addressed toward optimization of a system would offer improvement. A system must have an aim. Without an aim, there is no system.

A system must be managed. The bigger the system, the more difficult it is to manage it for optimization.

The performance of any component within a system is to be judged in terms of its contribution to the aim of the system, not for its individual production or profit, nor for any other competitive measure.

Optimization of a system should be the basis of negotiation between any two people, between divisions of a company, between customer and supplier, between countries, between competitors. Everybody gains under optimization.

Best efforts and hard work will not suffice, nor new machinery, computers, automation, gadgets. One could well add that we are being ruined by best efforts put forth with the best intentions but without guidance of a theory of management for optimization of a system. There is no substitute for knowledge.

It is a mistake to suppose that if you can not measure the results of an activity, you can not manage it. The fact is that the most important losses and gains can not be measured, yet for survival they must be managed. Examples of gains and losses are grades in school, from toddlers on up through the university; the annual appraisal of people on the job, even of teachers; ranking, with reward and punishment; incentive pay; monetary reward for suggestions; bonuses (to make sure that somebody does his job); quotas for production; gains from training, gains from education; business plans based on competitive measures.

The change required is transformation, change of state, metamorphosis, in industry, education, and government. The transformation will restore the individual by abolishment of grades in school on up through the university; by abolishment of the annual appraisal of people on the job, M.B.O., quotas for production, incentive pay, competition between people, competition between divisions, and other forms of suboptimization. The transformation is not stamping out fires, solving problems, nor cosmetic improvements.

The transformation must be led by top management.

—W. EDWARDS DEMING

Washington
23 June 1990

DEMING
MANAGEMENT
AT WORK

CHAPTER ONE

What You Need to Know to Read This Book

Transformation is required in government, industry, education. Management is in a stable state. Transformation is required to move out of the present state. The transformation required will be a change of state, metamorphosis, not mere patchwork on the present system of management. We must of course solve problems and stamp out fires as they occur, but these activities do not change the system.

—W. EDWARDS DEMING
"Foundation for Management of Quality
in the Western World"
October 10, 1989

I. W. EDWARDS DEMING: THE MAN AND HIS MISSION

On June 24, 1980, NBC-TV aired a documentary entitled "If Japan Can . . . Why Can't We?" that sought to discover how in merely thirty years the Japanese had risen from the ashes of World War II to economic gianthood with products that were far superior in quality to those of the United States and that were growing ever more popular.

That same year, the United States imported $30.7 billion in Japanese goods, mostly complex manufactured items such as automobiles, electronics and steel-mill products. It exported about two-thirds that much to Japan, $20.8 billion, mostly in raw materials such as lumber, seed grains, soybeans, coal, nonferrous metals and scrap. The relationship was one of a developed to an underdeveloped nation.

Notwithstanding the lopsided trade picture, Americans were wont to dismiss the Japanese juggernaut as accident or happenstance—a reflection of Eastern culture, perhaps. Low-paid workers whose slavish fealty to "the Company" was reflected in their willingness to wear uniforms, perform exercises and sing corporate anthems, while also working at breakneck speed, were said to be the reason that the U.S. relationship with Japan was topsy-turvy. The Japanese were also accused of "dumping"—selling products below cost to commandeer markets. Americans complained, moreover, that the Japanese didn't invent things. They merely copied our products, doing what we did better. They just didn't play by the rules—our rules.

The NBC White Paper, however, probed more deeply. In its final segment, it featured a seventy-nine-year-old American statistician named W. Edwards Deming, who had taught Japanese management and engineers quality as a system, how to pinpoint variation or swings in their processes, enabling them to detect and eliminate defects, thus cutting down on waste and reducing costs while simultaneously increasing productivity. These methods were referred to as statistical quality control (SQC) or statistical process control (SPC). They were not unknown in America. During World War II, Dr. Deming and others had taught them to technical personnel in the domestic wartime industries. But their use faded during the postwar boom when American business valued quantity over quality, and when there was no foreign competition to challenge the country's economic supremacy. Quality was considered the purview of inspectors, whose job was to sort out the bad from the good. Dr. Deming's mind went further.

Learning of Deming's work, the Japanese enlisted his aid in 1950 to teach them. Dr. Deming made repeated visits to Japan over the next two decades, not only to teach statistical methods but also to counsel the top managers. What he taught in Japan did not exist in America. He taught a new system, his product. Japanese management and engineers listened and learned, and put into practice what he taught. He taught also cooperation, though cooperation has always been a way of life in Japan.

In time his name became synonymous with quality, thanks in part to the Deming Prize established by the Japanese Union of Scientists and Engineers with the proceeds Deming donated from his publications. Since won by many major companies, the Deming Prize is today Japan's highest quality award.

Japan not only employed SPC in ever more sophisticated ways, but also developed a participatory form of management that drew on every employee's knowledge and abilities, at all levels, through teams and suggestion systems—and always focused on the customer. Companies called the new management system Total Quality Control or Company-wide Quality Control. Not only did the companies work continuously on improving processes to narrow variation and eliminate defects, they also sought constantly to innovate in order to get ahead, to leave the competition behind.

More than any other single event, that 1980 NBC White Paper set America on a new course toward quality, with Deming at the helm. Among the companies that enlisted his aid were Ford, General Motors and others. Some would fall by the wayside as the rigors of the task became evident. But others would take their place. Attendance at Deming's four-day seminars swelled from a dozen or two during the 1970s to hundreds.

Deming followed his own advice, to seek "continual improvement." "May I not learn?" he would frequently say. Over the years his lessons had evolved from the use of statistical methods into a full-blown guide to management. He was merciless in his condemnation of American management: "Export anything to a friendly country except American management," he said. He was also impatient with the pace of change, warning sorrowfully that any minute now America would be "down the tubes" as it fell further behind in the competition with Japan. In 1986 he published *Out of the Crisis,* a guide to the "transformation of the style of American management," which became a bible for Deming disciples.

Meanwhile, in 1984, I had been assigned by the *Philadelphia Inquirer Sunday Magazine* to write a profile of Dr. Deming. Afterward calls and letters poured in from readers wanting more information. There was a desperate, urgent tone to their requests. I myself sought to learn more, and in 1986 I wrote a book called *The Deming Management Method,* in which I gave an introduction to the man, his mission and his method, plus some brief descriptions of quality efforts underway in some companies. In America in the mid-1980s there weren't many.

The requests continued. People now wanted to know how to make Deming work. Who was doing it? Where could they get information? Or they'd been to a seminar; what should they do next? Because most of the companies in the Deming camp at that time were engaged in manufacturing, many of the requests came from service industries, whose leaders wondered whether his methods would work in their businesses. This book is in response to all those queries.

As I set about to find suitable subjects, I wrote to Dr. Deming for guidance. His response of May 20, 1989, read in part:

"A new book about companies that follow the fourteen points and adopt the new economics of cooperation, win-win, would be interesting. Unfortunately, I know of no such company. One finds here and there some glimmers of light."

Here, then, are some "glimmers of light"—my selection, not Dr. Deming's, who was not inclined to name names.

Many companies and organizations have, in fact, made great strides in a few years, and I am pleased to describe some of them here. These are not necessarily the "best" companies in America, nor the most "advanced" in quality. I present them because they have a track record, with both successes and failures from which others may learn.

The companies share a common approach. They are pledged to Dr. Deming's notion of continual improvement. The top management of each organization is committed to quality transformation. The people in these organizations understand who their customers are. They recognize the need to base decisions on data. And they are beginning to understand that there is variation in every process. The quality journey never ends, and people are at different points along the way.

Florida Power & Light in 1989 became the first American company to win the Deming Prize and is, from a quality standpoint, one of the most important companies in America today. In meeting the guidelines established for the granting of the prize, FPL demonstrated at once what American companies can do, and how far others have yet to go. The model developed by Florida Power & Light was also adopted by its insurance subsidiary, Colonial Penn, demonstrating that universal quality methods can be applied in different settings.

Hospital Corporation of America represents the best in the health care field, where soaring medical costs have fueled a tremendous interest in generating quality and productivity. Under the guidance of its vice president for medical care, Paul Batalden, the company has developed a thoughtfully orchestrated model for change that is winning followers among the chain's 270 owned and managed hospitals.

For those who doubt that quality methods used by the so-called smokestack industries will work in service industries as well, Florida Power & Light, Colonial Penn and the Hospital Corporation of America demonstrate otherwise.

It is essential to recognize that the Deming Method can transform not only the private but the public sector. When I was attending a Deming seminar in 1984 in San Diego, I met Laurie Broedling, a psychologist who was seeking ways to apply the Deming principles to the Navy, where she worked in personnel research. From the seeds she and others planted back then has come the Navy's involvement in what the Defense Department calls "Total Quality Management" (TQM), a term Dr. Deming himself does not use but that has gained widespread currency. Today Laurie Broedling is deputy under secretary of defense (TQM).

But what of small companies and/or local government agencies that cannot afford the high-priced consultants and training of which larger organizations avail themselves? With a helping hand from Tennessee Eastman Kodak, three small Tennessee communities—Kingsport, Johnson City and Bristol, in the heart of Appalachia—have joined forces in an effort known as Quality First. At the local community college, close to 300 teams from commerce and government were trained over four years in the Deming Method.

With even less support, another tiny company transformed itself into a quality organization worthy of the United States' new Malcolm Baldrige National Quality Award. The achievements of Globe Metallurgical Incorporated demonstrate that determination and the judicious use of training can do what a myriad of consultants often cannot.

Another Deming Prize winner, Japan's Bridgestone Corporation, the world's third largest tire company, bought an ailing, unionized Firestone plant in LaVergne, Tennessee, in 1983 and restored it to productivity, winning the hearts and minds of American workers. There are lessons here for American managers.

No issue in the Deming philosophy draws more attention than its creator's opposition to performance reviews, which rank people and reward them accordingly. I have departed from the single-company profiles to discuss how several organizations are doing without them.

At this juncture, we do well to remember Dr. Deming's admonition against the "search for examples," one of the "obstacles" to excellence he identifies in *Out of the Crisis.* Too often, he observes, Americans attempt to emulate what others have done, rather than map out their own route. Copying is not the answer. What works for one company may not work for another. One need only look at how the large corporations in this country latched onto quality circles in the early 1980s as a key to improvement. American executives did not understand that in Japan they were integrated into a very different way of managing. In this country quality circles became just another management "program," so poorly planned and executed that today their name has a negative connotation.

Deming says that "no number of examples of success or of failure in the improvement of quality and productivity would indicate to the enquirer what success his company would have. His success would depend totally on his knowledge of the fourteen points and of the diseases and obstacles, and the efforts that he himself puts forth."

II. THE DEMING WAY

The practice of management today, as taught in American business schools and as found in most companies, has changed little since the early part of this century, when the proponents of "scientific management," led by industrial engineer Frederick Winslow Taylor, left their mark upon industry. In their view, soon to grip the nation, man was merely a cog in the giant industrial machine, whose job could be defined and directed by appropriately educated managers, administering a set of rules. This notion of scientific management originated in industry but soon took hold in government and grew throughout the service sector. The management system that resulted is rigid and autocratic, as well as unresponsive to both workers and customers. Power and responsibility are lodged at the top. Change does not come easily.

W. Edwards Deming offered direction for the transformation of the static American style of management in *Out of the Crisis,* published in 1986 by the Massachusetts Institute of Technology Center for Advanced Engineering Study. In it he explained in detail the Fourteen Points, the Seven Deadly Diseases and Obstacles that embody his views, as well as the essentials of statistical quality control.

My own earlier book, *The Deming Management Method,* written with Dr. Deming's assistance, is a journalist's effort to deal in abbreviated fashion with the Deming theory of management. It is by no means a replacement for either Dr. Deming's book or his four-day seminar. But some have found it useful as an introduction to his ideas.

Because the companies I discuss in this new book are either direct followers or lineal descendants of the Deming Method, I include here a recapitulation of the Fourteen Points and the Seven Deadly Diseases.

The Fourteen Points

1. Create constancy of purpose for improvement of product and service. Dr. Deming suggests a radical new definition of a company's role: Rather than to make money, it is to stay in business and provide jobs through innovation, research, constant improvement and maintenance.

2. Adopt the new philosophy. Americans are too tolerant of poor workmanship and sullen service. We need a new religion in which mistakes and negativism are unacceptable.

3. Cease dependence on mass inspection. American firms typically inspect a product as it comes off the assembly line or at major stages along the way; defective products are either thrown out or reworked. Both practices are unnecessarily expensive. In effect, a company is paying workers to make defects and then to correct them. Quality comes not from inspection but from improvement of the process. With instruction, workers can be enlisted in this improvement.

4. End the practice of awarding business on the price tag alone. Purchasing departments customarily operate on orders to seek the lowest-priced vendor. Frequently, this leads to supplies of low quality. Instead, buyers should seek the best quality in a long-term relationship with a single supplier for any one item.

5. Improve constantly and forever the system of production and service. Improvement is not a one-time effort. Management is obligated to continually look for ways to reduce waste and improve quality.

6. Institute training. Too often, workers have learned their job from another worker who was never trained properly. They are forced to follow unintelligible instructions. They can't do their jobs well because no one tells them how to do so.

7. Institute leadership. The job of a supervisor is not to tell people what to do nor to punish them but to lead. Leading consists of helping people do a better job and of learning by objective methods who is in need of individual help.

8. Drive out fear. Many employees are afraid to ask questions or to take a position, even when they do not understand what their job is or what is right or wrong. They will continue to do things the wrong way, or not do them at all. The economic losses from fear are appalling. To assure better quality and productivity, it is necessary that people feel secure.

9. Break down barriers between staff areas. Often a company's departments or units are competing with each other or have goals that conflict. They do not work as a team so they can solve or foresee problems. Worse, one department's goals may cause trouble for another.

10. Eliminate slogans, exhortations and targets for the work force. These never helped anybody do a good job. Let workers formulate their own slogans.

11. Eliminate numerical quotas. Quotas take into account only numbers, not quality or methods. They are usually a guarantee of inefficiency and high cost. A person, to hold a job, meets a quota at any cost, without regard to damage to his company.

12. Remove barriers to pride of workmanship. People are eager to do a good job and distressed when they cannot. Too often, misguided supervisors, faulty equipment and defective materials stand in the way of good performance. These barriers must be removed.

13. Institute a vigorous program of education and retraining. Both management and the work force will have to be educated in the new methods, including teamwork and statistical techniques.

14. Take action to accomplish the transformation. It will require a special top management team with a plan of action to carry out the quality mission. Workers cannot do it on their own, nor can managers. A critical mass of people in the company must understand the Fourteen Points, the Seven Deadly Diseases and the Obstacles.

The Seven Deadly Diseases

1. Lack of constancy of purpose. A company that is without constancy of purpose has no long-range plans for staying in business. Management is insecure, and so are employees.

2. Emphasis on short-term profits. Looking to increase the quarterly dividend undermines quality and productivity.

3. Evaluation by performance, merit rating or annual review of performance. The effects of these are devastating—teamwork is destroyed, rivalry is nurtured. Performance ratings build fear and leave people bitter, despondent, beaten. They also encourage defection in the ranks of management.

4. Mobility of management. Job-hopping managers never understand the companies they work for and are never there long enough to follow through on long-term changes that are necessary for quality and productivity.

5. Running a company on visible figures alone. The most important figures are unknown and unknowable—the "multiplier" effect of a happy customer, for example.

6. Excessive medical costs for employee health care, which increase the final costs of goods and services.

7. Excessive costs of warranty, fueled by lawyers who work on the basis of contingency fees.

The Obstacles differ, Dr. Deming says, from the Points and Diseases in being somewhat easier to cure. Among them are the following:

—"Hope for instant pudding," the idea that "improvement of quality and productivity is accomplished suddenly by affirmation of faith";

—"The supposition that solving problems, automation, gadgets and new machinery will transform industry";

—"Search for examples," which companies undertake to find a ready-made recipe they can follow when they must instead map their own route to quality;

—"Our problems are different," the pretext managers raise to avoid dealing with quality issues;

—"Our quality control department takes care of all our problems of quality," another excuse managers use to avoid taking responsibility;

—"We installed quality control," yet another excuse that lets top management off the hook;

—"The supposition that it is only necessary to meet specifications." Not only may products meet specifications yet vary widely in quality, but in addition, "the supposition that everything is all right inside the specifications and all wrong outside does not correspond to this world."

In addition to the Fourteen Points, the Seven Deadly Diseases and the Obstacles, Deming teaches several other important principles.

The 85–15 Rule

Everybody works within a system, governed by conditions over which the individual has no control. A tire builder has to contend with the condition of a complex machine and the quality and coordination of sixteen incoming components, as well as lighting, heat and other environmental conditions. The speed with which a waitress delivers food depends less on her abilities and attentiveness to customers than on the performance of the kitchen, where cooks command an arsenal of utensils, machines and supplies and, of course, other workers. A nurse must deal not only with demands by patients, doctors and administrators, but also with medical supplies and equipment, paperwork systems and food delivery.

In the American style of management, when something goes wrong the response is to look around for someone to blame or punish or to search for something to "fix" rather than to look to the system as a whole for improvement. The 85–15 Rule holds that 85 percent of what goes wrong is with the system, and only 15 percent with the individual person or thing. In this connection, we do well to remember that in any group of people not all, nor even the majority, can be above average. In fact, exactly half will be below average.

Know Thy Customer

The quality effort requires a new way of thinking about the customer, and thinking as well about new customers. Spoiled by decades of success, when customers accepted whatever companies produced, American managers have yet to grasp that they *must* satisfy customer needs, because if they don't, their competitor will. With the customer as the reference point, priorities become easier to set.

In quality-minded organizations, the word "customer" describes more than a relationship in which money merely changes hands. It describes the exchange of services as well. For any given enterprise, there are two sets of customers: external and internal. The external customer is the end user of a product or service. The internal customer is the person or work unit that receives the product or the service of another within the same company. In a restaurant, for example, the waitress's customer is not only the patron but also the cook, who receives her order and whose performance is affected by whether or not it is written legibly. Once the order is filled, she becomes the cook's customer. The food must be well prepared with regard to taste and appearance so that she can serve it with pride. So it goes.

Too often one department does not understand how its work is used by the next, and thus cannot learn what things are important in carrying out its tasks. The notion of internal customers lends relevance to each employee's job and is absolutely critical to a quality transformation.

The PDCA Cycle

Americans are accustomed to seeing work projects in a linear fashion, with a beginning and end. The job is done; on to the next. Continuous or never-ending improvement requires instead a circular approach. Dr. Deming introduced the Plan-Do-Check-Act Cycle to the Japanese years ago. He called it the Shewhart Cycle, after the man who pioneered statistical quality control, Walter Shewhart. (The Japanese refer to it as the "Deming Cycle.")

The PDCA Cycle has four stages: Briefly, a company plans a change, does it, checks the results and, depending on the results, acts either to standardize the change or to begin the cycle of improvement again with new information. While many people engaged in the transformation may talk of "solving problems" or "working on projects," it is often because the terminology is convenient. The PDCA Cycle, in fact, represents work on processes rather than specific tasks

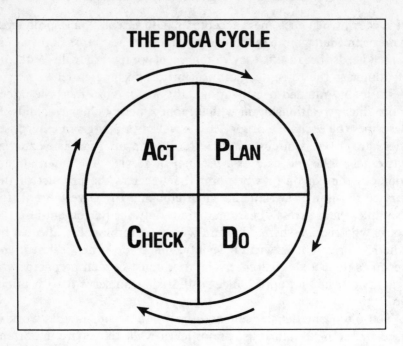

or problems. Processes by their nature can never be solved but only improved. In working on processes, one does, of course, solve some problems.

III. DOING IT WITH DATA

American managers pride themselves on hunches and intuition. When they succeed, they take credit. When they fail, they find someone to blame. But a quality transformation rests on a different set of assumptions:

—Decisions must be based on facts.
—The people who know the work best are the ones who perform it.
—Groups of people working in teams can have more success than individuals working alone.
—Teams need to be trained in a structured problem-solving process, which includes knowledge of how to conduct a meeting.
—It is helpful to display information graphically.

SEVEN HELPFUL CHARTS

CAUSE-AND-EFFECT

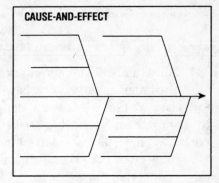

FLOW CHART

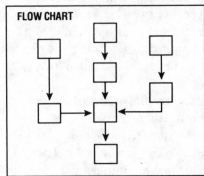

PARETO CHART

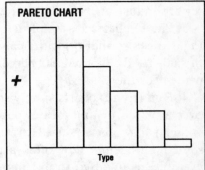

Type

RUN (TREND) CHART

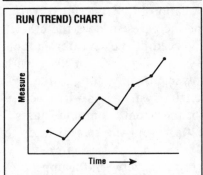

Measure

Time ⟶

HISTOGRAM

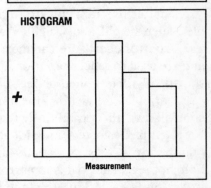

Measurement

SCATTER DIAGRAM

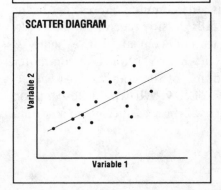

Variable 2

Variable 1

CONTROL CHART

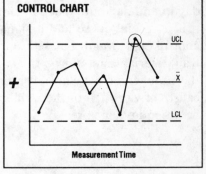

Measurement Time

©Bob King GOAL / QPC

The Seven Basic Tools

1. Cause-and-effect diagrams are also known as fishbone diagrams, after their shape, and Kaoru Ishikawa diagrams, after their originator. They are typically used to depict causes of a certain problem and to group them according to categories, often "method," "manpower," "material" and "machinery."

2. Flow charts or process-flow diagrams are the visual representation of the steps in a process. They are particularly useful in the service industries, where the work process involves unseen steps.

3. Pareto charts are simple bar charts used after data collection to rank causes so that priorities can be assigned. Their use gives rise to the 80–20 Rule—that 80 percent of the problems stem from 20 percent of the causes.

4. Run (trend) charts simply show the results of a process plotted over a period of time—sales per month, for example.

5. Histograms are used to measure the frequency with which something occurs, how often a train departs ten minutes late, for example, as opposed to five minutes or sixty minutes.

6. Scatter diagrams illustrate the relationship between two variables, such height and weight. As one increases so does the other.

7. Control charts are the most advanced of the seven basic tools and are used to reflect variation in a system. They are run charts with statistically determined upper and lower limits. As long as the process variables fall within the range, the system is said to be "in control" and the variation therein to stem from "common causes." To attempt to correct individual shifts within the system leads to "tampering"—overcorrection—and inevitably causes more variation, not less. The goal is to narrow the range between the upper and lower limits by seeking to eliminate the common causes that occur day in and day out. When a point falls outside the system, however, it is a special cause and a signal to management to investigate. A control chart might be used to track the arrival time of a commuter train. Variables could be the condition of the equipment, weather, the number of passengers or time of day. All would be common causes of variation in the train's arrival time. A special cause would be an equipment breakdown.

CHAPTER TWO
Florida Power & Light

Royalties due to Dr. Deming on his Elementary Principles of the Statistical Control of Quality . . . *were donated to Mr. (Kenichi) Koyanagi. With this as a basic fund, the JUSE Board of Directors in December, 1950, formally resolved to create the Deming Prize in commemoration of Dr. Deming's contributions to Japanese industry and for encouragement of quality control development in Japan. . . .*

—KENICHI KOYANAGI
"The Deming Prize"

The Deming Prize is an award presented by the Union of Japanese Scientists and Engineers for outstanding performance in achieving company-wide quality. This highly coveted award—ironically named in honor of an American—has never been won by a company outside of Japan. We have great hopes that FPL can become the first to do so.

—MARSHALL McDONALD
President, FPL Group, Inc.
October 18, 1988

I. THE LIGHTS GO ON

John Hudiburg would never forget that first meeting in 1985 with the counselors from the Union of Japanese Scientists and Engineers (JUSE)—the half dozen people who would shepherd Florida Power & Light through the process of applying for Japan's vaunted Deming Prize, the highest quality award in a country where quality is king.

It was a disaster.

As chairman of the board and CEO of Florida Power & Light, Hudiburg was to be the chief spokesman during this initial status report on the company's quality effort. He took the meeting seriously enough to be somewhat apprehensive. He had been the executive most in favor of going for the prize, because he believed it would expedite the work the company was already doing, and his reputation was on the line. Noting his apprehension, the head of the FPL quality improvement department reassured him, as Hudiburg later recalled, " 'Oh, don't worry, Mr. Hudiburg. We will prepare your presentation. You can read it on the plane going over. It's a sixteen-hour flight and you'll have plenty of time.' "

A North Carolinean by birth, who had started with the power company in 1951 as a student engineer and entered the executive ranks as vice president twenty years later, Hudiburg was accustomed to being treated with respect. Certainly he expected no less from the Japanese counselors. Though noted academics, they were nevertheless being paid by FPL to help the company prepare for the prize. They were consultants, in other words, and consultants didn't generally talk back to a CEO.

And so, the moment came for him to deliver the opening segment of the two-hour presentation. "It was a description of what we were doing at that time. And what we planned to do, and so on."

He had been allotted an hour or so. Even as he began, things felt wrong.

"I stood up and I started giving this very arcane, stilted, full-of-jargon presentation that I'd been handed and had rehearsed. . . . I was going on for about ten minutes when they stopped me, and said, in essence, 'Mr. Hudiburg, put that down. That isn't what we're here to talk about at all. . . . What is your problem? What's the problem of Florida Power & Light? What are you trying to achieve?' "

Fumbling for an answer, Hudiburg said something about the company's difficulties. Although FPL was the fastest growing utility in the U.S., it did face certain competitive threats. With electrical rates rising swiftly, industries such as steel and paper now found it economical to harness their steam by-products for their own electrical needs rather than to purchase them from utilities, and perhaps sell the excess as well. This was known as cogeneration. And cogeneration kits were making it easier for small companies to do the same thing. Moreover, federal law required utilities to buy excess production. There was also the specter of deregulation. If that were to happen, utilities wanted to be more prepared than the telephone giant, AT&T. They needed to be ready for the competition. Finally, FPL was also under constant surveillance by regulatory agencies and environmentalists.

Hudiburg had no sooner completed his first response than the Japanese came at him with more such questions. "What are your ambitions? What are your goals?" They wanted to know how the company measured its performance. "How do you know whether you're doing any good or not? Are you making progress?"

Said Hudiburg, "I felt like every time I got a question, I was an onion that had just had another layer peeled off of me. It was a very embarrassing thing, because I really floundered." He realized that these were questions "that I or any CEO should really have a firm grip on.

"After that we went through the motions of a few more presentations and left. And I vowed to myself that would never again ever happen to me. No one would ever prepare my presentation for me again. Whatever I was going to say, they would be my words and I would know what I was going to say and why I was going to say it. And I'd be right. And I'd be perfect. Because by damn, I wasn't going to be embarrassed like that."

Hudiburg's discomfort was soon felt at every level of the company as the Japanese counselors traveled to America repeatedly over the next two years, probing, teaching, scolding, and in all ways pushing FPL to quality levels heretofore reached only in Japan. On November 13, 1989, in Tokyo, Hudiburg accepted the Deming Prize for FPL, the first company outside of Japan to receive the coveted award. In that period, the Miami-based company was transformed at a dizzying pace into a data-driven organization with 1,800 teams, a suggestion system called "Bright Ideas" that had produced close to 20,000 ideas (6,284 of them useful) in the first nine months of 1989 and a sophisticated system of polling its customers and recasting their desires as company-wide goals.

By eleven different measures, the company's performance had improved dramatically under its quality improvement program. Among them were the following:

—Complaints to the Florida Public Service Commission had dropped from a high of 1.5 per 1,000 customers in 1984 to .24.

—Service unavailability had been cut from 75 minutes per customer in 1983 to 43.24.

—In the nuclear plants, violations cited by the Nuclear Regulatory Commission had fallen from 60 in 1984 to 20.

—Electrical rates, which in 1984 and 1985 had been rising faster than the Consumer Price Index, had now dropped below it.

—Lost-time injuries per 100 employees had been reduced from more than 1 per year to .5.

But the transformation that had enabled FPL to chalk up these gains had not been easy, as Hudiburg could attest.

In 1986, the year Hudiburg met with Japanese counselors, Florida Power & Light was not a company with a reputation for bad quality. Far from it. In the previous year the company had won the industry's prestigious Edison Award, thanks to gains from its quality improvement program, set in motion in 1981. Wall Street liked FPL. In 1986, *Wall Street Journal* subscribers named it the nation's "best-managed" utility.

A utility in a protected monopoly position might seem to have little incentive to improve its performance. Florida Power & Light was the fourth largest investor-owned electric utility in the United States and the fastest growing in number of customer accounts. It had a service territory covering 5.7 million people and 27,650 miles, approximately one-half the state of Florida. There were some 15,000 employees, 13 operating plants, 7 operations offices, 45 customer service offices, 72 service centers, 297 substations and 53,300 miles of transmission and distribution lines. All told, it had 3 million accounts.

Historically the company hadn't had to worry about keeping its customers happy. Founded in 1925, Florida Power & Light had gone forty-seven years without requesting a rate increase. Indeed, there were eleven rate *decreases* during the 1960s, while the company maintained a compound annual growth exceeding 13 percent. But after the oil crisis of the 1970s, prices gushed upward. The economies of scale and the technological advances that had long enabled FPL to hold down rates no longer sufficed. By the end of that decade, the rate-increase requests were coming one after another and customers were hostile. The company could no longer afford to be complacent. Moreover, through a quirk in technology, residential users had become particularly sensitive to vagaries in service. Even a momentary blip was enough to throw off every digital clock in the house, and there were more of them all the time. It irritated people no end to come home to a houseful of appliances with blinking zeroes.

There were other negative developments. The Three Mile Island nuclear accident in Pennsylvania prompted the Nuclear Regulatory Commission to increase its scrutiny of the company's two nuclear plants at Turkey Point and St. Lucie. Turkey Point, located south of Miami on Biscayne Bay, was the company's first nuclear power plant, built in 1972. It had become something of an embarrassment to the company, with recurring problems that experts would later conclude derived in part from FPL's inexperience and its defensive attitude toward regulators. Regulation increased in other areas of the environment as well.

But perhaps the greatest of the company's liabilities were internal. FPL had become apathetic and stodgy. "As the company had grown," confessed a 1988 brochure describing the origins of the quality effort, "it had become more bureaucratic and cumbersome. We were often inflexible in our operations and sometimes treated all customers the same regardless of their individual needs.

"Management could foresee no significant technological innovations to reduce the escalating power supply costs. We realized that a change in management philosophy was needed to achieve customer satisfaction and cost reduction through greater efficiency.

"We knew we had to change our way of thinking from supply-oriented to customer-oriented, from a power generation company to a customer service company. This new strategy needed to provide a means to address the key issues surrounding the satisfaction of our customers' needs and expectations."

Such a shift would involve "a radical cultural change to regain customer confidence and satisfaction. We also knew that this new strategy had to involve not only every employee, but also every vendor, consultant and supplier."

Then chairman of the board Marshall McDonald was the first FPL executive to perceive the need for change and to take action. He realized early on that such change had to be of a greater magnitude than in the past. "Rather than burn the toast and then scrape it clean," he was fond of saying, "it's time to fix the toaster." He was deeply concerned about what was happening in FPL's own backyard, where NASA was experiencing repeated delays and quality problems in its missile launches. He told people he didn't want that sort of thing to happen at FPL.

In 1981, McDonald formed a quality council of top managers, which assigned itself the task of writing a vision statement.

It took at least four meetings to produce the following 27 words:

> "During the next decade, we want to become the best managed Electric Utility in the United States and an excellent Company overall and be recognized as such."

They agonized over every word—"best," for example. Was it overreaching to use such a superlative? Hudiburg recalled the managers asking themselves, "Do you say you want to be a 'good' company? Or do you want to be the 'second-best' company? Those were the kind of discussions we had. We said, 'No, if we're going to do anything like that, we're going to be the best. We're not going to shoot for mediocre. . . .'"

Having chosen to say "best," he continued, "we were a little worried how other people might look at that, think we were cocky or something. We decided, 'What the hell. If they want to be the best, they can try too. We don't have to win by default.'"

Initially, they set themselves no time frame for becoming "the best managed utility." But they subsequently decided they needed a deadline—1992—hence, "in the next decade."

Explained Hudiburg, "We said, 'If we don't set a deadline or a time period, it becomes nothing but sort of a vague hope or a wish. When you have a hope coupled with a deadline, it becomes a goal.'"

How would they know when they were the best? "We argued about that. How do you know when you're the best? Do you measure the number of softball championships you've won, or what? And so we decided that we couldn't absolutely determine if we were the best, so we said, 'We will let those outside our company decide if we're the best or not.'" Hence the phrase "and be recognized as such."

They decided to call theirs a "vision" statement, even though everybody else was writing "mission" statements in those days. Explained then senior vice president Leland "Bud" Hunter, "Ours was unlike a mission, which says what you're going to do, not what you're going to be." It was a small distinction, but important to those involved. FPL was talking about transforming its identity, not merely taking certain actions.

When the quality council finished its work, said Hudiburg, "We were really proud of our vision, for a little while, and then we looked at it again. We said, 'My goodness, we've really put a load on our shoulders. Because if we are going to be the best we're going to have to do something different. That means we've got to help our employees with some sort of management system that's better than what we have now.' "

Accordingly, the quality council fielded a team to scour the country for a shelf-ready quality model the company could adopt. The team visited a number of companies, including IBM, General Electric, Xerox, Ford, General Motors and Consolidated Edison. Instead of finding one to copy, however, the team concluded that FPL would have to put together its own model. It turned to the leading gurus of the day, principally W. Edwards Deming and Joseph W. Juran, both of whom had been influential in Japan's postwar economic recovery.

Deming at that point was known principally for his statistical instruction, including the PDCA Cycle that carried his name, and for advocating the critical importance of using data in all decisions. He lectured repeatedly on the need to have top management involvement, without which there could be no transformation. FPL sent hundreds of people to his four-day seminars, which were becoming increasingly popular in the early 1980s, as the country sought remedies for its economic losses to the Japanese. A demihero in Japan, Deming had labored as a statistician in the United States in relative obscurity until 1980, when he was featured on the fateful NBC special entitled "If Japan Can . . . Why Can't We?" Over the years he had developed a mature philosophy of management that went far beyond statistical methods alone.

Juran was known for his *Quality Control Handbook,* published in 1951 and popularized by the Japanese. He had also consulted extensively on how to establish and direct the work of teams in the transformation, and he was a frequent visitor to FPL during the early 1980s. Neither Deming nor Juran, however, offered specifics on how to structure a quality improvement program. In that regard FPL was on its own.

Marshall McDonald, who had a degree in law from the University of Florida and an MBA from the Wharton School at the University of Pennsylvania, lodged responsibility for FPL's fledgling quality improvement program with his management services department, which had previously been responsible for establishing work standards and keeping the staff lean by monitoring the budget process.

(QIP eventually became a separate department.) Many people were suspicious that the new program was really more of the same. The company had already tried MBOs (Management by Objective), and when that didn't work so well, there were "enhanced MBOs."

A bigger mistake than relying on management services, however—and it was common to many companies—was to try to work from the bottom up, bypassing middle management to form teams among workers, who were generally delighted at the prospect of being able to improve the caliber of their work. Middle management, however, tended to view the change as a threat to its authority, with the result that the teams were often working in a vacuum, without support from above.

Bill Ellis, the general manager in the West Palm Beach District, remembers what it was like to be in middle management in those days. "When we started, we trained top management, then we trained employees. We left out the middle management, we left out the supervisors. We realized employees were talking a language, top management was talking a language, but not the people in between."

Moreover, FPL had plunged into forming teams before training a sufficient number of team leaders or facilitators—people who could guide the teams through the problem-solving process. The accomplishments of the teams were uneven. In those days, FPL was more likely to boast about the number of teams they had—470 in 1983—than about their successes.

Jimmy Braddock was the leader of a team that was struggling to clarify and streamline the way customers secured electrical service for new homes in the St. Augustine area. "It took us eighteen months. We really floundered. We weren't structured to follow through. We didn't have enough facilitators. We didn't have the buy-in from middle management." But they came up with a new procedure nevertheless, and Braddock, who had initially been suspicious that QIP "would be another fly-by-night program," was a convert.

Braddock himself became one of the company's first facilitators. He was assigned to thirty teams, which meant he attended all their meetings, helping them stay on track with their projects, coaching them in the appropriate data collection, and running interference with management. At that time that was about three times more teams than what came to be the accepted load for facilitators.

As FPL continued to lurch forward with quality efforts, Marshall

McDonald often was away visiting the Kansai Electric Power Company in Osaka, which in 1983 had decided to compete for the Deming Prize.

Prior to seeking the prize, Kansai, like Florida Power & Light, had a good record. Its rates were the lowest among Japan's nine electric power companies, and it also claimed to have the shortest outage rate in the world. But forces outside of Japan had made the company aware of the need to improve. Heavily dependent on nuclear plants, Kansai like FPL had experienced a loss in customer confidence with the Three Mile Island accident. The Japanese, of course, were particularly sensitive to the danger of nuclear holocaust. In addition, the rapid increase in oil prices had forced Kansai, like oil-reliant companies everywhere, to look for ways to cut costs. The company also felt it needed to do a better job meeting customer needs. "Our company had tried to improve its operations and work procedures by reflecting the customers' needs or requirements, but it was seldom made in a systematic way and with sufficient analyses," confessed Kansai's president.

The decision to try for the Deming Prize made the difference. By 1984, Kansai could point to rapid improvement in every major area, from cost reduction and reduction of job-related accidents to customer confidence, as measured by answers to the question "Is our company trustworthy?"

FPL executives realized that as recently as 1981 the two power companies had been in pretty much the same position. But by 1984, John Hudiburg said, it was clear that Kansai "had left us pretty far behind."

Looking back on his campaign to win over others at FPL in those days, McDonald said that "I sometimes felt as if I was engaged in a holy war against ineffectiveness and inefficiency . . . and some compared my appearance to that of a Southern preacher spreading the corporate gospel of quality. Of course, there were others who questioned exactly what it was that I was spreading. Those were the same folks who insisted that the only function of our quality program was to make astrology look good."

One of those skeptics was senior vice president Bud Hunter, who had headed every major operating area and every staff group except finance in his thirty-eight years at FPL. He was also its chief labor negotiator. Hunter was extremely popular in both the company and the community, so much so that when he retired in 1987, 1,148 people attended the farewell bash. If Bud Hunter couldn't be convinced, he'd have a lot of other people on his side.

Hunter was proud of the company's accomplishments, which had been emulated by others in the industry. FPL was a pioneer in preformed splices and emergency restoration procedures during hurricanes. A joint apprenticeship program that Hunter had helped originate was used as a model by the U.S. Department of Labor. And the Port St. Lucie nuclear unit had come on line at a savings of more than $500,000—after only six years of construction, which was more than three and a half years faster than the industry average.

Hunter was suspicious of McDonald's efforts to foist a Japanese-style quality strategy on the company. As far as he was concerned, McDonald was "not really a utility man." McDonald had come to FPL from the oil industry and Hunter didn't think "he knew enough to make judgments" about utility issues. So when McDonald returned from his Japan trips full of enthusiasm, Hunter's reaction was predictably quite negative.

When John Hudiburg went over to Japan and came back similarly enthused, Hunter was forced to reevaluate his position. Not only was Hudiburg a certified utility man, with more than thirty years at FPL, but he seldom registered emotion of any kind. On one occasion the company had won a $400 million lawsuit that had long worried the executive leadership. Hunter, rushing to tell Hudiburg the news, located him in the company cafeteria. "That's nice," Hudiburg said. "What are you going to have for lunch?" The words "excitement" and "enthusiasm" came under "e" in most people's dictionaries, Hunter said. In Hudiburg's they were somewhere back "with x, y and z."

So when Hudiburg got excited, Hunter listened. Finally he went to Japan himself. "I swaggered into Japan," he was fond of saying years later. "I staggered out a bent and humble man."

At that time, he said, "I was planning on retiring, and being happy in the thought that I was a good manager. And I go over there and I find out that there are things being done so much better."

In the mid–80s, the average outage rate in the U.S. utility industry was 125 minutes per year. At 85 minutes, FPL's rate was cause for pride. But, Hunter said, "I go over to Japan and they've got it down to 7 minutes." A mere 7 minutes! He also learned that the Japanese had built a plant very much like that at St. Lucie in just 40 months.

And then there were the transformers.

On one Kansai visit, Hunter walked through a room where twenty transformers were sitting forlornly in one corner. He had never seen so few stored in one place. At FPL they sat around in batches of a couple hundred. He asked what they were for.

"They said, 'Those are when a lightning storm goes through this district, to replace the transformers that are burned up by lightning.'

"I said, 'Well, where are the rest of them?

"They said, 'That's all we have.' "

That particular Kansai district was roughly the size of Coral Gables, where the FPL vice president knew a lightning storm could take out one hundred transformers in one swipe, at $1,000 apiece. And some parts of Japan were just as subject to lightning as Florida. Hunter marveled at how they could get by with just twenty transformers in reserve.

"I wanted to believe those people, but I have to admit that every place they took me for the rest of that trip I was looking around for more transformers somewhere. And I never found them."

The Japanese said they had learned that transformers were vulnerable to lightning because their employees were not grounding them properly. Once they taught them how, fewer transformers blew out. Hunter was not surprised. "Grounds require you to pound an 8-foot rod, or a 6-foot rod . . . , then couple another rod on top of it, and drive it into the ground, and mankind just doesn't like to drive rods into the ground, and who was around to see how many they ever drove into the ground? You'd only be able to tell by pulling the damn thing up."

Even though workers had a measuring device to test the resistance of the ground rod, it was easy to manipulate the results. In Florida, Hunter later learned, and perhaps in Japan as well, "Many crews of men were able to drive the improper number of rods and still get good readings because all they did was urinate on it. And it gave you a good reading for that moment. Of course, urine has a habit of drying out and going away. And then you do not have a proper grounding. Alternatively, you could pour water on it. Or you could just lie about the reading, or you didn't have to take the reading."

The Japanese evidently had come up with a way to overcome such resistance. And that was just one of many improvements. In all, Hunter said, "The things I saw made me very dissatisfied with my management career, a career that I thought to this point was pretty distinguished in the utility business." Hunter finally was persuaded to take charge of FPL's quality improvement program rather than retire.

At Kansai, quality went under the name of Total Quality Control. The president of Kansai explained this to employees as a major shift in thinking: "If you just consider the ordinary ideas or usual ways of doing things, it would be a task of extreme difficulty. . . . Any judgment based on subjective elements or past experiences would never do."

In 1984, Kansai won the Deming Prize. The company offered to help FPL do the same thing. It was up to Hudiburg to decide whether or not to go for it. That same year Florida Power & Light had reorganized. FPL Group, Inc., became a holding company, with Florida Power & Light Company as its chief subsidiary. Marshall McDonald took over as Group chairman, turning the reins of the utility over to John Hudiburg. He admonished the new CEO that he was at a turning point on the quality issue, that he was "going to have to go a lot farther with this or let it go."

As Hudiburg weighed the direction in which to take the company, he was influenced by the enthusiasm employees had shown for the teams, even though results had been mixed. There were around 400 teams at the time. "Half of them were doing some pretty good things and about half of them were floundering." In 1985, Hudiburg announced that the quality improvement program would go company-wide. And he accepted Kansai's offer to help.

The electric utility industry was different from others in that there was no international competition. Moreover, lessons learned at Kansai were very nearly completely applicable to FPL. Explained Hudiburg, "The electric utility is exactly the same the world over. Electrical measurements are metric measurements. . . . We measure everything the same way. We use the same equipment. . . . You study electrical engineering in Japan, Germany or the United States, it applies equally well. Transmission lines, distribution facilities, customers and problems and everything are all virtually identical."

Hudiburg had learned that the Deming Prize had an international category, which no company had entered. In 1986, Hudiburg inquired of JUSE whether the Florida utility would be eligible. The answer was yes.

"We were just crazy enough to try something different," said Hudiburg, a man who seemed anything but crazy. At the same time, he said, "We weren't sure we had the ability, that union employees would be receptive." Paradoxically, FPL executives thought they could do it with less effort than the Japanese. Kansai talked about 80-hour weeks. "We thought it wouldn't be necessary. That's because the Japanese are such 'Type A' people. We were wrong there."

Hudiburg would remember being asked around that time, "Mr. Hudiburg, how much of your time does this cost? And I gave him an answer, 'Maybe 45 or 60 days a year,' and I said 'I'm ashamed to be able to answer the questions, because it implies that I separate quality from everything else. And really it should be—as far as everyday activities go—the way we run the company, the way we manage the company and not a thing apart. And my ambition would be not to be able to answer the questions because it's so much a part of everyday activities there's no way to separate it out."

To make quality an everyday thing called for a top-down approach—but one that consisted of more than the typical American style of issuing orders. Management would have to set priorities, so that the heretofore random work of teams would from now on advance company goals. The teams would have to be reinvigorated and given more education and direction. Middle management would have to be trained and brought into the process. Finally, the company would have to work not just on obvious problems—the iceberg tips—but it would also have to standardize and monitor the day-to-day processes of generating and selling electrical power: the thousands of systems that made up its business.

Team members were by now familiar with problem-solving techniques, but the company would standardize them in a seven-step procedure that became known as the Quality Improvement Story. In time, the QI Story became more than just a team problem-solving procedure; employees used it in all manner of situations as a systematic way to analyze, act and follow up.

FPL's new quality improvement program was symbolized by the quality improvement triangle that began to appear throughout the company's literature. The program incorporated policy deployment, quality improvement teams and quality in daily work. And it rested on four principles:

- Customer Satisfaction
- Management by Fact

- Respect for People
- Plan-Do-Check-Act Cycle

The notion of customer satisfaction was a new one for FPL. There were the external customers, of course—the people who bought electricity. But as redefined by FPL, the term was now more far-reaching. It meant internal customers as well—the person who received another person's work. Usually when employees were asked to name their customer, they would answer "My boss," because that was the person they had to please. Now they were coached to think of their job as part of a process and the customer as the next person down the line.

Customers and suppliers could sometimes be the same people. The customers of a word-processing pool, for example, were those who received letters and memos that the pool had typed. But they were also the suppliers, which meant that those in the word-processing pool were their customers as well. A mechanic's customers were the guys who drove the trucks he serviced.

Management by fact meant eliminating the "gut-feel" decisions on

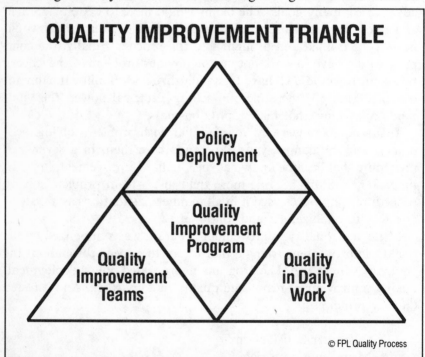

QUALITY IMPROVEMENT TRIANGLE

**Policy
Deployment**

**Quality
Improvement
Program**

**Quality
Improvement
Teams**

**Quality
in Daily
Work**

© FPL Quality Process

which many managers prided themselves. "We Western managers love to brag about our 'gut feel' and our 'instinct' and our 'experience' that we fall back on when we make some of these marvelous remarkable decisions," observed Bud Hunter, explaining this point. In managing that way, he added, "you will find that you are only wrong about 50 percent of the time."

The notion of respect for people meant that everyone in the organization would be invited to participate in QIP on an equal footing. It was both the simplest and clearest of the four planks—and the hardest to achieve because it meant giving up stereotypes about education and position. Even the lowliest employee had something to contribute.

PDCA, Plan-Do-Check-Act, was the Shewhart Cycle that W. Edwards Deming had introduced to the Japanese in his lectures in the early 1950s.

The "Plan" phase called on people to plan a change by collecting and analyzing data on the reason for doing so. The plan was carried out in the "Do" phase, "preferably on a small scale," as Dr. Deming always suggested. In the "Check" phase, workers were to analyze the results to find out whether in fact the change had accomplished what was planned. In the "Act" phase, participants decided whether to keep the change, refine it or in some other way take action aimed at improvement.

It is impossible to overemphasize the importance of the PDCA Cycle. In its literature, Florida Power & Light would note that "the PDCA Cycle is a concept that can be applied to any process, from planning your annual vacation or preparing supper to intricate technical work procedures. It is also the concept that underlies the QI Story—plan for improvement, institute improvement, check the results and act to further improve or standardize. It helps us keep on track as we solve problems and make continuous improvement."

That PDCA is always represented as a circle and not a linear process underscores the reality that improvement is neverending. Some users preferred to draw the circle rolling up an incline to suggest the ascendant nature of improvement.

The very notion of continuous improvement was a radical departure for FPL, and for Americans in general, who were used to "solving" problems and moving on to other things. Said Hunter, "As managers we kind of love problems. Somebody who works for us says that they have a problem, we run in there and we solve the problem. . . . The minute we solve the problem, we turn our backs on it and we never want to hear about it again. We want to go on to the next problem. Our employees know that, and if our solution does not work, they make pretty sure we don't hear about it again."

That negative pattern would have to change.

II. POWER TO THE PEOPLE

Florida Power & Light's quality improvement triangle was no meaningless graphic. Each piece was critical to the journey the company would take in the coming years. As complex as the three sectors might seem, at the end of the journey people throughout the company would speak of policy deployment, teamwork and QIDW with the intimate understanding that came from practicing them day in and day out.

Policy Deployment

Tacked up to office walls throughout Florida Power & Light were copies of a somewhat mysterious 23- by 14-inch black and white chart entitled CUSTOMER NEEDS TABLE OF TABLES. Indeed, this chart looked like the table to end all tables. It was divided down the middle, with each half further divided into subsections and each subsection harboring from 5 to 38 categories. Each half could be read across or down, with alternate lines shaded to make this easier. Squares formed by the vertical and horizontal intersections were occupied by triangles, circles and circles with big black dots. The Table of Tables looked a little like the charts in the magazine *Consumer Reports*. And it was, in fact, a consumer report on a massive scale. It was the visual depiction of FPL's annual customer survey, carried out in interviews and focus groups.

This survey was the key to FPL's policy deployment, which perched at the top of the QIP triangle.

Deployment, of course, is a word commonly used in military circles to refer to troop assignments. If an army's top command plans an enemy strike at a certain time and place, its forces are deployed at strategic points with assigned duties to support the overall mission. In policy deployment, if the management of Company X decreed that employee safety was the goal, then each unit of Company

X would work on safety as it pertained to that unit. That in its simplest form is what began to happen at Florida Power & Light.

Policy deployment simply meant that the company had a policy, consisting of a set of goals to be used to guide improvement. Each division, district and department developed, in turn, its own consistent version of those goals.

It is one thing to set goals, of course, and there is scarcely a company that doesn't take a stab at it at one time or another, usually in the CEO's annual message. It is another to devise methods for carrying them out, then hew to them. Making policy deployment work hinged on where the goals came from, whether they were reasonable and whether the organization was sufficiently disciplined that all employees worked on them.

People tend to think that improvement comes from everyone "doing their best." Dr. Deming agreed—but only partially. "Best efforts are essential. Unfortunately, best efforts, people charging this way and that way without guidance of principles, can do a lot of damage. Think of the chaos that would come if everyone did his best, not knowing what to do."

Today in corporate America the clarion call for improved customer service is as sacrosanct as motherhood. But unless a company knows what its customers want, and unless each of its employees understands how to improve customer service on the job and has the wherewithal to do so, then such a goal is mere lip service.

That was where the FPL's Table of Tables came in.

On the left side of the chart were listed the users: residential, commercial/industrial and sale-for-resale (wholesalers). On the right were listed the regulators: the Nuclear Regulatory Commission, the Florida Public Service Commission, the environmental regulatory agencies, state and local governments and the Federal Energy Regulatory Commission. FPL considered them spokesmen for the customers as well. Two pie diagrams at the bottom showed the weight given each customer, according to numbers and revenues, and the weight given to regulators based on their impact on the company's operations.

The chart translated what customers said they wanted into the things FPL actually did. John C. Evelyn, manager of research, economics and forecasting, whose task it was to explain the "electric behavior" of FPL customers, drew an analogy with the auto industry, which must relate the desires of would-be buyers to how a company builds cars. "When we shop for a car, we might tell the salesperson we like 'red cars,' 'really fast cars,' 'cars that handle well' and 'don't break down,' 'really comfortable cars.' We are talking in terms of our wants and needs.

"But as a car manufacturer, we don't 'really fast,' we don't 'really comfortable,' we don't 'red.' What we do is, we roll steel, we set torque, we paint, we buff, we polish."

FPL labeled quality elements its version of red, fast and comfortable. Thus, when FPL customers said they wanted to be able to make payment arrangements on past due bills, the company checked off the quality element "considerate customer service" on its Table of Tables.

Customers might also say that doing quality repair work was important to them. This translated, in FPL terms, to quality elements that provided continuity of service and public safety. Commercial users wanted the company to restore power quickly. For FPL this meant, once again, continuity of service and public safety but also concern for community.

On the right side, the FPL chart revealed that the number-one priority for the environmental regulatory agencies was that the company meet health standards for air. FPL activities to carry out that priority were continuity of service, capacity, employee safety, preventing pollution/protecting public health, and protecting the natural environment.

The triangles and circles represented the relative strength of the relationship between the customer's need and the company's quality element. In the example of the regulatory agencies that wanted the company to meet health standards for air, the phrase "protect the natural environment" got a heavily weighted circle with a dot, while "employee safety" got a lightly weighted triangle.

After analyzing the results of their survey with formulas that assigned weights based on customers' numbers and revenues, FPL determined which were the top-ranked categories. These were translated into priorities for one-year plans. In 1988, for example, there were thirteen. One was to improve the reliability of electric service. Among other one-year plans were: to improve customer satisfaction, develop a vendor quality improvement program, continue to improve employee and contractor safety and increase profits without a rate increase.

Thirteen plans might be considered a lot for a small company whose work force is engaged in making and/or marketing a single product. Such a company could have a fairly simple set of goals. But FPL's 15,000 employees were divided into five geographical divisions and several major departments. Neither every division nor every area functioned under the same conditions, so in practice each would be working on a subset of goals, rather than all thirteen.

The policy deployment process was developed with the aid of Kansai Electric Power. From the Japanese FPL learned the adage that "If you put one hundred rabbits in a room, you will be chasing all the rabbits. You will be lucky to catch one. You are better off to have only four or five rabbits."

Armed with the information gleaned from their survey, anyone in the company could now see how his or her job related to the overarching company policy. Decisions were no longer made at "gut level . . . somebody's rubber ducky," as Evelyn observed. Making decisions based on customers' needs and wants was far different from the self-serving "product out" approach to which Americans were accustomed: "I'm going to build this and you're going to use it the way you get it."

In addition to a yearly survey for policy deployment, FPL did four quarterly phone surveys that measured current levels of satisfaction with its performance. However, as FPL learned so well from the Japanese (and as Dr. Deming said so often), it did no good to have goals if there were no method or plan to carry them out, nor any way to measure progress toward those goals. Thus each goal was accompanied by an implementation plan and a set of outcomes the company called indicators.

To improve the reliability of electric service, a 1988 goal, the company's implementation plan called for a reduction in the frequency and length of outages, collection and analysis of data on their causes and preventive maintenance on the machinery and processes that could make the most difference. Improvement could be measured in two ways: whether service was interrupted less frequently and whether the total time customers were without service decreased.

Florida Power & Light used the word "catchball" to describe the give-and-take that went on up and down the managerial hierarchy as goals and targets were set. The power resources area, for example, deployed its goals to power plants, asking each to submit business plans for carrying them out. From those, it drafted its own overall business plan. The ideas flew back and forth—hence "catchball." This process mimicked the budgeting process in place in other companies, but was broader.

How did this work in practice?

In both 1988 and 1989, FPL power plants were asked to develop business plans focusing on three areas: reliability, safety and budget. In 1988, there was no question that reliability would take precedence at the Martin Power Plant. Situated 40 miles northwest of West Palm Beach on windswept former marshland surrounded by citrus groves and cattle ranches, the Martin Plant consists of two 783,000-kilowatt oil/gas-fired units built in 1980 and 1981.

In 1986, one generator had failed on one unit and a high-pressure boiler component made of the wrong material caused problems on the other, propelling the Equivalent Forced Outage Rate (EFOR) upward past 60 percent. EFOR was the ratio of two figures: the number of hours the plant lost generating capacity divided by the number of hours it needed to produce electricity. Martin's problems were a major contributor to the overall company EFOR rate of 14.02 percent that year. And though both problems were remedied that year, the EFOR rate for the two units in 1987 was still on the high side at 6.38 percent and 5.0 percent.

The Martin business plan laid out the plant's objectives and the indicators that measured success or failure. It listed actions to carry them out and the person who was responsible. It also listed teams, their projects and the processes they would work on. The plan was a working document, used as the basis for weekly management meetings at which it was reviewed and updated—one section each week on a rotating basis.

Operations superintendent Jim Keener considered it an invaluable resource. "If you were to ask me two years ago what my policies were," he said, "I wouldn't have any idea what you were talking about. I'd come up with something. Depending on the month, they'd change."

In 1988, with reliability as a beacon, and an improvement plan in place, Martin went to work. Every time there was an accidental outage, plant management assigned a team to look into the cause. In FPL lingo these were called "task" teams, as opposed to "functional" teams of people who worked together in the same area, and were akin to quality circles.

One task team discovered cracks in low-pressure turbine blades. The cracks were repaired while the team worked on a redesign. Another found that fan blades were also cracking. In this case the team came up with a written procedure for welding them and recommended a regular inspection schedule. Engineers and union employees worked side by side on the teams.

Meanwhile, employees alerted to the plant's reliability campaign made suggestions through FPL's newly invigorated Bright Ideas suggestion program. One worker, for example, realized that a set of critical dampers kept sticking because there was no way to lubricate them. He suggested drilling holes for grease fittings, then adding the dampers to the maintenance schedule.

From above, the power resources group developed a set of inspection procedures for all its plants designed to head off potential problems. Following these procedures, inspectors at Martin found a piece of equipment called a reheat header that had cracked from thermal shock. The workers at the plant repaired the crack and modified the drain system to keep it from happening again.

"In the past," said maintenance superintendent Tim McCartney, "you'd get the maintenance supervisor who had the most experience and ask him what kind of maintenance he thought we should do on this piece of equipment. . . . That's not all bad but it's certainly not systematic. There's now a process for making sure you address the critical issues.

"We used to focus on just fixing things. Now we try to start early in the process with our planning group and say, 'What is the objective of this job? What are we trying to accomplish by this job? And how are we going to know if we are successful or not?' "

Plant personnel did more than make sure equipment was in good working order. They also questioned how effective it was. That, too, was different from the past. "Before," McCartney said, "we might do a complete inspection of a cleaning device and never verify that it's doing the proper job."

After reducing ongoing problems, plant management found that unanticipated events were still causing trouble. To deal with these first-time instances, they gathered data on similar situations at other plants. "Instead of just looking at the things that happened on this particular unit, we looked at all of them that happened on sister units, adjacent units and other like units," said operations superintendent Keener. If equipment like theirs failed elsewhere, they searched for the cause and sought to counteract it at Martin before it happened there.

Technical superintendent Joan Stuart, meanwhile, was using statistical formulas that could predict when a failure would take place based on past history, sometimes called prevention through prediction. This information was fed into what was called the RAMP (Reliability Availability Management Plan) profile. RAMP was aimed at making aging plants more reliable, so that FPL would not have to construct costly new plants to take their place. "The goal here," said a piece of company literature, "is not to simply be the best at making repairs following failure, but to see failure coming and prevent it."

Explained Stuart, "We say these are the top fourteen hitters on this unit that are going to affect us and this is what we have to do to fix those problems. Based on the downtime those things will cause, we calculate a projected reliability impact." That figure, in turn, determined its priority on the RAMP list.

On unit one, the forced outage rate was sliced nearly in half by the end of 1988, to 3.42 percent; on unit two, it dropped to .56 percent, the best record of any unit of that megawatt class in the country in 1988. The following year, when the policy deployment directive came down, reliability had improved to 1.22 percent on unit one and .36 percent on unit two. With such progress, safety rather than reliability then emerged as the number-one priority.

Once again, FPL used the same methodical approach to an issue. In the past, Stuart said, "We did not think safety was an issue. We thought our performance was okay. 'Accidents happen. You can't do anything about it.' Now we look at it as if everything you do is controllable. You can plan for the future. We can plan and prioritize our work—not just go to work every day and wait for things to happen.

"A fellow walked out, he stepped on a rock and he twisted his ankle. We used to say, 'Oh, those things happen.' Now we say, 'Hey, that really was within our control. We're asking this fellow to walk out and service a piece of equipment and monitor it in an area where there's nothing but a bunch of rocks and grass and weeds and he's got to walk out there once per shift, so sometimes he does it in the dark, so it is within our control to prevent that. Give him a nice spot to walk out onto.' "

Until recently, the only indicator for safety that the Martin plant used was the number of employee lost-time injuries. "We learned that isn't the way to do business," said Keener, "because lost-time injuries are the tip of the iceberg." According to one analysis, for every lost-time injury, on the average, there were ten cases where people must see a doctor. And for every "doctor case" there were ten minor injuries, and for every minor injury there were ten "unsafe acts and conditions". How much better it would be to eliminate unsafe acts and conditions before they escalated into doctor cases.

Martin did so with a program developed by Dupont. Known as S.T.O.P. (for "safety training observation program"), the plan called for training people to spot potentially dangerous situations. Supervisors were asked to rank unsafe acts on a bar chart and take corrective action, rather than wait for injuries to occur and then to analyze their cause.

Jim Keener learned to evaluate his own actions as a supervisor more closely. "In the past I'd walk out and a guy would put his hard hat on when he saw me coming and I'd never say a word to him. I learned that I was giving him the signal that I approved of that action. I know now I have to approach that individual and say 'What if . . . something fell from the sky? What if this happened? Why don't you wear a hard hat?' In other words, try to get his buy-in from a very personal point of view.

"We used to have up to four lost-time injuries a year and twenty-four doctor cases a year—no big deal. The old way of doing things—and we did it this way even two years ago—we'd stratify the injuries by categories like back strains or legs or eyes, and then we'd do something like have back-injury prevention training. We didn't do anything about unsafe acts. Guess what? As soon as we got through all our training we'd have another lost-time injury."

(Elsewhere an FPL service depot addressed this issue by color-coding equipment according to weight so workers loading trucks knew instantly whether to hoist an object without help.)

The people at Martin also helped FPL develop a safety management protocol for all the plants, which set forth procedures and checks to be carried out at every level. In 1989, Martin had zero lost-time incidents. Its 15 doctor cases represented a better than 36-percent improvement. Unsafe acts and conditions increased to 313, but Keener interpreted this as evidence that people were now taking matters seriously enough to report them. "The plant population is spotting things, we're working on potential problems and correcting them."

In places where accidents had previously occurred, drawings of little tombstones were pasted. Every doctor case now required an investigation. And just as the plant used statistical analysis to predict equipment failure, it was now using an "error modes" analysis to pinpoint the most dangerous areas of the plant to come up with countermeasures.

Teamwork

In 1984, FPL's quality improvement department began to address the gap in middle management that had opened up between the teams at the line level and management at the top.

In the beginning, to get QIP moving, FPL had created a shadow organization, with team leaders advised by facilitators. Now that was proving to be a problem. Managers felt threatened by the activities of the workers, because they weren't involved. If quality improvement was to be truly integrated into the company, then it had to be done the way FPL did business day in and day out: managed by managers like everything else.

In 1984 and 1985, a course called "Leadership for Managers" was offered to the company's 400 middle managers. In 1986 and 1987, the company's 2,400 supervisors were run through a similar course, retitled "Supervising for Quality." The graduates were sometimes jokingly referred to as "supertators"—a combination of supervisor and facilitator. That was in fact an accurate description of their new role. Middle management now was equipped—and expected—to both lead and facilitate teams as a regular duty. Full-time facilitators were gradually reduced in numbers. Today every manager and supervisor at FPL is required to take three days of team leader training. Team members get two days of training.

At each level—departments, divisions and area offices—managers and those who reported to them were organized into lead teams. A manager would chair the lead team below and serve on the one above. It was the job of the lead team to assign quality improvement projects consistent with the company's policy deployment objectives and to review them each step of the way.

By 1987, teams were popping up all over, tackling all kinds of problems. The visitor to Florida Power & Light could see their work displayed in offices and hallways on what were called "story-boards"—42- by 48-inch visual displays of the seven-step problem-solving process. The Japanese tractor company Komatsu is generally credited with developing storyboards. And FPL's storyboards have since been widely copied by other companies.

The teams followed this seven-step analysis:

1. Reason for improvement: To identify a theme (problem area) and the reason for working on it.

2. Current situation: To select a problem and set a target for improvement.

3. Analysis: To identify and verify the root causes of the problem.

4. Countermeasures: To plan and implement countermeasures that will correct the root causes of the problem.

5. Results: To confirm that the problem and its root causes have been decreased and the target for improvement has been met.

6. Standardization: To prevent the problem and its root causes from recurring.

7. Future plans: To plan what is to be done about any remaining problems and to evaluate the team's effectiveness.

The corporate library had its team of "Happy Bookers," who decided to take a look at the haphazard way in which publication requests came in from other departments. Until that point, anyone who wanted to order a book was likely to scribble the name of the author or the title on a piece of paper and thrust it under the nose of a library staffer. Using their new quality improvement tools, the team established procedures and a three-part order request form. It was not a complex project, but it helped them learn the process.

The library soon moved on to weightier matters; for example, revising its method for routing periodicals and other materials to groups of employees. Sometimes material took so many weeks to reach people at the bottom of the lists that they resorted to ordering their own subscriptions at company expense. By revising the sequence of names on the list, ordering additional subscriptions for popular titles and educating users about the constraints of the service, the team was able to satisfy users and discourage them from ordering their own copies.

Meanwhile, another team called "The Clippers" addressed an even greater issue, library service 100 miles north for the company's

Juno office, where almost half the general office staff had moved in 1982. (See QIP Stories, pp. 71–73.)

In the accounting department, a team tackled difficulties that had arisen when engineers needed to retire an obsolete piece of equipment. In such instances, the engineers were required to fill out a retirement document that accounting used to keep property records up to date. Eighty percent of the documents were improperly prepared.

The accountants and the engineers would argue with each other over who was to blame. "They used to tell us, 'We're not accountants. We're engineers,' " said Leo Quintana, an accounting analyst. "They wouldn't return our phone calls." For their part, the accounting staff was unhappy at having to continuously correct the forms, which they regarded as the job of the engineers.

Still, when the accountants said they were setting up a quality improvement team and began using such magic phrases as "customers' valid requirements," the customers—in this case, the engineers—were willing to help.

As a result of the team's recommendations, the accounting department began to prepare semiannual compilations of property records that had the accounting information the engineers needed to fill out the document; in addition, accountants gave engineers an eight-hour course on how to fill out a retirement document using historical data from their files.

The relationship between the engineers and accountants changed dramatically. The trust level was eventually such that the engineers believed the accountants weren't out to hinder them but were genuinely interested in improving the process. "Now they're calling us to find out how many mistakes they've made," Quintana said.

In customer service and sales in West Palm Beach, teams tackled everything from dog bites to delinquent customers angered by demands for additional deposits. (See pp. 69–71.) Over time, as all departments became familiar with the quality improvement process, lines of communication opened up. "Through quality improvement, there's been a culture change," said Quintana.

As time went on, the teams became more and more sophisticated. Where once they had sought to identify improvement opportunities with the question "What prevents you from doing your job right the first time?" they learned that that only lead to shifting the blame and months of indecision. Recalled Caryl Cullen, then a facilitator at the

West Palm Beach office, "First we selected a problem, then tried to figure out who the customers were." They learned it was more helpful to begin with a definition of who the customers were and what kinds of things upset them. Those then became the processes to work on. Customers, of course, could be either internal or external.

So it went, with hundreds of teams throughout the company. Their completed stories were summarized in "improvement action memorandums," which were computerized for access throughout the corporation. All the teams could see what the others had done; they need not reinvent the wheel.

It was not always smooth sailing, to be sure. In its zeal to win the Deming Prize, FPL moved very rapidly to develop teams and introduce statistics. Resentment over what some thought of as pressure tactics was strongly reflected in a 1988 employee survey about the quality improvement program. Only 31 percent of respondents on QI teams said they had volunteered to be on a team because they really wanted to be. Half the respondents felt team participation should be given less emphasis. Fourteen percent said they had joined because they did not want to be downgraded on their performance appraisal. And, 90 percent of all managers and executives thought "My career advancement depends upon my participation in QIP." Depending on how you looked at it, this was not all bad. It meant that quality was becoming FPL's way of doing business.

Employees were also critical of the recognition process. In the beginning there had been small monetary rewards for teams whose work was judged to be superior. FPL discovered, though, that people were less eager for money than appreciation. Although teams were treated to banquets with company dignitaries, the survey disclosed that what people wanted most of all was to see their solutions in place. They felt that the evaluation process for selecting "winning" teams placed too much emphasis on the physical appearance of the QI stories. Hours and hours were spent on polishing graphs and charts. Employees protested that QIP was interfering with their regular duties. And they felt that many of their activities were being "backfitted" to double as QI stories.

FPL President Robert Tallon took on some of the questions in the July 1988 issue of the employee newspaper, *Sunshine Service News*. Tallon begged for patience, noting that some earlier excesses already had been addressed. At one point, for example, the company had set an eight-month deadline for projects. That had been rescinded. "Instead of quotas, we want to look at a team's progress," Tallon said. A suggestion system was being revamped so that people could contribute ideas without being on teams. Perhaps what was most remarkable about Tallon's plea was less its content than its tone, which was neither defensive nor obfuscatory. He simply acknowledged that all was not perfect and that the company was still working on the problems.

True to form, FPL organized several teams to address the issues raised by dissatisfied employees, such as the recognition procedure. Employees had let it be known that their idea of a good time wasn't necessarily a fancy dinner with John Hudiburg. As a result, events were introduced in the workplace to honor teamwork. One was the "expo fair"—an idea borrowed from Xerox—that gave employees time off to mount exhibits of their QI stories for friends and family to see.

Such changes were applauded in places like the Martin Power Plant. In the initial stages of QI story development, said technical superintendent Joan Stuart, the relationship between management and the teams had become rather adversarial because the recognition process called on managers to take a very critical stance in evaluating a team's work. "Whether it was moving the water cooler or not, it was difficult to learn the process and solve the problem. And then we proceeded to put the team through a difficult recognition process, which involved a lot of additional work and rework of their solution."

Managers learned to ease up, and the more informal recognition events proved popular. Said Stuart, "What we found out was that we could improve that recognition by allowing the team to just show their peers throughout the company what they had done. The real payback is that they made their own job easier. It was more important to them that their solutions were implemented, not just that 'We know what the solution is, and some day we'll get around to putting it in,' but actually implement the solution and let them just show what they did." The expo fairs, she said, had been a "giant stride" in awarding teams recognition.

Quality in Daily Work

Reconstituting and redirecting the teams, while also drafting middle management into QIP, was one corporate chore. The other was introducing the concept known as Quality in Daily Work. Together, they were the base of the QIP triangle.

A pioneer in this area, Kansai Electric, had described QIDW in its Deming Prize summary of Total Quality Control: "To supply electricity and other services of good quality to as many as ten million users, it was required to have not only the system of policy control (policy deployment), but also the system of control of daily or routine work which concerns the construction, maintenance and operations of huge facilities and the services for users. Our company, therefore, introduced and has promoted control of daily or routine works as one of the most important TQC activities. It is the most important point that through control of daily or routine work we should prevent any crucial accident, since any trivial trouble in the power system could result in a crucial one."

QIDW was consistent with the Japanese conviction that constant, ongoing improvement, no matter how small, was more valuable than the great leaps forward favored by Western corporations. The Japanese called their approach *kaizen*. *Kaizen* was process-oriented; the latter was results-oriented. In his book *Kaizen: The Key to Japan's Competitive Success,* Masaaki Imai defined the word as "continuing improvement in personal life, home life, social life and working life. When applied to the workplace, *kaizen* means continuous improvement involving everyone—managers and workers alike."

In the fifth of his Fourteen Points, Dr. Deming instructed: "Improve constantly and forever the system of production and service." The notion of quality in daily work life was FPL's version of *kaizen.*

The job of any person or department could be viewed as a collection of processes. Each process could be measured. If your job was mowing the lawn as quickly as possible, the time could be measured from when you took the mower out of the garage until you returned it to the same position after finishing the job. If it was to mow as much lawn as possible in an hour, you could measure how much territory you covered in that time. Or if your job was to mow the lawn thoroughly, you could, in theory at least, count the number of blades of grass left standing when you had finished. Once you defined your job and the standard of measurement, you could begin to look for ways to improve it, always referring back to that standard.

In a company the size of Florida Power & Light, there were thousands of processes—lawns to be mowed—carried out by many individuals and groups of individuals, and many ways to measure how well their work was being done. Simply by monitoring those processes and attempting to standardize them—make them the same day in and day out—glitches would become apparent. Some would be small enough that an individual could take care of them. Others would be fodder for teams. In this sense, improvement would bubble up from the bottom through hundreds of QIDW activities.

Supervisors had gotten a taste of QIDW in their "Supervising for Quality" training. Through the use of control charts, they had learned how to select out-of-control processes for improvement and to develop indicators. Now the division lead teams began to identify the processes in their departments and to select those important enough to monitor on a frequent basis. At the Martin plant, operations superintendent Jim Keener eventually would have his people tracking 123 processes.

In the district customer sales and service offices, meter reading errors were one important indicator that manager Vic Arena could monitor on a monthly basis. In 1989, for example, errors per 1,000 meters were perking along at about two a month. They began to edge upward in May, hitting three in June—a 33-percent increase. A simple one-sheet "process control investigation" disclosed that one new employee was responsible for 33 of 79 total errors. It was clear the employee hadn't mastered all the procedures. She was given additional training; her errors dropped and so did the overall indicator. Arena's other indicators, or "triggers" as they were called in-house, included the number of uncollectible accounts, how long customers waited in line at the front counter, how long it took to make an appointment with a customer who had complained and the number of employee injuries that required a visit to a doctor.

One of Arena's responsibilities was to oversee the training of his staff. A strong supporter of quality, he had no objection to that. Whenever he was notified of openings in the various training sessions, he would consult his records to see who had not yet attended a particular session, then enroll whoever was able to go and needed to do so.

Although well intended, his was a fairly random selection process. And there were several things wrong with it. For one thing, it didn't seem to be working. Supervisors did not have the statistical tools they needed, and some had never been given team-leader training. As a result, there was a distinct shortage of team leaders. And for another, if someone dropped out at the last minute, the slot usually remained empty. "There was no way to fill the places if they were going to miss, and no system as to who went." This meant Arena got calls from Organization Development and Training wanting to know where his people were. "The people in ODT were always upset. They would complain to the division and the division would complain to the district." To Arena, in other words. Meanwhile, employees who chose not to go to training sessions were not held accountable.

No team was necessary to tackle this job. Arena simply made a list of his employees and the training they needed, along with a three-year plan for who would go when. From then on, he said, whoever couldn't attend had to let him know why. The idea made so much sense, he said, that "you would think this is obvious. But we didn't do it." In 1988, thirty-one slots had been available but only nineteen were filled. In the first nine months of 1989, however, his staff had not missed one training session.

In the library, supervisor Caryl Congleton began to chart the number of days it took to process an order for a publication. It wasn't so much that people were complaining, she said. But the usual delivery period of six to eight weeks seemed excessive, particularly given the atmosphere of quickening change.

So, the library staff began to ask its customers how badly they needed the material and then to negotiate with vendors for priority treatment when speed was important. Charting the data where all could see it reminded the staff to be certain to process publication requests at the beginning of each day. If someone was absent, a substitute was designated to handle the requests to prevent a backlog from forming.

Library assistant Susan Johnson began sending copies of the orders back to the person who made the request, stamped with the date the order was processed and an approximate date of delivery. "That way they won't wonder what happened to their requests," she said.

In another instance, a library vendor complained that he was not receiving his payment within the required thirty days. Working with the accounting department, the library drew a flow chart of the process, indicating the amount of time each step took. Examination of the process revealed that accounting prepared a check and sent it back to the library, one of whose people would then send it to vendors. It had been done this way for years so that the library staff would have a record of the check number and mailing date. But the people in accounting now had an automated check preparation and tracking system that the library could use for verification. "There was no real need to do that other than that's the way we'd been doing it," observed Congleton. Eliminating that step saved at least three working days. In addition, Congleton reassigned part of the payment process to another staff member, Josephine Snider, who further streamlined the library's work flow. The result was a drop from 23 to 6.5 days on average to process an invoice. To continue monitoring the process, Congleton added vendor payments to her QIDW indicators.

Senior library assistant Jean Dingee similarly charted the processes of on-line literature research, securing loaned materials and requesting documents from other sources. She stressed that timeliness was not the only criterion for improving service. "Customers of literature searches want the product to be comprehensive and appropriate to their needs."

Up in the systems and programming department, as people set out to document and standardize the repetitive tasks, the technical center—the office that offered technical support for programming— began to track incoming calls on one chart and the time it took to respond on another. One measure was the number of calls answered by a recording machine. The callers, in this case the center's "customers," were often people with pressing computer problems that couldn't wait—but had to. To their surprise, the technical center staff discovered they had a business meeting scheduled at the busiest time of the week. It was rescheduled.

Quality improvement at FPL had begun in 1981 with Marshall McDonald's enlightenment, followed by fitful starts that gradually became more evenly orchestrated as the three areas of the QIP triangle were introduced. Beginning in 1986, FPL had the assistance of counselors from the Union of Japanese Scientists and Engineers. On July 25, 1988, John Hudiburg announced to employees that their counselors from JUSE advised FPL that "we have made enough progress in the QI process to begin our challenge for the Deming."

III. GOING FOR THE PRIZE

During the week of August 10, 1987, Wendel Sauer from the Miami district office of FPL stepped up to the podium in a hotel conference room furnished with flip charts and an overhead projector for presentations such as the one he was about to make. Although the room was packed, he was in fact primarily playing to an audience of one, a diminutive Japanese academic named Noriaki Kano.

Kano was one of five counselors from the Union of Japanese Scientists and Engineers helping FPL prepare for the Deming Prize, but he was the one who would assume a lead role and, in just a brief time, become a legendary figure at FPL, appreciated for his acumen and humor. It was not hard to see why.

He was the master of an interrogative approach the Japanese called "single-case bore questions." The name derived from the relentless nature of the questions, which began as broad exploratory queries and eventually homed in on weaknesses and omissions.

Sauer was about to become a target.

Sauer's office processed the flood of bill payments that arrived daily from FPL's Southern Division customers—close to 400,000 a month, totaling $61,600,000 in revenue. As the district sought to bring its processes under control, it focused on its failure to credit payments to customer accounts the day they arrived. Data showed that during 1986 an average of 18,000 payments a month were not credited for at least a day. This both reduced the company's cash flow and increased collection procedures for overdue bills. Most important, the customer who was being dunned for a payment that had just been mailed was distinctly annoyed, and might even complain to the Florida Public Service Commission.

Although the problem had persisted for some time, a supervisor in the Miami office had not found it difficult to arrive at a solution. Much of the backup occurred on Monday mornings, when employees struggled to catch up with mail that came in over the weekend. At the supervisor's suggestion, a new Sunday-to-Thursday shift was added to the work week, and the Monday schedules of four other employees were rearranged so they had free time in the morning to help out on an as-needed basis. By April of 1987, the carryover time for crediting payments had been reduced to zero.

After proudly presenting this successful solution, Sauer rested his case. Kano began his "boring" questions.

In halting English, Kano at first sought to clarify for himself what others may already have understood. The solution to the problem had been found by a highly motivated supervisor. "What kind of thing did she do? . . . How to find these countermeasures?"

Sauer explained again about the added shift and the borrowed workers.

"Do you have data about how many mails did you receive on Monday?"

"Yes, she had that data. I'm sorry I don't have it here to show you."

"By these first actions, how was this situation then changed? Number of receiving mail by weekdays . . . how to say? How did this become homogenous . . . uniform? So do you have data?"

Once again, Sauer said, "I don't have it to show today."

"Another thing," Kano asked, "if you make a graph of job route to the time—7:30, 8, 9, so on—how much inventory of the job to be processed?" In other words, Kano wanted to know how much mail was processed on an hourly basis.

Again Sauer came up short. "Now, I don't believe that was ever done. The amount of work load by hour that was being processed—I don't believe we've got that information."

Kano continued. "Now you have solved the problem. My question is that this is a problem of quantity . . ."

"Quantity, yes," Sauer replied eagerly.

"Problems of quantity can be easily solved by increase of the number of people."

"Surely," Sauer agreed.

"Okay? So, of course, some time we need the increase of people. But the important point is, is it economically efficient? Now I see you increase the number of employees . . . is the increase reasonable or not? How do you explain why you increase four (employees) instead of three or five?"

Four were available, Sauer said. And sometimes not that many were pressed into service. It depended on the volume of mail. The supervisor was the person who decided how many workers to add.

"How does she judge?" Kano asked. Was there a relationship between the pieces of mail and the number of extra people assigned to open and process it? How many pieces of mail did the people process on average? Perhaps the efforts of an industrial engineer were in order, to measure this. Not, Kano stressed, as a way of determining compensation as was so often done in the United States, where performance measurements were "too much closely linked with salary." But in this case, he thought it was appropriate to "consider how

much time is necessary to open one mail. . . . If you have such data
. . . you can more easily plan the necessity of your work force."

In addition, Kano remarked, "If you have such kind of standard
of time based on actual calculation, you can improve how to reduce
each of this time."

Kano's English may have left something to be desired, but his
intent was clear. The Miami office had a problem of too much work,
so it recruited more staff to do it without first collecting sufficient
data that might have suggested other, less costly ways of solving the
problem. Without the data, too, there was no way to further analyze
the process for continual improvement.

In closing, Kano related a parable of a wealthy man who lived in
a beach house behind high walls. His private beach was covered with
gold. One day, losing interest in his money, he opened the walls to
the public for an hour, inviting people to carry off as much gold as
they could. His guests that day carried off all the gold they saw. They
got "big results without any effort." The next day he did the same
thing. Now people were forced to sift through sand for the gold that
had filtered beneath the surface. On the third day, when he again
issued his invitation, that shallow gold too had been scooped up.
Forced to work in deep areas, the scavengers "need some equipment—X rays or ultrasonics. The effort is so big, the results are
small." Still, no one believed it wasn't worth doing.

Kano turned to Sauer. "What you have shown me is something
like the first day."

Sauer laughed. "You want the second or third day."

Kano laughed too. "On the second day," he said, "you need more
scientific approach, in terms of data and QC tools. I suggest you
study i.e. (industrial engineer) techniques about how to prepare standard time."

It was through grueling sessions like these, during which people
were grilled and coached, that FPL learned what to prepare for the
Deming Prize audit. Though the five Japanese counselors visited just
twice a year for several weeks, their visits were highly leveraged. FPL
filled hotel meeting rooms for the sessions and videotaped them for
later study. American managers became adept at the same kind of
inquisitions. As the audit approached, they, too, grilled employees
repeatedly. When the actual audit took place, said one presenter, it

was in some ways a relief. The pace was slower than the practice sessions because the Japanese required translation. "It gave us more time to think."

Though Kano and the other counselors often cloaked their remarks with humor, they had the same devastating effect on lower-level managers that John Hudiburg had experienced on his first humbling trip to Tokyo.

There was the time one had asked a manager, "What is your job?"

"I'm district manager of_____."

"No, that's your title. What is your job?"

The man repeated his answer. The counselor turned to the man's supervisor. "You pay this man money? He doesn't even know what his job is. He should be errand boy." Another man used the word "liaison" in describing his job. "Oh, you are a gofer," said the counselor. The Japanese were not interested in job titles. They wanted to know what people actually did, and then they wanted to ask them about it.

They were not easily impressed. During a presentation brimming with paper and classy overheads, a counselor quipped sarcastically, "Let me ask you, you have stock in Xerox? Too much paper."

Another such incident became famous throughout FPL when Dr. Kano visited the Port St. Lucie plant in early 1986 to hear its first presentation. During several trips to Kansai and other Japanese companies, plant manager David Sager had been impressed with how extraordinarily polite his hosts were. Given Japanese civility and the track record of Port St. Lucie, of which everyone was truly proud, he felt comfortable assuring his staff they had no reason to be apprehensive about their presentation. But he was not prepared for Dr. Kano, who "can be a little direct, to say the least."

At the outset a bulb burned out in the overhead projector—bad form for an electric company. Sager said the presentation "went downhill from there." The schedule that day called for an overview of the organization, before moving on to what the plant was doing with teams and policy deployment. Officials never got beyond the organization chart, some thirty pages of diagrammed names and titles. Kano spent two hours trying to understand it. Next, on a plant tour, he repeatedly asked employees for their process flow charts. "I didn't know what he was talking about," Sager said. And neither did anyone else. The whole day was clearly a shambles.

Things got even worse. Later in the week there was a briefing in

Miami, attended by the company brass. Kano critiqued all that he had seen, lambasting the company for poor management. "He said he had seen better management in Third World countries," Sager recalled. As for the accomplishments of Port St. Lucie, which had beat the industry record in the time and cost of construction, Kano dismissed them with the offhand remark, "You were lucky." Only it came out "rucky."

The news got back to the plant in about a nanosecond. By the next morning, a crop of colorful stickers had blossomed on hard hats and briefcases. They bore the emblem of the Japanese flag—the orange sun on a field of white—with the words "We are rucky." And in one corner "Prant St. Rucie."

In retrospect, Sager, who was still wearing the sticker on his hard hat in 1990, believed Kano wanted to "take the best of what we had and show us we didn't know anything." And although "it wasn't funny at the time," he could see later that the incident "turned out to be a great motivator." In the three years following his visit, the plant made great strides in quality. And the organization chart they presented to the examiners during the Deming Prize audit was a one-page summary, with backup material at hand in boxes. The plant was also using the summary for visitors such as those from the Nuclear Regulatory Commission and the Public Service Commission. Sager now realized that the Japanese didn't "want to know every detail," and neither did anyone else. "I would never show a thirty-page organization chart today."

Port St. Lucie was not the only site to be "accused" of good luck. Managers long accustomed to being praised for good results might find themselves asked to explain how they were achieved. Often they wouldn't know. "You were very rucky," a counselor would comment. It became an oft-heard quip in-house at FPL.

The counselors demanded data for every activity. And as Wendel Sauer had discovered, it was uncomfortable not to have it when pressed. Data in hand, the Japanese were certain to ask where it came from and how it was used. "When they ask a question in a review, there's not much point in saying anything unless you have the documentation," librarian Caryl Congleton observed. The library was hit doubly hard. As a department, it not only had to prepare for its own potential inquisition by Deming examiners, but it was being inundated with requests for information by other departments in the midst of preparations.

Manager Bill Ellis would not forget the first day Dr. Kano came to the West Palm Beach district office: September 1, 1987. Said Ellis, "We thought we were doing very well. We had our indicators in line. We were getting 2-percent improvement. We thought we were all prepared and had every answer in the world."

They were not prepared.

"The depth that he would go in his area of question! 'Why are you doing that? What is it telling you?' The most important thing I learned was the verification of the root cause. I've heard more people say that what appeared to be the obvious cause or problem turned out to be something different."

The effort encouraged FPL offices to cooperate—in self-defense. Where once one district office was reluctant to adopt an improvement pioneered by another—the "not-invented-here" syndrome—they became eager to help each other. Said Vic Arena, second in command at West Palm Beach, "We realized if we could put these things in place, we wouldn't have to spend hour after hour to get ready."

The sessions with the Japanese counselors contained not only critiques but instruction in such matters as the use of statistical tools. One could take a flow chart, for example, and add a vertical time line to show how long each step took. Often a team's flow chart might be too detailed for a presentation to management. In those cases, Kano suggested a simpler, general flow chart might be more appropriate. There were times when a scatter diagram that measured two variables could be more useful than a histogram. Above all, the Japanese emphasized the need to circle round and round the Plan-Do-Check-Act Cycle. Before, said Arena, "We were really not into PDCA. We had a plan in '86, we did it in '86. We didn't check on it in '87. We just assumed that it would work."

Said Bill Ellis, "We became painfully aware that we many times looked at twelve-month ending data. You could have a terrible month, but it would get lost. You wouldn't see it till it was too late. We learned to look at our indicators daily or monthly or year-to-date."

In the old days, a customer would complain; the company would take care of the problem. "But," Arena said, "we wouldn't put anything in place to keep it from happening again. We didn't really have the tools. We weren't tracking anything. We'd just hope it wouldn't happen again."

When, for example, a tree falling on a line caused an outage, an emergency team would repair the damage and a treecutting team would come into the area to trim others so it would not happen again. Kano, Arena said, wanted to know what kind of trees the company was dealing with and how fast they grew. A team was formed to study the tree situation. It consulted with foresters, among others. Subsequently trees were classified and put on routine treecutting cycles, reducing the chances of sudden outages and emergency repairs.

The on-site examinations for the Deming Prize were to take place in July and August of 1989, a year after the counselors told the company they were ready for the final stage of preparation. Like FPL's five counselors, the examiners were academics. Based on material submitted in advance, they would decide which operations to audit. No division would be informed, however, until June, so everyone would have to be prepared. The audit itself was divided into two parts, Schedule A and Schedule B. In Schedule A, company managers made presentations. Afterward, the auditors could ask questions. Schedule B was a review and questioning session.

There were ten examination criteria: policy; organizational structure; education and dissemination; collection, dissemination and use of information; analysis; standardization; management system; quality assurance; effects; and planning for the future. A guidebook for managers prepared by the Quality Improvement Department warned that "examiners question participants to verify that implementation of QIP is occurring through the organization with confidence, understanding and enthusiasm."

The guidebook emphasized what Hudiburg and other executives had tried to stress all along: that the true value of the prize was in the preparation. "The Deming Prize challenge has been proven as a means to gain rapid improvement within organizations as they are preparing for the examination." It noted that earnings for Deming Prize manufacturing companies in Japan had been nearly twice that of the industry average. But even if the value was more in the race than in winning, to go for the prize and lose would be a severe disappointment.

Years of effort would be crammed into a few hours spent with the auditors. The guidebook devoted several pages on how to answer their questions. It advised people "to be honest at all costs. Things that are not being done or not completed should be honestly admitted. This demonstrates that there is an awareness of the weakness. In this situation, documented plans should be presented.

"If you try to hide things you have not done, eventually these things will be uncovered by the examiners because they will ask single-case boring-type questions until they discover the 'facts.' "

In that final year, rocky marriages of workers and spouses would crumble. Anxiety would reach crisis proportions. Ninety-hour work weeks would not be uncommon. Some people would quit. And when the audit was over, employees would not wait to hear the results to celebrate. Such was their relief that there were parties everywhere the minute the examiners were done.

Once the auditors announced their site visits, most of the company was off the hook. At the target sites, however, the pressure increased. The company assembled mini-teams of statisticians and other company experts, all of whom descended on the target sites twice a week to conduct mock audits. Months later people were still catching up on other work that had been postponed.

In the organization development and training department, said trainer Caryl Cullen, who taught a team-leader course, suddenly "it seemed like everybody in the world needed training." Moreover, the Deming examiners always audited the training department, so organization development and training was struggling to align its own systems and to produce a measurement system. They didn't have much to go on. Said Cullen, "Even the Japanese didn't have a good handle on systems to measure people at different periods." They came up with several before-and-after training surveys.

On the eve of the audit, the Northeastern division received a letter from Kano, wishing them luck and reassuring them. "You should go with confidence and adherence. You need not now create anything because all the answers to the questions from the examiner exist in your packages, files and data bases."

The audit itself was similar to the counseling sessions with which FPL staff had grown so familiar.

The examiners complimented John Evelyn's office of research, economics and forecasting, which had devised the "Table of Tables." They made copies of it to take back to Japan, along with other customer-related materials and models. "We blew them away," Evelyn said happily. "It went far beyond anything they had seen."

Immediately following the audit, people were "almost disappointed," Cullen said. " 'Is that all there is? We had so much we wanted to show them and they didn't see it.' "

The announcement on October 18, 1989, that Florida Power & Light had indeed captured the award was oddly anticlimactic. President Robert Tallon held a press conference to announce victory. Reporters were underwhelmed. FPL had been a favorite whipping boy for years, and the press still found it hard to believe the company was doing anything right. "A winner!" the *Miami Herald* business-page headline crowed the next day. "FPL earns Deming." But much of the story was suggested by the subhead: "Critics say prize wasn't worth cost." The consultants and ancillary expenses had cost $900,000.

There was some favorable coverage several days later in the form of a story on the company's troubled nuclear plant at Turkey Point, the source of much bad press over the years. The *Herald* reported that the Nuclear Regulatory Commission had upgraded the plant in all but one category in which it had previously been deficient. Security remained a problem. Jerry Goldberg, FPL's executive vice president for nuclear energy, sounded a familiar refrain: "We will not be satisfied until Turkey Point is recognized as one of the best plants in the region with solid performance throughout."

But other than the Deming Prize press conference that was beamed over scattered monitors throughout the day, it was business as usual at headquarters, which was festooned with banners for yet another contest. FPL was a 1992 Olympics corporate sponsor, a move meant in part to keep spirits from going flat in the inevitable letdown following Deming.

The quest for the prize was already becoming a memory. In the company cafeteria, John Hudiburg lunched on overcooked vegetables and recalled the terrible embarrassment of that first meeting in Japan three years earlier. Many times since, he had watched other managers go through a similar experience, as powerless to save them as he had been to save himself. "You can't stand up there and just dance your way through a presentation, because it doesn't work and they really embarrass you. They really embarrass you so bad that you just want to . . . die." Hudiburg knew the feeling. So did Wendel Sauer and countless other FPLers.

Hudiburg had come to appreciate the Japanese style and to see its merits. "They're very methodical and very precise and very careful. They do not pick on little people. . . . They don't ask you anything that you shouldn't know. In other words, they don't expect you to be an expert on statistical quality control. That isn't the kind of questions they're asking.

" 'What is your job? Where is your data?' They will ask questions until you can't answer them, and then they tend to stop. They'll make a few comments about where you need to go from there, and that's it. You learn from your own hands-on doing."

In the library, assistant Susan Johnson reflected on how the quality movement at Florida Power & Light had changed her attitude toward work. How different she felt, for example, about the people who used the library. "Before I was doing good just to process their orders." Back then she would think to herself: "This is a benefit to them. Now, I feel that it's a privilege. . . . My whole outlook has changed through the last three or four years." A new team was forming in her department and she hoped to be its leader. "I want to grow within the company and I want to make an impact within my department." Recently, she said, someone she met from AT&T had congratulated her on FPL's Deming Prize victory. "I had a sense of ownership over all that. He said, 'Congratulations for your efforts.' It was a pat on the back for me."

And Caryl Cullen recalled how unsettling it had been to work for FPL a decade earlier. Were she to forget to remove her company I.D. on leaving, she was certain to be nailed in a grocery-store line by unhappy FPL customers who said things like "Oh, you work for Florida Power & Light? I've got to tell you about my bill." Or "I got a late notice."

"People were embarrassed to work there," Cullen recalled. "At a party you might say 'Well, I'm a supervisor.' But you weren't too quick to say of what and for whom." In recent years, however, the public attitude became more positive. "It was good things they were saying."

Cullen left FPL two months after the audit to work for its training subsidiary, QualTec, which had been established to market FPL's quality model. In retrospect, she said, there was no question in her mind that the final year preparing for the Deming Prize was worth the effort, "even the eighty-hour weeks. Looking back now there's a sense of camaraderie that's phenomenal."

John Hudiburg, too, left FPL, retiring after thirty-eight years with the company to become a QualTec consultant. There was no shortage of clients. In the aftermath of victory, the company was getting seventy calls a week.

"There's nothing exceptional about us," he said. "Any company can do it if they choose to. The rest of them can do it too."

IV. QUALITY STORIES

West Palm Beach: Deposit-related Complaints

Although customers of Florida Power & Light really had nowhere else to go for electrical service, they could—and did—make their feelings known when they were unhappy by complaining to the Florida Public Service Commission (FPSC). Complaints did more than tarnish the company's image. A company representative had to contact the complainant within twenty-four hours and file a written investigation of the incident to the FPSC within ten days.

It was possible to categorize the complaints by subject. In the West Palm Beach district, a team was assigned by the customer service and sales manager to "reduce deposit-related complaints to the FPSC." In other words, it would analyze why customers complained to the Public Service Commission on matters related to the deposits the company required for electrical service.

The team summarized its effort using the seven-step improvement process.

• *Reason for improvement:* Complaints from the district had already dropped sharply since 1985, when they numbered 131. In 1986 there were 83; in 1988, 64. The team believed they could further reduce them by 8.

• *Current situation:* Data spelling out the current situation from January to September 1988 showed that 23 complaints were directed at customer service and sales, while 18 involved construction services—the people who laid the lines. Of the complaints to service and sales, 8 dealt with high bills. The decision had already been made to form a division-wide task team with members from each district to address this category. Seven deposit-related complaints constituted the next highest category. Further analysis showed that only 1 of these complaints was from a commercial customer. Of the 6 others, 4 arose when the company requested an additional deposit.

"Let's look at the additional deposit billing process as it exists now," the team declared in this stage. The process was depicted on a flow chart. FPL customarily issued a warning letter to customers who were behind on bill payments. After 100 days with no payment, the company requested an additional deposit.

• *Analysis:* The team contacted each of the four customers who had complained and was successful in reaching two. Interestingly enough, none of the four had been a customer for less than two years.

In tracing the process, the team made the important discovery that bills for additional deposits were being sent to customers who had, in fact, made extension agreements but were waiting for the due date to make their first payment. The customer service representative was interpreting procedures to mean that the additional bill should be sent if no payment had been made, regardless of whether there was an extension agreement or not. Further investigation showed that although just one such customer in this position had complained, many more had cause for unhappiness. In all, the team said, "This represented 46 customers in the month of November 1988 alone who should not have been billed an additional deposit." That accounted for 8.2 percent of all the additional billings. This was labeled Root Cause #1.

The team also noted the negative ramifications of requiring long-term customers to ante up additional deposits. One complainant had been a customer 87 months, which analysis showed was 66 percent longer than the average customer base; another, 171 months, a period longer than 90 percent of all other customers. These people told interviewers they felt they had been treated unfairly because the company had given no consideration to the length of time they had been conscientious bill payers. The team concluded "No consideration for long-term customers is a root cause" of the complaint situation. This was the second root cause.

• *Countermeasures:* The antidote for Root Cause #1 was to clarify the process and review it with the customer service representatives so no bills were being sent to customers with extension agreements before the first payment was due. As for Root Cause #2, the team decided to defer billing an additional deposit to customers with more than 48 months of service and to call or write them before doing so.

The 48-month level was not selected arbitrarily. Three-quarters of those billed had less than 48 months of service. The potential financial impact of not billing the remaining 25 percent was a loss of $31,622 a month in additional deposits, which represented 32 percent of the dollars collected in additional deposits. In terms of dollars that were never collected, however, they contributed only 13 percent. The team concluded that "Therefore this group can be shown 'special consideration' with very little risk to the company."

• *Results:* The number of incorrectly billed customers immediately plummeted to zero for late 1988 and early 1989, except for the month of February. In that month, a customer had paid in person, but the payment had not been processed in time to halt the additional bill. An investigation of that complaint led to a countermeasure—to have a clerk check for in-person payments before sending out a bill.

The company also stopped billing large numbers of customers with 48 months or more of service. Figures showed no increase in revenue loss. Meanwhile, from January through April 1989 there were no complaints to the FPSC related to additional deposits bills.

• *Standardization:* The countermeasures to the two root causes became standard operating procedure for the West Palm Beach district. At the division level, a customer satisfaction committee recommended adopting the procedures in all districts and the division management ("lead team") was considering endorsing it for the entire system. A revised flow chart incorporated the additional steps that now had to be followed before a bill would be sent out.

• *Future plans:* In this section, the team listed "lessons learned":

1. "We learned a higher level of statistical analysis."

2. "We learned to orient our customer attitude in a more positive 'win/win' direction."

3. "Our analytical minds were fine-tuned."

4. "We learned that frequent facilitator review saves a lot of time."

In addition, there would now be customer satisfaction committees at all levels, poised to investigate FPSC complaints as they occurred.

West Palm Beach: Dog Bites

• *Reason for improvement:* One of FPL's policy deployment goals in 1989 was employee safety. Although the West Palm Beach customer service employees had no lost-time injury cases, they did have the largest number of cases in which an employee needed the services of a doctor in the division—a total of fifteen from January to September 1988, compared to just one in the Delray district and three in the Treasure Coast district. If the trend continued, there would be twenty-four doctor cases in 1989, ten over target. A team of nine was assigned to investigate.

• *Current situation:* The team got to work in October. There had been four more doctor cases. Of the total of nineteen, fifteen were wounds, three were sprains and one was a case of electrical shock.

Of the fifteen wounds, two were from nails, three were from miscellaneous causes and fully ten were from dog bites. The team therefore focused on how to reduce doctor cases due to dog bites. It decided there was no acceptable level, and set its target at zero.

• *Analysis:* FPL meter readers carried with them a hand-held electronic meter reader (EMR) on which they entered readings. The EMR was a small computer containing a log of their households, with information on each, such as whether there was a dog and whether that dog was "good" or "bad." It might even advise the meter reader to "bluff dog."

The team brainstormed for possible causes of the high number of accidents and came up with four. Perhaps the meter reader didn't know there was a dog because he didn't have his EMR with him, or it didn't contain a dog warning. Or the customer may have assured the meter reader that the dog was friendly and harmless when the opposite was the case. Finally, the company itself could be at fault because there was a performance award system in place for a low number of "can't get ins" (CGIs)—cases in which employees were unable to get into a home to read a meter. The employee with the lowest number of CGIs for the month got a $50 dinner certificate. Competing for the award might prompt meter readers to take chances with unfriendly dogs.

Next the team surveyed the ten victims. In four cases, the customer had held the dog and assured the meter reader it was all right to come in. Two other cases were related to the company's can't-get-in policy: One reported that there was no dog message on his EMR device; another was an odd circumstance deemed unlikely to recur (a special cause). The last two cases involved a category of employees called bill deliverers, since eliminated.

• *Countermeasures:* The team felt it had three root causes to counteract. Meter readers would now be told to regard all dogs as a risk, regardless of customers' assurances to the contrary. They would carry with them plastic meter reading cards to hand dog owners. The customer could either secure the dog in a room or other enclosed area when the meter reader came or use the card to position movable needles to the proper place on a dial and display the card through the window. The meter readers would be trained to explain the policy to customers who might be offended.

In order to guarantee that the electronic meter readers would carry the appropriate information, dog messages would be standardized and all those in place would be reviewed.

As for the can't-get-in policy, the $50 incentive award was dropped. Instead, management merely calculated the average rate of CGIs per meter reading, making that, in effect, a QIDW indicator to be monitored for sudden changes.

To carry out these countermeasures, the team drafted an action plan with a timetable for ordering the plastic cards, training the meter readers on when to use them, developing and reviewing the dog messages and monitoring the results.

• *Results:* In January of 1989 plastic cards were issued to employees, who logged the number of times they used them. In February, March and April, some 500 dog messages were added to the electronic meter readers. By April there had been five dog bites.

• *Standardization:* The new procedures were incorporated into a flow chart and a training checklist. The new dog messages were: "Dog (Dog OK)"; "Bluff Dog"; "Bad Dog."

• *Future plans:* Clearly something wasn't working right. An investigation of the 1989 dog-bite situation showed that in two cases the message program hadn't been installed in time to protect the workers and that the plastic card employees were supposed to carry was too large to fit in a pocket and wasn't being used. The card was modified to fold in half.

The team decided to continue investigating dog-bite cases. Team members said that they had learned a lesson from setting an overly optimistic target of zero: "When developing a target, make sure your countermeasures will get you to that target."

Corporate Library: Juno Branch

• *Reason for improvement:* Until 1982, the primary patrons of Florida Power & Light's corporate library were the 1,733 people in 36 departments housed in the Miami headquarters. Beginning in the summer of that year, however, the company moved 830 people in 17 predominantly research and engineering departments to Juno Beach, some 100 miles north of Miami. It became apparent to the library staff that they were no longer meeting their departmental objective: "To provide an access or referral point for the timely and centralized acquisition, organization and distribution of library information materials."

A cross-functional team, with members drawn from the general office and Juno departments, was organized with this theme: "Transfer of users to Juno facility causes the need to revisit existing library services."

Calling themselves "The Clippers" (Corporate Library Information Planning Project Evaluating Resources & Services), the team consisted of librarian Caryl Congleton as team leader, plus workers representing staff and engineering departments at each facility.

• *Current situation:* People from Juno either had to make a special trip to Miami or resort to the mail, fax or phone to get information. The team surveyed the departments located at Juno to find out whether these logistics caused a problem for them. Sixty-three percent of the respondents said it did. The team decided to try to cut that amount in half.

• *Analysis:* The cause-and-effect diagram revealed that Juno employees had no research materials on hand and no one to ask in person for the information they needed. Moreover, there were no procedures for the long-distance use of the library, nor was a list of its holdings at hand.

• *Countermeasures:* The team considered a number of countermeasures. Perhaps each department at Juno could have a library representative who would function something like the departmental credit union representatives—as a contact working on behalf of the department's particular library needs. Or maybe there could be a vehicle such as a bookmobile to visit Juno with materials. A third alternative—an electronic network—was beyond the library's technological reach. A fourth alternative was to establish a satellite operation at Juno, either transferring someone from the general office or hiring a new employee. This was clearly the most effective, but also the most expensive, alternative. Moreover, no one knew of any space available for this purpose at Juno.

The effort, however, had attracted widespread support at Juno. Among those operations located there, the Quality Improvement

Department was particularly sympathetic to the cause and set aside a small portion of its office space for a rudimentary library collection and customer service area. Other departments soon followed suit and agreed to provide funding for a trial of the proposed satellite library. Armed with funding and space, the Clippers developed an action plan for setting up, staffing and publicizing the mini-library.

- *Results:* The team monitored usage at Juno for four months and found the new service was definitely proving useful. "There were more than 1,000 visitors during that trial period and nearly that many requests for information," reported Pat Fraga, who had become the library's Juno liaison. Fifty percent of the departmental representatives now said they were satisfied with the facility; the remainder reported they had not yet paid it a visit.

- *Standardization:* The team recommended that the Juno satellite become a permanent fixture with corporate funding.

- *Future Plans:* The team recognized the need to familiarize people with the new service. The satellite library could also serve as a model for other outlying areas in the FPL system.

V. COLONIAL PENN: QUALITY TIME IN THE FAMILY

The team had been moving in that direction and today they decided to go for it. From now on, Colonial Penn would do as most other insurance companies were doing, charging customers for a heretofore free duplicate policy. But what would the customers think about suddenly having to pay $10 for one?

"I think it's somewhat predictable, isn't it?" said Douglas B. Pierce, president and chief operating officer of Colonial Penn Group, Inc., and also the team leader. "They're not going to like it."

As an alternative, the company would issue free a one-page certificate describing the policy and its benefits. That was all many policyholders wanted anyway to give to their lawyer or family. Pierce suggested that rather than be apologetic about charging for duplicates, Colonial Penn should emphasize that the service of providing a certificate *was* free. "Be positive. Tell people we are happy to provide this document at no cost." While there was of course a cost to the company to dispense the certificates, about $5 apiece, it would be far less than the $165,000 it spent on duplicates each year.

For eight months Pierce, a lifelong insurance man, had been chairing this team, composed of himself and upper-level managers from health actuarial, marketing, sales, policyholder services, health underwriting, management services, data and research. Its purpose was to look into why customers dropped their health insurance policies, a phenomenon known in the business as "lapse." Imposing a charge for duplicate policies had emerged as a side issue, but it was one the team felt was too important to postpone.

A diversified insurance company catering to a post-fifty age group, Colonial Penn was headquartered in Philadelphia, Pennsylvania, on Market Street, the city's main east-west thoroughfare. Across the street, in adjunct offices, on the same day Pierce and his team came to their decision, a supervisory team was meeting under Darrell Robertson, manager of telemarketing sales, to examine the issue of employee turnover in that department. For two hours they struggled with a fishbone (cause-and-effect) diagram, shaping the entries to read in a logical sequence.

It was rare enough in many companies to find a team of mid-level managers at work on process improvement. But it was even more rare to find a company president like Pierce chairing a working, nut-and-bolts team. But then, a total quality system in this sort of business environment was another rarity. Even Florida Power & Light, Colonial Penn's sister company, though essentially in a service business, produced something: electric power. You could see its effects. But selling insurance revolved around a commitment. You couldn't see it, let alone measure it. Or could you? Surely there was no more challenging—some might say difficult—setting than an insurance company for instituting the quality methods pioneered in manufacturing. But day in and day out, as on this particular day in February of 1990, Colonial Penn, in two meeting rooms in the heart of Philadelphia, was proving that it could be done.

Given the way FPL was charging ahead on quality, no doubt it was only a matter of time before Colonial Penn would be pressured into doing the same. As it happened, no pressure was necessary. Scarcely had the FPL Group purchased Colonial Penn on December 31, 1985, than Colonial Penn's vice president of organizational development, Tom Berry, was on a plane to Florida.

Berry spent a few days talking to people at FPL and touring operations, then drove to Tampa, where his friend Sigmund Brody headed Colonial Penn's southeast regional office. They agreed that office would be an ideal pilot site for a quality movement, which was eventually christened "Commitment to Excellence" (CTE).

About the time Berry toured FPL, the utility company was in the midst of restructuring its training, having recognized that its failure to involve middle management and supervisors in its Quality Improvement Program was holding it back. Berry wanted to avoid that pitfall by involving middle management at the outset. He recruited nine middle-management people, including two from the Tampa office, for a design team, and took them to see what FPL was doing in Florida. They came back as enthusiastic as he was.

But they realized they couldn't do everything all at once. The Colonial Penn design team agreed it made sense to begin in a limited fashion with the Florida pilot site, "to get the test out of town," in Berry's words. "That had the advantage of insulating the quality effort from corporate headquarters," where the aftermath of the acquisition was producing a lot of turmoil. Indeed, by the end of 1986 there had been a nearly total turnover in top management, including those who approved the quality initiative a few months earlier.

The second decision was to begin with teams rather than the other two elements of the FPL triad. "That's what gets people involved and teaches them the new skills," Berry explained. But unlike those at the parent company, these teams would at the outset be drawn from management.

In October of 1986, the Florida office of Colonial Penn had its first training, a three-day workshop for every person with a management title, thirty-six in all. Their "graduation," attended by FPL chairman Marshall McDonald, took place in a glassed-in atrium. As mystified employees gathered on balconies to watch their bosses, a flock of balloons rose in the air. Afterward, managers met with their people to tell them what was happening.

The Florida management selected six projects and appointed six teams of managers to work on them. A few months later, the first nonmanagement teams were set up. Thirty-six volunteers were needed. There were 136. "Nonmanagement people were dying to do something like this, to actually have a say in what gets done and how it gets fixed," Berry said. To help, Colonial Penn borrowed a facilitator from FPL. Although the Florida office had only 300 employees during 1989—one-tenth of Colonial Penn's work force—there were 45 teams at work.

By then, the Philadelphia offices had joined the effort. "As soon as we knew this was seeming to work, at least in Florida, we faced the challenging experience of bringing it to corporate headquarters," Berry said.

In mid–1986, Colonial Penn's president, Richard W. Ohman, agreed to set up a quality council of his direct reports. Berry advised them that "to know about what you ask others to do, you need to know the language. And by the way, you're going to be on teams." The first training session for the half dozen top people took place in Philadelphia's preeminent hotel, the luxurious Four Seasons.

Eventually Colonial Penn evolved a system of training teams as they were formed, dividing the curriculum into three modules that would be taught "just in time"—as each team worked its way through a project. The advantage was, Berry said, that "they already know the project, so they can relate it to the problem they're going to solve." The quality trainers were plucked from the corporate training office. Already skilled at teaching, they just needed to know what to teach, and that was easily learned from FPL.

A dozen or so facilitators were trained as well. "The ultimate objective," Berry said, "should be not to need facilitators, and it will be our ultimate objective. But this is so different you really do need a set of crutches. At this stage facilitators are very useful. They're aligned with the organizational chart and owned by the areas they serve."

Beginning in 1987, teams were formed from the top down. The flagship team was the one that included Ohman, now Colonial Penn's CEO and chairman, with a membership of three executive vice presidents, the corporate council and the chief financial officer. It met for the first time that April to select a project, eventually opting for one involving the high cost of nonregular salaries—for overtime, parttime and temporary help. The issue was chosen, in part, because it seemed big enough to warrant management's attention. Those costs were projected to total $5.5 million in 1987. Of that, overtime payments were the highest ($3 million), followed by temporary ($1.5 million) and parttime costs ($1 million). In addition, the company, which had offices in several suburban locations in addition to two downtown, recruited workers from twenty-three temporary-help agencies.

Although overtime ranked highest of the three expenses, the team decided that to change that policy could be too disruptive. Moreover, it was better to have extra work performed by experienced people than by temporaries who didn't know the business. For that and other reasons, the team decided to focus on the costs of temporary workers, which were averaging almost $10,000 a month over budget.

The problem statement cited the need to reduce the 1987 expenditure of $1.5 million for temporary help. The team flowcharted the process for hiring temporaries, brainstormed possible causes for their heavy use and surveyed the people who hired temporaries. Their analysis led them to two potential root causes: Because the issue was not viewed as a priority by management, there were no clear guidelines on when and how to use temporaries; nor were managers aware of alternatives to selecting such help.

The team decided it might get better service and less variation by using just one temporary-help agency. Orders went out to put a contract up for bids. The agency that won the contract agreed not to charge for the first three hours a temporary spent on the premises learning the job. In addition, in return for all of Colonial Penn's business, it would give an up-front 10 percent discount—and it would also conduct an evaluation on each employee.

In 1988, the team was rewarded with a drop of $458,000 in the cost of hiring temporary help. That experience made a believer out of Doug Pierce, one of the executive vice presidents on the team, and the man who became Colonial Penn's president in 1988.

Pierce was captivated by the statistical tools. He had spent some of his formative years as an apprentice to a master carpenter whose simple code, he joked, was "to wear a red shirt and work hard." From him, Pierce had also learned it was better, and easier in the long run, to take time to do the job right the first time. "People always know *how* better than they *do*," the carpenter was always saying. Wasted effort bothered Pierce. "I have always hated to redo things."

Perhaps that explained the appeal of structured problem-solving, which promised real answers. Some years earlier, while with another insurance company, Pierce had taught a problem-solving method that required matching up a problem to one of an inordinate number of models that had to be memorized. The beauty of this new approach was that it afforded "a field day for asking questions" and relied purely on logic. To begin, one need only say, " 'I believe this is a problem' . . . then follow up with 'Well, why is this a problem? . . . What are the consequences of this?' You get into this iterative process. That's when you really just flair all these things out . . . and everyone can participate."

Pierce asked Tom Berry to give him additional tutoring in the use of problem-solving tools. Berry agreed, but Pierce soon grew impatient with their weekly meetings solving hypothetical problems. "I said, 'It's fun to practice. But I need a real problem, which when solved would really be meaningful to the company.' "

That "real problem" turned out to be the lapse rate among health insurance policyholders.

Insurance companies typically spent a large amount of money to land a customer. And in the direct-response end of the business that amount was significantly higher than for policies sold through agents. In health insurance, for example, the costs included not only direct mail and TV advertising followed up with telephone calls, for what was known as the acquisition cost, but also the subsequent costs of processing the application, obtaining medical information and issuing the policy. It could take five or more years to recoup those costs and begin making money. That was why it was so important to hold onto customers. Some policies would always lapse, of course, if for no other reason than death. Those lapses were built into the premiums as "pricing assumptions." But when more policies lapsed than had been projected, a company made less than anticipated and in some cases lost money. That was what was happening at Colonial Penn.

To increase prices would jeopardize the company's competitive position. Nor did it make sense to grow by simply attracting new customers. Because of the large front-end costs, it was more profitable to keep the existing ones. Reasoned Pierce, "By retaining more of your current customers, you can keep costs down. . . . That means you can keep your premiums down even more. Soon you become the low-cost producer, and by doing the best job among your competitors of keeping your customers, you can put more money into providing a better product and better service."

There was always the possibility that a certain line of insurance no longer offered the potential to make money and that the company might be better off if the policy did, in fact, lapse. That too required analysis.

The issue was complicated because the company's health insurance was sold by agents as well as by direct response. Agents handled more than one company's insurance. And, unlike Colonial Penn, the agents collected the majority of their commission in the first year. Insurance companies were always suspicious that agents were encouraging people to switch policies so they could sell them another.

Pierce chose his team members and called them together to select a meeting time that all could make without fail. Eight to ten A.M. worked well because no one would be delayed by a prior meeting. They also agreed that no meeting would take place without an agenda; assignments would be completed and distributed forty-eight hours in advance, and minutes of the meeting would be distributed within forty-eight hours after adjournment. When Pierce couldn't be there—he was the chief operating officer, after all, with a busy schedule—David Schobelock would chair. He was from management services, on a two-year assignment from FPL.

After nearly five months of concentrated analysis, the team came up with a problem statement reflecting the three areas in which the discrepancies between projected and actual lapse rates had the greatest premium impact. The first involved agent-sold policies up for renewal after the first year; these were lapsing at more than twice the pricing expectation. If that rate continued, the company would experience at $63 million premium shortfall over the next five years. The next highest category consisted of direct-response policies when the first mailed-in payment was due; these had a lapse rate of 1.5 times the pricing expectation, with a potential five-year premium shortfall of $27 million. The smallest category dealt with some policies dating from a period when the company had been affiliated with the American Association of Retired People; these policy lapses could earn the company $24 million less premium than projected over the next five years.

The team divided into three subteams, one assigned to probe each type of policy. Their first tasks were to draw cause-and-effect diagrams and gather further data within each of the three problem areas.

If Pierce had desired more real problems to solve, he was getting them in spades. "There are a lot of times, when you've been in the business for a long time, that when somebody says 'That's a problem,' you say 'Yeah, I know the answer to that problem. I've solved the same problem 87 times.' You just kind of reach into your hip pocket and pull out a standard solution. And the longer you've been in the business, the longer your lists of standard solutions."

But being on the team opened his eyes to things he never suspected about certain facets of the insurance business. "I've probably said more times than at any other time in my career 'I can't believe that.' We would develop this data and people would say this is how we do that, or this is how we treat that transaction and I would say, 'I can't believe that this is how we do that.' "

That was precisely what he said when one team member mentioned that Colonial Penn issued a lot of duplicate policies. "I said 'Well, how many duplicate policies do you think we issue?' and she says 'Gee, I don't know. A lot.' I said 'Well, why don't you come back next week and tell me what a lot is.' A lot turned out to be a very, very big number, something like 16,500 copies a year, at about $10 apiece. . . .

"I said 'Before we take off running and charge all these people, let's find out why they order so many. Let's look at everything that we send them. And let's look at the telephone scripts.' And do you know what our reps would say? One of their sign-off scripts said—if someone called in with a question—'By the way, do you have a policy? Would you like another one?' Reps were *offering* policies to people. It was just incredible!" Likewise, one of their form letters invited customers to *ask* for a duplicate policy. Needless to say, those two invitations were immediately rescinded.

Pierce was surprised that the largest request for duplicates came from direct-response customers. He was almost certain that policies being replaced by competitor's agents was causing problems. "I would have bet a lot of money that it would have been our agent-sold business that was causing most of the requests."

As the team returned to its original theme of lapsed policies, Pierce experienced similar revelations. "Your first thought was . . . lapses were caused by lousy service, poor handling, something like that. Then you find out that billing records were lost during a process changeover and you didn't send your customers bills. And then you say 'My God, I don't believe that.' . . . As soon as you called them and told them that their policy had lapsed, they said 'I wondered why I hadn't received any premium notices.' "

Pierce bought himself a Colonial Penn life insurance policy, then purposely failed to make payments, "just to see what the system would do to me as an individual policyholder, and I got some real surprises." The policy was supposed to lapse after thirty days. "Colonial Penn never said it lapsed, just kept sending premium notices. . . . These systems are kind of strange things." It caused him to wonder "how many executives of companies really know what the bill looks like that they send their customers." Time after time, as the team continued meeting, he found himself just "diving into the depths of the organization."

Over in telemarketing, meanwhile, Darrell N. Robertson, serving on a team for the first time, and also its leader, was going through the same process as his boss several times removed. Meeting since March 1989, he and his team, composed of two supervisors from sales, one from service and others from human resources and payroll, and aided by a facilitator from property and casualty sales, had begun with this initial problem statement: "Turnover rate in the Philadelphia telemarketing division exceeds the corporate goal of 20 percent, as stated in the TAI (Tactical Agenda Item) 2.1, resulting in additional cost associated with hiring, training and productivity."

The situation was not unlike the insurance policy lapse rate, with its high initial costs. In telemarketing, Colonial Penn hired many talented people and pumped them full of enough training to pass a licensing examination as well as to sell all over the country. The estimated cost of this training was $10,000 per person. That money was out the window if they left after a short time. The break-even point, in terms of the money the telemarketers generated, was between eighteen and twenty-four months.

Two of Robertson's team members had served before on teams. Others like himself were learning as they went. After eleven months, they had collected a thick sheaf of data on who left and why. In the majority of cases people quit when they had new jobs. The team wrote this modified problem statement: "The New Job category dominates all reasons for turnover, 32% in '87 and 40% in '88. YTD (Year to Date) results as of 7/15/89 reflect a similar trend of 31%; corporate goal is 20%. Data indicates the greatest impact is in salary grades 7 and 8, resulting in increased hiring and training costs."

During this particular February meeting, Robertson had the Commitment to Excellence Guidebook open to cause-and-effect diagrams, coaxing team members through their own chart. The guidebook was a step-by-step presentation of Colonial Penn's problem-solving process, modeled after FPL's.

"If your chain of logic is unbroken, the diagram should make equal sense read down or up," the guidebook said. "Ask 'Why?' or 'What causes this?' to break effects down. A useful formula for

reading up is 'When I have this (bone), I get (the next bones up).' "
The "bones" were entries on the cause-and-effect "fishbone" chart.

The overall effect that the team was attempting to break down into causes was "Salary Grades 7 and 8—New Job Dominates All Reasons for Turnover, 32% in '87 and 40% in '88." As Robertson asked questions, people offered suggestions for rearranging entries and wording them to read easily or, in some cases, diplomatically. The team did not want to sound accusatory. They changed "outmoded recognition" to "insufficient recognition." They picked apart the "communication" cause, delicately wording entries that dealt with management failures to relay information. Focused on the chart, the discussion went smoothly for the most part. The closest thing to a disagreement was over whether one bone should read "company instability" or the "perception of company instability." FPL Group had just announced it was considering selling Colonial Penn, and one team member believed the company truly was unstable. Others who had survived previous sales held out for using the word "perception."

Robertson said the process made him appreciate the benefits of working together with facts "rather than trying to find a solution and not knowing whether the solution will work. . . . CTE will not solve every problem. It will identify what is a problem and what is not."

Robertson had been assigned by his boss to lead this particular team. Not so with Douglas Pierce, who was the boss. No one told him he had to join a team. He had chosen to get directly involved in the lapse team not only because he believed "the best way to learn anything is by doing it" but also because the issue was too important to delegate. "There were so many disciplines involved . . . and they all report to different people, all of whom had lots of things on their platter. I felt my position was needed to get a focus because, quite honestly, we had been losing money on this line of business."

In addition, Pierce wanted to send a message about how seriously he took this quality business. Given his hands-on participation, it would be pretty hard for others in the company to say he didn't mean it.

CHAPTER THREE

Hospital Corporation of America

Well here I am, flat on my back literally and in other ways, right ankle resting on three pillows. Gravity is vital to treatment. . . .

Dr. Sch . . . ordered from the drug store (in the hospital) a paste for the itch that had set in in Minneapolis. The drug store was out of one of the ingredients: must order it from the wholesaler, and can not make it up till Monday, as this is Saturday, no delivery from the wholesaler till Monday. I need it tonight. On prodding from Dr. Sch . . . the drug store sent someone out to another drug store to fetch the missing ingredient. The paste came up that evening.

Unbelievable: the same scenario took place some days later. . . .

I wonder why is a registered nurse making beds? It seems to me that making beds is not good use of her time. Her education and skills could be put to better use, so it seems to me.

The chair in this room is huge, would seat two people, takes up an exorbitant amount of space, heavy to move. . . . The coat hangers here are that maddening kind, found in most hotels. . . .

My nurse of the moment put on a hot towel this afternoon. 'I'll be back in twenty minutes, and if I don't come, please ring.' Sixty-five minutes later I pressed the button. A helper came in; explained to me that this was not her kind of job, so she cancelled the light for the nurse, and went off. Thirty minutes later I rang again for the nurse. The same helper came and observed again that the job was not in her line of duty, so again she cancelled the light and went off. The solution was simple, for me, merely discard the towel and insulation myself with the rules or against the rules. The same event recurred another day.

What is the moral of all this? What have we learned? One answer: the superintendent of the hospital needs to learn something about supervision. Only he can make the changes in procedure and responsibility that are required.

Talks between physicians and nurses, even with the head nurse, accomplish nothing. The same problems that I have noted will continue. A physician cannot change the system. A head nurse cannot change the system. Meanwhile, who would know? To work harder will not solve the problem. The nurses couldn't work any harder.

W. EDWARDS DEMING
"Notes on Management in a
Hospital (excerpted)
September 20, 1987

I. CHARTING THE COURSE

One bright October Wednesday in the Nashville, Tennessee, head-quarters of Hospital Corporation of America, nine executives from hospitals around the country met to discuss the introduction of a hospital quality improvement program. Their assignment was to construct a flow chart to show the chronological sequence of steps in the conversion to quality management. Time was short. They had just forty-five minutes to get the chart done.

A recorder took notes on a flip chart, as people suggested various steps. Several voices dominated the discussion, which tended to wander off into individual experiences: "At my hospital . . ."

"Let's get on with it. We're losing time," muttered one of the participants, who had barely spoken until then.

The dialogue lost momentum. The team leader, appointed by acclamation, rose impatiently and started to draw the flow chart with quick stabs of a marker. "I think we should . . ."

Now, two people were standing at flip charts. No one was leading the meeting. Silence descended on the group. The leader threw his flow chart on the floor. He laughed as if joking, but he looked tense. The recorder sat down.

No one could argue that the meeting was anything but a shambles. That was no surprise to a man sitting on the sidelines, an HCA consultant leading this workshop on team skills. The reason these people had volunteered for this painful exercise was their belief that up to 90 percent of the time they spent in meetings was wasted. They wanted to learn a different way.

Over the course of the next three days, these workshop participants—hospital administrators, physicians and high-level managers—would hold four additional meetings, gradually incorporating new techniques as they learned them. By the final meeting they had learned to agree in advance on an objective, develop an agenda, set time limits for discussion and critique their meeting. They would be changing positions without yielding their views, listening more and resolving conflicts.

Elsewhere in the building during the same three-day period, another group of HCA managers engaged in W. Edwards Deming's famous "red bead experiment." One by one, four volunteers—"willing workers," Dr. Deming called them—dipped a paddle with fifty holes into a container that held both red beads and white beads as an HCA trainer pretending to be an employer exhorted them to collect only white beads. Her commands were futile, naturally. Red beads in varying numbers always turned up in the count. Performed four times by each of the four volunteers, this exercise made the point that verbal exhortations are futile when workers are saddled with conditions beyond their control. It also demonstrated that variation is inevitable, despite all efforts to the contrary.

These senior HCA employees were in "Q101," HCA's initial three-day course in quality. Q101 covered Deming's Fourteen Points, customer-supplier relations and useful statistical charts. In the final sessions, participants practiced HCA's nine-step process-improvement procedure, which was called FOCUS-PDCA. Graduates of Q101 would go on to the team-skills course—Q102—and others, if they wished, such as Q103—a more advanced course in statistics. In time, HCA would combine all three into a single course, with two consecutive three-day sessions.

So it had gone, month after month since 1987, as the nation's largest hospital chain methodically trained hundreds of hospital executives in the basics of quality. Only after a CEO and his direct reports had attended the Nashville sessions would the HCA Quality Resource Group in headquarters dispatch trainers to do on-site training in hospitals, and then only when the CEO agreed to teach part of the course.

As the '80s drew to a close, this disciplined quality effort had begun to show results for the chain. By 1990, HCA teams were at work on virtually every administrative process from billing to bed assignments to budgeting, and some clinical processes as well. HCA Chairman and CEO Thomas Frist Jr., himself a doctor, had become a fan of total quality and mandated that headquarters begin to form teams. And the quality office had emerged unscathed in a major restructuring that pared down other administrative units.

In the health care field, HCA had long enjoyed a good reputation as a well-managed provider of professional care. Now it was a trail-blazer in the total quality movement. The hospital company's efforts were also a model for the service industry, in which examples of total quality control had been notably lacking.

It might seem odd that HCA, a private money-making chain with a conservative Southern white male–dominated hierarchy, would emerge as an early leader in the quality movement. But as a for-profit operation, the chain lacked the financial cushion of subsidized public hospitals. Thanks to a crisis in the health care industry, there were sound financial reasons for its pursuit of quality.

Hospital Corporation of America was founded in 1968 by three people—father-and-son physicians Thomas Frist Sr. and Thomas Frist Jr., and Jack C. Massey, a Nashville venture capitalist who had pioneered the fast-food market with Kentucky Fried Chicken, but who also had been involved in the hospital business.

Massey, of course, had experience with retail outlets. And Frist Jr. had a college acquaintanceship with Kemmons Wilson, founder of the Holiday Inns. "It made me think about hospitals," Frist once told an interviewer. "Why should there be 7,000 independent hospital companies, like a cottage industry?" In an age when chains of restaurants, hotels and stores were girding America, the three men reasoned, why not hospitals?

Many of the first HCA hospitals were in underserviced rural areas. Tom Frist Jr. was an avid pilot who could go where scheduled airlines did not. A company history says the young doctor undertook "an odyssey of barnstorming airplane flights to spread the word about HCA and its philosophy of hospital management."

The fledgling company grew rapidly. By 1973, HCA owned 51 hospitals with 7,900 beds. In 1977, having acquired a reputation for expertise in both medicine and business, HCA got into hospital management, typically dispatching a CEO and a controller to run what were mostly nonprofit institutions owned by counties, cities and charitable organizations. In 1988 HCA either owned or managed 390 hospitals in 47 states and 8 foreign countries. It also had plunged into diversification. The corporation owned a television station and a data-processing center. It bought into medical supply companies, nursing homes and psychiatric care facilities.

From its entry onto the stock exchange in 1969 and all through the early 1980s, the company posted a continuous record of earnings, with profits in some years as much as 35 percent.

But HCA was changing. In 1987 the younger Frist, now firmly in charge, had begun planning to dismantle the hospital empire he and his father had built. By the mid–1980s, profits were on a downward spiral, owing in large measure to the way the federal government had revamped its costs-plus Medicare payment system. Since 1983, the government had paid fixed prices for each medical procedure—so much for a gall bladder operation or a broken arm, regardless of complications or length of hospital stay. These set prices were assigned for various diagnosis-related groups (DRGs). Unlimited Medicare funds had underwritten much of HCA's growth in the go-go years. Now, the fixed fee payments for DRGs would prompt radical surgery.

But that was just one problem. The words "health care" were now often paired with a third word, "crisis." Runaway costs not only jeopardized the financial health of hospitals but also inflated the total cost of the nation's goods and services. Employee health-care costs added $700 to the cost of a Ford Taurus, but just $200 to a car manufactured in Japan. Dr. Deming saw fit to include "excessive medical costs" as the sixth in his list of the Seven Deadly Diseases afflicting American businesses.

Unlike the crisis in U.S. manufacturing triggered by Japanese competition, the one in health care originated within the industry itself. In 1989, health care expenditures were rising at 12 percent a year while Medicare increased its payment schedule to hospitals by less than 4 percent. Sixty percent of the hospitals in Massachusetts were operating with deficits.

Hospitals were hurting for help. Nursing school enrollments declined by a third between 1983 to 1987, and RNs were deserting the profession in droves for higher-paying, less stressful jobs. The malpractice crisis had not abated, and doctors felt increasingly alienated and maligned. The profession was less and less attractive. Medical school enrollments in 1987 hit a six-year low of fewer than 66,000.

Equally troubling was an acute shortage of medical technicians. A 1988 survey of 7,000 hospitals by the American Hospital Association disclosed that staff shortages had forced 25 percent to cut services— and 15 percent to close altogether.

Meanwhile, payers were seeking ever more rigorous means to keep costs down. But nothing seemed to work. The average cost for employee medical benefits in 1989 rose more than 20.4 percent, to $2,600 per worker—more than four times the inflation rate for the year.

Critics of the health care system could point to its uneven application. Depending on where she lived, the odds on a woman's avoiding a hysterectomy up to age seventy-five ranged from 35 to 75 percent; a Boston resident was three times more likely to undergo bypass surgery than a resident of Hartford. Citing these comparisons, Glenn Laffel, leader of the quality effort at Brigham and Women's Hospital in Boston, observed that "there's extraordinary variation across the system." At the same time, he said, "We are obsessed with trying to show that the performance in our organization conforms to standards."

The public response to health care slipups was to adopt an ever more vigilant regulatory posture. Lamented HCA's quality czar, pediatrician Paul Batalden: "In the state of New York the health commissioner believes that the best way his office can improve care is to engage in a program of surprise inspections. They're wonderfully spectacular media events, because they show up unexpectedly, and then they're always investigating some spectacular thing. I was told that it costs each hospital in New York State that wants to be ready for those inspections about $75,000 a year. So they develop an inspection process to deal with the state health commissioner. . . . It's a stupid way to go about improving care, once you understand a different way. But if you don't understand a different way, it seems like he's just doing his job. He's finding all these problems. Somebody fell out of bed. Nobody checked on something. It's great. It's vintage Americana."

The chief regulatory watchdog was the Joint Commission for the Accreditation of Health Care Organizations, which fielded teams of inspectors to wade through hospital records seeking documentation that hospitals were meeting its standards, spelled out in a 289-page code. Woe to the malingerers, who at worst could lose their accreditation and with it perhaps their eligibility for federal and private reimbursement, not to mention the tidal wave of bad publicity that would follow. That seldom happened, of course, but the prospect produced a state of panic in hospitals for weeks before a Joint Commission visit was due. The standards left much room for discretion to the examiners. Once they received the customary six-weeks notification of a visit, hospitals called other hospitals to gather information on what their particular inspection team had been like—not only where they probed most deeply, which sometimes reflected the specialty of the physician on the team, but also what they liked to eat and do, so that their personal whims could be indulged, hopefully putting them in a good mood. HCA hospitals were in a better position than some, since they could check with headquarters on the experience of sister hospitals in the chain.

The army of regulators produced a siege mentality. A hospital might have as many as four employees churning out the required paperwork. Donald M. Berwick, a physician and executive with the Harvard Community Health Plan, noted that inspection riddled the medical industry as much if not more than any other. Writing in the *New England Journal of Medicine* in January of 1989, he said, "It predominates under the guise of 'buying right,' 'recertification,' or 'deterrence' through litigation. Such an outlook implies or establishes thresholds for acceptability, just as the inspector at the end of an assembly line decided whether to accept or reject finished goods."

In that article, entitled "Continuous Improvement as an Ideal in Health Care," Berwick declared that "practically no system of measurement—at least none that measures people's performance—is robust enough to survive the fear of those who are measured." People play a deadly game to distort data or change measurements. "The signs of this game are everywhere in health care."

The Health Care Financing Administration, for example, published yearly mortality data by hospitals; hospitals, in turn, deluged the agency with thousands of pages of defensive responses. Wrote Berwick, "The same game is being played between aggressive Boards of Registration in Medicine and other regulators that require hospitals and physicians to produce streams of reports on the contents of their closets."

Hospitals and physicians had no choice but to comply. The Joint Commission required, for example, that in every unexplained death there be an attempt to secure an autopsy, duly documented in writing. If that meant asking the family of a ninety-year-old grandmother who had faded away in uncertain fashion to permit an autopsy during this time of grief—and foot the $1,200 or $1,400 bill for it—so be it.

A small industry had sprung up to aid hospitals in complying with the Joint Commission standards, which were not always clear. Hospitals were required to monitor indicators for surgery, for example. A company called InterQual had produced generally accepted criteria for various procedures. In the case of a tonsillectomy, InterQual posited that four episodes of tonsillitis in the preceding twelve months was justification for a tonsillectomy. Doctors who could not document four cases would be subject to review for having performed unwarranted surgery. Of course, once that requirement was made known to physicians, records that once mentioned "several" episodes of tonsillitis suddenly said "four." That was how the system worked.

While there was nothing wrong with measurement per se, Berwick emphasized, it was dangerous to believe "that the assessment and publication of performance data will somehow induce otherwise indolent caregivers to improve the level of their care and efficiency."

Berwick believed that the techniques used to improve quality in manufacturing could also be applied to hospital processes. He was the director of a pioneering 1987 study called the National Demonstration Project on Industrial Quality Control and Health Care Quality that paired twenty-one hospitals with companies such as Xerox Corporation, Corning Glass Works, AT&T, Hewlett-Packard and Ford Motor Company. The industrial experts assisted the hospital teams, with many positive results.

When it came to introducing quality, however, the medical field had certain advantages over other industries. Many of its scientifically trained professionals looked with favor rather than fear on statistical methods. Nor was the notion of continuous improvement foreign to medicine. On the contrary, physicians and others in the health field were continually looking for new advances to improve care. Moreover, people in clinical settings were used to working in teams, albeit ones where the doctor was in charge.

The historically dominant position of doctors in the medical industry did pose a problem. In manufacturing, no equivalent class of individuals had such a privileged status. From medical school on, doctors were trained to be the ultimate arbitrators of patient care; all responsibility rested with them. This training made it difficult for them to give up power. How to persuade doctors to participate in egalitarian team efforts was a major theme in the hospitals' struggle to achieve a quality transformation.

Physicians, for example, had a hard time with the notion of a supplier-customer relationship with underlings in which they were the supplier rather than the customer. Berwick, a pediatrician who had undergone a revelation on this point himself during a four-day Deming seminar, once described to a group of doctors a paperwork exchange with his secretary in which she was the "customer." In order for her to perform her own job well, it was his job to give her the information that she needed in an intelligible state. One of the doctors confided afterward that this was a novel idea. "I always see myself as the customer," he said.

Doctors tend to be strong individuals who dominate their interactions with others, but who seldom behave like members of a larger community. In a sense, Berwick said, they were like a "cottage industry." Total Quality Control, however, with its emphasis on group decision-making, required cooperation among people on an equal footing.

Doctors aside, care of patients did not always lend itself to traditional measurements of outcomes used in manufacturing. In medicine, the results of treatment might not be known for a long time.

But some hospitals were coming around to the view that all these obstacles were not insurmountable. At HCA, Frist was growing concerned that adverse forces in health care not diminish quality, the way they seemed to have done in Great Britain. "It wasn't so much my concern of improving quality as maintaining it, with the new pressures, the new environment in which we were living for the first time. Our world had changed overnight unexpectedly, not just for us but for the whole health care system."

Frist had other reasons for being concerned about quality. HCA was about to undergo a major upheaval, spinning off 100 hospitals to an employee-owned company called HealthTrust. And Frist did not want to open himself up to charges that he was sacrificing quality for profits. In 1986 he hired Paul Batalden to create a quality model for the chain.

Before coming to HCA, Batalden had been a practicing physician and the chief operating officer of a Minneapolis medical group of 280 physicians. In the 1960s, he had been a clinician at the National Cancer Institute, medical director of the federal Job Corps and, finally, director of the Community Health Service, which oversaw neighborhood health centers, migrant farm-worker activities and the Appalachian Regional Health Commission. CHS was also the agency that set standards in those days for Medicare and Medicaid.

In 1980, Batalden was one of many people whose world changed because of W. Edwards Deming. That was the year Deming was prominently featured on the NBC special "If Japan Can . . . Why Can't We?" Millions of Americans learned that the father of the Japanese quality movement was actually an American.

For all their vaunted success in manufacturing with TQC (Total Quality Control), the Japanese had not applied the same strategies to health care. In 1990, according to Dr. Kozi Morooka of Tokai University, a reported 60 percent of Japanese hospitals, which were headed by physicians, faced bankruptcy. The average hospital stay for surgery was thirty days, compared to six in the United States.

Batalden subsequently read an interview in which Deming talked about how people wanted to do their best, but that systems got in the way. Deming also talked about meeting the needs of customers. The quality expert's remarks struck "two resonant chords" for the Minneapolis physician. "It was a new way of thinking about the workplace." Batalden read Deming's book *Quality, Productivity and Competitive Position,* attended a four-day seminar in Atlanta and developed a medical version of the Fourteen Points that Deming would include in the book he was writing at the time, *Out of the Crisis.*

Batalden saw a "paradigm shift" in health care that "required a profound commitment to the customer." In an earlier "Samaritan" era of treatment, when technology was nonexistent, practitioners cared for people as best they could. Then, beginning in the mid–1700s, medicine came to be dominated by scientific diagnoses and treatments. In the decade of the 1980s, there was—for want of a better word—"social accountability." The idea of "caring" never faded away. Indeed many hospitals made it their marketing pitch. But increasingly the new measure was scientific treatment at best value.

As the Deming philosophy germinated in the years that followed, Batalden began to search for a way to develop a quality model for health care with the aid of a small interdisciplinary group of colleagues. But neither universities nor public agencies seemed to have the resources or the inclination to experiment.

Enter Tom Frist. Frist, however, was not prepared to hire Batalden without doing some research on the Deming philosophy. Through membership in industry groups, he knew the CEOs of companies such as General Motors, Ford, Xerox and Monsanto, and what they told him was that they believed Deming had something to offer.

"They all to the person said, 'Yes, there's a practical aspect to it.' " But Frist still had reservations. He was talking to people from "smokestack America." To himself, he said, "That's fine for manufacturing, but how in the world are we going to do this in the service sector?"

Frist hired Batalden with the proviso that he launch the effort in a handful of hospitals. "Pick seven or eight hospitals. Let it prove itself." What he had in mind, he would later say, was "not so much prove it to them as prove it to me."

Frist was aware that he and his new quality czar did not quite see eye to eye. "Paul will tell you that the responsibility starts at the top—chairman and CEO. That's nice, that's wonderful to say that. I don't know any chairman and CEO who wouldn't agree with that. On the other hand, they would tell you, they've got a thousand other pressures on them, and if they don't have able staff there to keep them focused, to bring them back, it would be lost."

Among Frist's other concerns at the moment, of course, was the restructuring of HCA. As the corporation shrunk, management sought to reduce corporate overhead by 50 percent. "Each department," Frist said, "had to stand the rigorous process of scrutiny: whether it brought value to the table." At that point, he decided not to reduce the quality commitment, primarily for "psychological and cosmetic reasons." Frist didn't want to open up HCA to accusations that the company was being driven by the profit motive at the expense of quality. "You have to be very careful what kind of message you send." And he was also concerned that employees would regard the quality initiative as just another fly-by-night program, of which HCA had had its share. Frist was still slightly embarrassed about a highly touted but short-lived "chaplaincy" program. That, too, had been designed to prove the chain was concerned about more than just money by assigning a chaplain to each hospital.

In 1988, Frist engineered a leveraged buy-out of the company he had founded, which now numbered 270 medical/surgical hospitals—79 of which it owned and another 191 that were managed by what was now a separate company, HCA Management—plus 50 psychiatric hospitals. The firm was concentrated in the South. Fifty-six of the owned hospitals were in Florida, Georgia, Tennessee, Texas and Virginia. Two layers were sheared off at the management level, so that hospital administrators now reported directly to a group president who reported to Frist himself. Four regional group presidents replaced twelve regional division heads.

To buy the company back and take it public, Frist had assumed a huge debt burden. Once again each headquarters operation underwent scrutiny for possible savings. And once again the Quality Resources Group was spared the scalpel. But this time the reasons were more than cosmetic. By now a track record showed that hospitals involved in quality improvement were making significant gains. Frist was especially impressed with the way a regional effort in Florida had enabled the company to meet its five-year quota for purchases from its chief supplier, Baxter Health Care Corporation, earning a $50-million rebate.

Things like that made Frist a believer. He was even using the new quality language. When it came time to decide the budgetary fate of the quality office, he said afterward, "We asked the customers—not the patients, but the hospitals, department heads, doctors. I sent staff out as well as inquiring myself. Many of the senior members of management were surprised by what they heard." The hospitals wanted more, not less, support for quality. "We found out, not only could we afford to have it, we couldn't afford not to have it." Batalden's office got more money, not less. Its budget of $2 million did not even include the money the hospital themselves spent. The costs of training and staff came out of their budget and not headquarters'.

The Quality Resource Group was staffed with a statistician, whose job was to simplify statistical concepts for use in the hospitals, a writer to disseminate information, a marketing expert to develop information on customers and a medical peer-review director to help bring physicians into the process. Batalden's job, as he saw it, "was to try to knit all this together and nurse it along."

Just as Florida Power & Light several years earlier had searched for a "shelf-ready model," in 1986 Batalden looked to "see who had this developed, a way to help us make this happen." He himself had difficulty trying to figure out how to proceed. Because health care seemed so different, on the surface, from manufacturing, "it was hard to conceptualize. There was no simple way to do it."

FPL had a training arm called QualTec in West Palm Beach. The University of Tennessee offered classes in statistical quality control. And there were other training outfits, some either expensive, hacks or both. But no one had a track record in health care.

Finally, Batalden reached the same conclusion as FPL years earlier: The hospital chain would have to come up with its own strategy and training. By the end of 1986, the first courses had been designed.

The HCA model called for hospital CEOs to designate a chief facilitator called a "coach" and for both to undergo the Q101 and Q102 training in the Deming philosophy, process improvement and team skills. Each participating hospital was assigned a mentor from headquarters to offer guidance and gentle nudging. Batalden would mentor the first hospitals on board. As HCA trainers became more skilled, and the hospitals more numerous, they would take on that role.

Only after the CEO had been trained would other high-level managers be invited to attend. And only then would HCA conduct on-site training for middle managers. When that happened, the CEO was required to teach part of the course. "No exceptions," Batalden said. The CEO and his top management would constitute the hospital's Quality Improvement Council, which would charter and monitor teams.

"It's very purposeful on our part to not make it so readily available," said Batalden, explaining the reasoning that went into developing the model. The CEOs "have some work to do and they don't like that. It's a very conscious adult education strategy. They say 'You mean I actually have to learn this stuff?' They don't just turn the key and these quality educators come in. They have to go through this learning process and their senior leadership has to go through this learning process and then they have to work on the formulation of the quality policy of that organization—what its mission statement is, what it means by quality, what kind of guidelines or principles they're going to use. And then they have to practice some of this." The process was laid out on a "roadmap" for hospitals to follow. (See p. 97.)

The planners at headquarters also had to make sure that the

training was affordable. Each hospital paid the course fee, plus expenses, per participant.

No hospital would be compelled to enroll. HCA traditionally allowed its administrators a great deal of autonomy. To do otherwise in this case would not be consistent with the corporate culture. Moreover, so much commitment was involved in the transformation, Batalden said, that "I knew anything less than volunteers wouldn't survive. Nobody can be ordered to do this. It has to be made attractive."

Just as Frist had once barnstormed for new hospitals, Batalden made the rounds of the HCA institutions to drum up business.

II. WEST PACES FERRY HOSPITAL: SEEKING PATIENCE

Chip Caldwell, the tall, soft-spoken CEO of West Paces Ferry Hospital in a well-to-do section of Atlanta, stepped to the front of a classroom filled with new employees and introduced himself. Then he posed a question.

Who in the group, he asked, had ever heard of W. Edwards Deming? Blank faces greeted the question. No hands went up. How many in the group could recite the mission statement of any company where they had worked? Caldwell did only slightly better: One person raised a hand.

In the next hour and a half, Caldwell identified Deming and shared West Paces' mission statement with them. He told how hospital teams were laboring with some success to cut down on unnecessary cesarean sections, invoice discrepancies in purchasing and antibiotic waste. He pointed out an enormous flow chart displayed on one wall—the work of a team on food service that had discovered there were "twenty-two different ways that a patient gets a Coke at West Paces' Hospital." (Atlanta was, of course, the home of Coca-Cola.) Caldwell's conclusion? "It would be a lot cheaper if we just gave everybody a six-pack."

Teams, the West Paces CEO said, were for everyone. One team trying to expedite the delivery of medications recruited a maintenance man when it discovered the seventeen-year-old pneumatic tube system had never worked correctly. "The problem now is that too many people want to be on a team, and there are too few teams."

HOSPITALWIDE QUALITY IMPROVEMENT ROADMAP

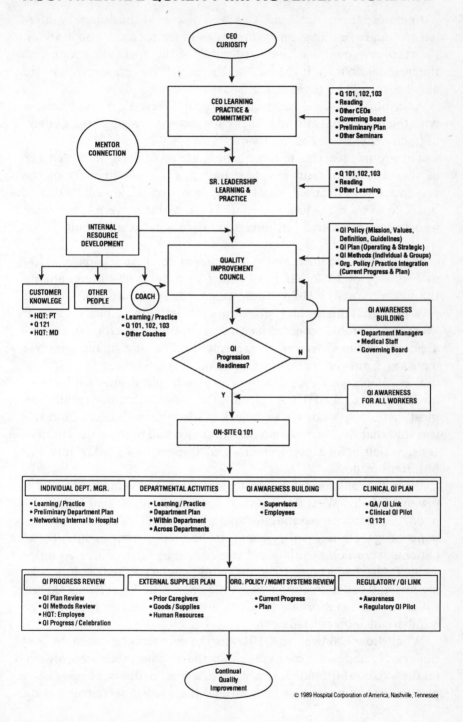

© 1989 Hospital Corporation of America, Nashville, Tennessee

In a more theoretical vein, Caldwell discussed the notion of internal customers, citing as an example a gall-bladder operation in which the recovery room was the "customer" of the operating room, and the medical floor, in turn, the "customer" of the recovery room. He also broached the topic of statistical tools.

As a hospital, Caldwell told the group, West Paces had broken with the traditional attitude "that patients never existed before entering and ceased to exist afterward."

The group's reaction to this quality blitz was mixed. In one corner of the classroom a drowsy new hire dozed through most of the presentation. Enthused, another approached Caldwell during a break to ask for reading material. The remainder were somewhere in between, interested but uncertain as to what it all meant.

When Paul Batalden and others taught the first session of Q101 in February of 1987, Charles ("Chip") Caldwell was there, among the first recruits to HCA's new quality drive. It was not financial pressures that made him susceptible to Batalden's pitch. Indeed, West Paces profits reflected its location in the prosperous Buckhead area, where the Governor of Georgia dwelled in a plantation-style mansion. Caldwell had come there from a small hospital in Florida.

West Paces was founded by a group of physicians who subsequently approached HCA to take them over. Architecturally, its most distinctive feature was its lack of distinction. Indeed, Caldwell was told that the hospital had been designed and built by the Holiday Inns, which at one point entertained thoughts of getting into the hospital business.

With 294 beds on its main site, and 60 in a psychiatric facility a few miles away, West Paces served not only its immediate neighborhood, but it also served the client population of a large health maintenance organization with whom it had an arrangement. These patients were not wealthy, and came from as far as 50 or 60 miles away. It also had a competitor that could not be ignored, a bluestocking hospital called Piedmont, with 425 beds. Still, West Paces did not suffer the financial pressures of inner-city hospitals with their large numbers of indigent patients.

What drew Caldwell to Q101 was the emphasis he heard on customers. He had never cared much for the way hospitals were always on the lookout for faddish new ways to attract patients. Seeking new, profitable treatments, hospitals around the country were trumpeting their clinics for sleep disorders, depression, addictions and weight loss. Critics called it the "disease-of-the-week" approach or "boutique medicine." In an industry where salt was once regarded as a much-prized amenity, valet parking, luxury rooms and gourmet menus were becoming commonplace. Gone was any hesitation to advertise in newspapers or on television.

Complained the West Paces CEO, "I'm always getting all this pressure from my staff to spend more money on advertising. It just doesn't make sense to me. It doesn't feel right. Why is it we advertise all this garbage, when we haven't the faintest idea if anybody wants it?"

Batalden offered an alternative to the marketing wars that were costing the hospital industry more than $1 billion a year. What he said was, as Caldwell remembered it, " 'We're going to design our services based on needs and expectations of customers, we're going to put it into service, we're going to measure it against those expectations, we're going to repeat the cycle again." When Caldwell heard that, "My thought was, what a wonderful integration between marketing and operations. We're going to make a better product . . . make a better meal delivery system . . . make a better admissions process . . . make a better emergency room process, and once you've done that, ask again, how can we improve? So I saw it really as more of a marketing thing."

When Caldwell returned from his first session of Q101, he dispatched his ten direct reports.

Their reaction to the course was mixed. "Twenty-five percent became champions, twenty-five percent skeptics, and the others just sort of hid out." Caldwell grew to appreciate the skeptics. "A lot of times when I talk to an audience about rolling this thing out, people ask about skeptics, and it's always in a negative way. But I think the skeptics help bring the champions back to reality. I need that. I can get off on a target very quickly."

In time, several of the disbelievers would leave of their own volition, uncomfortable with the new way of doing things.

Once his managers were trained, they formed a seven-member quality improvement council, consisting of Caldwell, an associate administrator, two assistant administrators, the chief financial officer, the executive assistant and the coach, Vicki Davis.

Davis, who had formerly been materials manager, was not Caldwell's original choice for the position of coach. After taking Q101, he had appointed another manager who worked part-time during the six months when the hospital was just beginning its quality movement. But that first part-time coach was unwilling to give up his other job to work full-time on the quality transformation. In retrospect, Caldwell said he had moved too quickly in that and other respects. Batalden had cautioned him to wait for "the cream to rise to the top" before making hasty decisions. But Caldwell had been eager to get on with things. Now he realized it would have been better to wait than to rescind such a key appointment.

In June of 1988, Paul Batalden and other members of HCA's Quality Resource Group conducted West Paces Ferry's on-site training for several dozen department managers. In addition to learning the FOCUS-PDCA process, the trainees brainstormed words that could be incorporated in a quality statement. Caldwell drafted the statement. This was the final version:

"At HCA West Paces Ferry Hospital, achieving quality means adding value to all that we do through a commitment to the continuous improvement of services that meet the needs and expectations of our patients, physicians, payers, employees and the community we serve."

In the next year and a half, West Paces launched twenty-two teams. Eight were cross-functional, spanning different departments. Eleven were centered in single departments. And three dealt with clinical processes. Thanks to Caldwell's early involvement, West Paces became the hospital where visitors from other hospitals inside and outside the chain were steered for inspiration.

What they saw immediately was a CEO who had in small and not-so-small—but always very visible—ways devoted himself to spreading the word.

On his way out to lunch one day, for example, Caldwell took a detour through the hospital emergency room. The reason: "Sometimes our ER nurses are not as friendly as they should be, and I make it a point to cheer them up."

Another day, he presided over a presentation by four of the hospital's Quality Improvement Teams, held monthly in the cafeteria. He was not happy that almost none of the department heads had turned up. "I ask them to come if only for ten minutes. I think it means a lot to the people presenting to have the leadership of the hospital here." Still, he did not plan to make attendance mandatory. Sooner or later, he hoped, they would understand how important it was to put in an appearance.

And once every two weeks on average, Caldwell taught the ninety-minute quality segment of new employee orientation, galloping through a summary of Deming's Fourteen Points, describing how teams worked at West Paces and touching on the notion of internal customers.

Caldwell first delivered this capsule version of Q101 to some 600 West Paces staffers on all shifts. "I came in on Sundays, I did them from the crack of dawn to late at night." He began to burn out. But when he appealed to the new quality improvement council for some help, they turned him down. "It took them all of three minutes to vote that it was just the right thing to do." So he kept on going.

Later, he could see that they were right. "If the administrator is visible in it, then the organization from bottom to top will understand its importance. If the administrator's nowhere to be seen, it's not going to be considered a high priority for the organization."

West Paces' first team had been the "nourishment team" that constructed the enormous flow chart on food delivery, including Coke. Later, this would be seen as a largely unsuccessful practice effort. But soon other teams enjoyed more success.

A team working to reduce turnaround time in the operating room—the "Tator" team—focused on the amount of time consumed by the admission process. A flow chart showed that a patient was asked for substantially the same information by three different people. The bulk of the delays, however, were created by tests on patients that could be performed on another day. Based on the team's recommendations, the hospital increased its preadmission rate—those people who came in on a prior day for tests—from 17 percent in August 1988 to 73 percent in July 1989.

Another team decreased waste of IV medication by 44.5 percent, resulting in a potential savings of $22,755 per year. And a third team seeking to reduce delays on stat medications—ones that weren't administered on a regular schedule—decreased the number of unnecessary trips to the pharmacy by 79.5 percent.

An "appearance" team recommended a schedule for painting and repairing walls in patients' rooms, with wall washing done on a regular basis, and the hiring of two new painters to handle the additional work.

Meanwhile, back at HCA headquarters, the Quality Resources Group was developing a set of surveys that would aid its hospitals in the quality transformation. These were called the Hospital Quality Trends system—HQT—and they were quite unlike any the hospitals had used before.

For one thing, there were four of them: for patients, physicians, employees and payers. For another, the surveys gave very detailed information. The physicians survey, for example, had 118 questions, plus verbatim comments, covering such categories as doctors' perception of the hospital's image in the community and their opinion on the quality of its nursing staff and administration and on how it scheduled patients. When the results came back, the answers were broken down by physicians' specialties and by the frequency with which they used the hospital. The patient surveys were broken down by age, education, form of payment and unit where they were lodged.

Typically, hospitals sent out questionnaires to patients after they had been discharged. The HQT survey differed in that there was a broader sampling base, and follow-up with telephone queries when patients didn't respond. The data from the survey highlighted areas for improvement, but it was still not fresh enough for changing trends. At West Paces, Sandra Walczak, assistant administrator for marketing, developed an even more detailed patient questionnaire as a supplement.

West Paces had not previously done a physician survey, but the information gathered from it was clearly just as important as that from patients. Doctors were the "gatekeepers," the people who made decisions about which hospital to use for their patients more often than patients themselves did.

After receiving the results of the first surveys of patients and physicians, the West Paces quality improvement council set out to develop a set of goals or indicators for the hospital—their version of policy deployment used by Florida Power & Light.

Some survey questions had used the phrasing "brag about." For example, physicians were asked to "Brag about nursing: Extent to which the medical staff is prepared to brag about nursing at this hospital." There were six possible answers, from "not observed" to "excellent."

The hospital used the "brag about" phrasing in setting forth its list of fourteen indicators. For example, the statement "A physician brags about West Paces Ferry when . . ." was followed by certain indicators: "scheduling needs are met; nurses are responsive, informing and accessible; state-of-the-art equipment is available." Or "A patient brags about West Paces Ferry when . . ." was followed by these indicators: "the expected clinical outcome is achieved; living arrangement needs are met; admission procedures are understandable, quick and efficient." Departments in the hospital were asked to relate their activities to the fourteen indicators.

Other hospitals owned by or affiliated with HCA were also hard at work. Here are just a few examples from a November 1989 compendium:

—At Glover Memorial Hospital in Needham, Massachusetts, a management team led by the marketing director developed criteria and a request form for capital expenditures where none had existed before. Equally if not more important, the team also developed a long-range capital plan that set forth priorities and a procedure for monitoring purchases. In the past, the team said, the process had been "short-sighted, arbitrary, uncontrolled and without standardization." Another Glover team working in a different area had targeted the lost-and-found storage system for improvement, to stem the tide of patients' possessions that were being lost or broken.

—Midlands Community Hospital in Papillon, Nebraska, had teams working to arrange supplies so that nurses could find them; to revise time cards so they would be more accurate; to make certain that conference rooms, audiovisual equipment and refreshments would be available when meetings were scheduled and that the furniture was properly arranged. Said the team: "The current process is confusing, time-consuming, labor-intensive and ineffective."

—A number of hospitals had targeted the admission process, which in many hospitals seemed to break down at the point of locating a bed and transferring the patient. HCA Portsmouth Regional Hospital in New Hampshire was working on delays in admitting patients from the emergency room. In its flowcharting, City Hospital in Martinsburg, West Virginia, had identified seventeen persons or departments contributing to preadmission testing alone.

—At HCA Wesley Medical Center in Wichita, Kansas, a team

assigned to outpatient registration under the director of admissions had revised forms, rescheduled the receptionist for peak hours and established the order in which to call patients.

—HCA Lawnwood Regional Medical Center in Fort Pierce, Florida, was working on room assignments. Greater Laurel Beltsville Hospital in Maryland was piloting a multi-copy discharge form that would notify admitting, the cashier and the pharmacy when a patient was leaving, in order to maintain an accurate bed count and to arrange payment. After several modifications of the form, the hospital found the departments were being notified 95 percent of the time, up from 25 percent when their team began its data collection.

—At HCA North Florida Regional Medical Center in Gainesville, where teams delighted in selecting names, one called "Rambo" decided to develop a policy for dealing with potentially violent situations. Another named "Hot Wheels" zeroed in on a chronic shortage of wheelchairs and stretchers. It conducted a "round-up" of stretchers to clean, label and inventory them, as well as to check them for repair or replacement of IV poles, rails, mattress pads and patient-belongings baskets. After also looking at ways to store and distribute oxygen, the team realized the staff needed in-service training on the proper use of tanks and regulators.

In social services a third team, which selected lost calls to staffers as a process to improve, conducted a survey that disclosed the surprising information that there were, in fact, very few lost calls. A subsequent survey of regular callers revealed that they had not noticed a problem. What appeared to be the case was that conscientious social workers had overreacted to the few calls that were, in fact, lost. "Very surprising to team and happy that internal problem only perceived by in-hospital staff," the team leader reported. Nevertheless, a new beeper procedure was introduced to make it easier for social workers to get and return calls.

—At Tuomey Regional Medical Center in Sumter, South Carolina, a "potty chair" team planned to make sure that clean commode chairs were available for each patient.

—A team at Parkview Episcopal Medical Center in Pueblo, Colorado, realized computers were proliferating with no standards for avoiding duplication of purchases, maintenance, training and usage. Another Parkview team was attempting to redress problems in the distribution of payroll checks.

Hospital food service was another promising area for the quality transformation. Patient surveys frequently disclosed that patients were unhappy with food service.

—At Portsmouth Regional, complaints about items missing from trays diverted nurses and the dietary department from other tasks while hungry patients grew irritated. A team's first step was to collect data on whether patients forgot to write down the items on their menu or whether dietary workers inadvertently forgot them.

—A team at HCA West Florida Regional Medical Center in Pensacola, where patients frequently complained their food was cold, found that nurses were often busy with a variety of tasks when the trays arrived, particularly during the breakfast hour. Changing the time and sequence of delivery resulted in a decrease from thirteen to five minutes from the trays' arrival on the unit to their delivery at bedside.

—At Brazosport Memorial Hospital in Lake Jackson, Texas, food preparation for special hospital functions often hit snags. A team's initial solution was to post a notice of such functions on a bulletin calendar so employees could plan their schedules accordingly.

Among clinical processes, the use of IVs—a prime source of infection and discomfort for patients—attracted the efforts of teams at Portsmouth, Greater Laurel Beltsville and North Florida Regional. A Portsmouth radiology group wanted to reduce the need to repeat chest X rays. A North Florida Regional team from the transcribing unit sought ways to make sure X-ray reports got to their destination within three hours after dictation; at Brazosport, it was the timely charting of lab reports that was targeted for improvement.

Supplies came in for close scrutiny at many hospitals.

—A team working under the materials manager at Portsmouth found that nursing carts on the surgical unit contained 36 items that had not been used over a 120-day period. At the same time, the carts often ran out of crucial supplies, prompting many time-consuming trips for more. Space on the carts was at a premium. Therefore, the team decided that all items not used in 60 days should be stored. Teams in several hospitals were working on problems with representatives from Baxter Health Care Corporation, which supplied the chain through contracts negotiated by HCA headquarters.

Other brave quality teams tackled processes dealing with payers. A half dozen hospitals were looking at their billing procedures. Four were seeking to decrease emergency-room delays. Employee orientation, suggestions, recruitment and turnover were other issues being explored. There was, in short, no shortage of things to work on, no area that would not benefit by improvement.

Three times each year coaches from HCA-affiliated hospitals met for two days to share their experiences and learn new skills. CEOs joined them at two of the meetings.

In the beginning, when only a handful of hospitals were involved in the quality movement, these meetings were tiny. But as word spread of successes, and it became clear that HCA headquarters looked with favor on the effort, more and more administrators saw fit to involve their hospitals. A 1989 meeting drew more than 100 coaches, CEOs and other HCA staffers to a woodsy conference center outside Atlanta to both formal and informal meetings on quality. That a morning-long session on the intricacies of flowcharting was well attended showed just how dedicated attendees were to process improvement. Flowcharting had proved to be a highly useful tool, perhaps more so in the service industry than in manufacturing because service processes often were less visual and it was thus helpful to trace them on paper. Many hospitals were now two years into the quality process, with experiences to share that could be helpful to others.

At a session for CEOs, there was a lively give-and-take on the subject of teams. John Kausch, administrator of HCA West Florida Regional Hospital, urged his colleagues to "avoid cross-functional teams at almost any cost early on. They're just so much more complicated to manage. I was frankly very surprised at the types of dynamics that went on between department heads that I thought were totally cooperative with each other."

Glover CEO Frank Niro agreed. "I think single-department teams are an accelerator. People learn best by doing. People also learn better, I think, in an environment where they're comfortable. When people are engaged in a team looking at a process with people they're always working with in that process, they tend to be more comfortable and more productive and get practice and then our experience has been they then seem to be ready to work on something with people from another department."

Others disagreed, saying that cross-functional teams played a useful role in breaking down barriers between traditionally hostile departments. One said they worked best where there was widespread recognition that a given process needed fixing.

Several talked about how hard they had worked to build understanding of the new quality philosophy from the top down. Said John Trezona, head of HCA Lawnwood Medical Center in Fort Pierce, Florida, "It was almost a year to the date from the time that I was first introduced, born again, etcetera, until we rolled it out to our management team. But it's not that we didn't do anything in between. We had monthly meetings where we began introducing various parts of the philosophy of the quality improvement process to our management team—meaning all the department heads, head nurses, major supervisory posts."

Trezona's quality improvement council assigned itself reading, watched videos and talked about Deming and the Fourteen Points. "At the next session, we had little quizzes, like 'My favorite of the Fourteen Points of Deming's is . . .' They had to fill in the blank . . . they got scared to death."

There were other exercises. " 'I *will* learn more about this new philosophy—true or false.' " Or the multiple-choice question: " 'Dr. Deming is (a) the new medical director of the psychiatric hospital; (b) a cardiovascular surgeon; (c) a genius who revolutionized Japanese industry following World War II.' " In short, Lawnwood didn't take itself too seriously to have some fun with educating its staff.

But there *was* a serious side to the levity. "It was a great opportunity to break down the barriers, open up the lines of communication that had really not been explored before." People from different departments were deliberately seated next to each other.

Lawnwood held its training offsite because, Trezona said, it was "really important to show the commitment that you can put your beepers away—you're not paged away from the session."

Although he wouldn't do it differently now, he said moving slowly was at times difficult because people were so excited and eager to get started.

HCA Wesley Medical Center in Wichita was also going slow, spending a great deal of time drawing up a set of "guiding principles." The discussion had moved from top management to the departmental level, where a debate was taking place over such apparent inconsistencies as the performance appraisal system. "Basically," said administrator Jim Biltz, "I said, 'This is what we believe in and if we don't follow it, you need to ask why.' Well, now they're asking why."

William Corley, president of Community Hospitals in Indianapolis, recalled how a medical student had once told him that surgeons learn to "See one. Do one. Teach one." In the same fashion, he thought it was helpful for a manager to see quality at work in another hospital, or even industry, then to be on a task team and finally to teach. Not that the HCA model permitted the CEO any choice on that matter. Nevertheless, he thought it was, in Paul Batalden's terms, a "major accelerator." There was, he said, "nothing quite like being up in front of your entire administrative staff just petrified, saying 'Oh, gosh, I hope they don't ask me a question about this.'"

It was also important, Corley said, to make sure "that you had true knowledge and excitement in the level of top management before you went to the department director." And so on down the line. "That anchoring is crucial."

At the last minute, the man who was to be the chief speaker at the Atlanta conference sent his regrets. HCA chairman Tom Frist was ·tied up in financial negotiations over the chain's psychiatric hospitals. Some participants were disappointed at what they saw as a lack of commitment.

Frist said otherwise. In an interview several weeks later, he struggled for an analogy to describe his role. "It's a little bit different from maybe some of the stories where you see a chairman and CEO who says 'Gosh, this is something we've got to do' and all the sheep fall into line." In this case, he said, the sheep fell first, meaning the hospitals, "dragging the shepherd along.

"But I can tell you I've been in fifty-one hospitals in the last six months. And I've visited with the administration, employees and clinical staff. And I could see the difference in those institutions that had implemented the program. And I could see a difference in the institutions depending on what stage in the implementation they were in. And I have yet to find a hospital where we tried this and it didn't work and they said 'It's not for us.'"

III. QUALITY STORIES

The core of HCA's quality improvement methodology was a nine-step process-improvement method called FOCUS-PDCA. HCA training emphasized the need to improve processes rather than to undertake improvement "projects" with mere problem-solving methods. Process improvement was viewed as both broad and never-ending. It would involve problem-solving, but problem-solving alone might not improve the process. Indeed, problem-solving could have adverse effects on some departments, solving one group's problem while creating havoc for others. Process improvement never did.

To make an analogy, process improvement was like the holistic approach to medical care. For a patient with multiple problems, one doctor's "cure" could be another's bane. It was important to treat the entire patient, not simply one organ or one set of symptoms.

FOCUS-PDCA was an acronym with the following meaning:

—Find a process to improve
—Organize a team that knows the process
—Clarify current knowledge of the process
—Understand causes of process variation
—Select the process improvement
—Plan the improvement and continue data collection
—Do the improvement, data collection and analysis
—Check the results and lessons learned from the team effort
—Act to hold the gain and to continue to improve the process

The final four steps were, of course, the PDCA Cycle.

A process was defined as "a series of actions which repeatedly come together to transform inputs provided by a supplier into ouputs received by a customer." It consisted, then, of the following chain:

Suppliers→Inputs→Actions→Outputs→Customer→Outcome

Usually each process had an owner. The owner was the person who had "responsibility and authority to continually improve the inputs, actions and outputs of the process."

In selecting a process to improve—the beginning "F" step—team members were asked to write a simple statement describing the process, its owner, how suppliers and customers fit into the process and why it represented an opportunity for improvement within the context of the hospital's quality objectives. This was called an "opportunity statement."

Because processes were long chains of interactions, teams chosen in the "O" step would in the "C" step put "boundaries" on that part of the process with which they would concern themselves. With rare exceptions, this involved flowcharting the current process. Often at this stage team members saw duplication and other forms of waste. And just as often facilitators would have to deter them at this point from immediately trying to "solve the problem." Sometimes that proved impossible, and the team would plunge ahead, only to discover it had acted in a shortsighted fashion. In cases where it was, in fact, appropriate to introduce a solution, the PDCA Cycle still applied.

In the "U" step, the team needed to describe the customer's needs and expectations. How well the process satisfied those needs and expectations were the outcomes, and how they were measured were those points on which the team could collect data in the "U" stage. HCA called them "key quality characteristics." In this stage run charts, control charts and cause-and-effect diagrams were all useful.

Finally, in the "S" stage, the team would select the change, then follow it through the Plan-Do-Check-Act sequence.

At West Paces Ferry Hospital, the administration applied four mandatory criteria before giving a team the go-ahead to improve a process.

—The improvement had to support a set of hospital objectives determined by the surveys.

—It had to be process-related.

—The improvement had to be measurable.

—The team had to fill out a "blueprint" describing how the preceding three conditions had been satisfied and submit it to the Quality Improvement Council for review.

Only after the blueprint was reviewed and approved would the Quality Improvement Council select a team leader and a facilitator to undertake FOCUS-PDCA.

The following two cases from West Paces illustrate FOCUS-PDCA in practice.

The GMT Story

It would come as no surprise in West Paces' first HQT: Physician Survey that doctors were not very happy with the quality of nursing care. Earlier, in a remark circulated among hospital executives, one doctor had commented that he seldom saw the same faces twice. And he was right. Owing to a severe nursing shortage, West Paces, like many hospitals, relied heavily on the use of temporary nurses hired through an employment agency.

If doctors weren't happy, neither were nurses. Many had left hospitals for better-paying jobs with less stress. Nursing school enrollments were down. That was one reason for a statewide shortage of 3,000 in 1988. The profession had a bad image that discouraged recruits.

In April of 1987, the West Paces Ferry Quality Improvement Council used its new blueprint procedure to charter its first team, one composed initially of four nurses, to look at the shortage. Later the team grew in size.

The nurses' team drafted the following opportunity statement: "The objective is to assure optimal levels of patient care, and to meet the needs of all customers at the most reasonable cost through the continuous improvement of the patient care delivery system through: enhancement of utilization of the clinical skills of the RN; enhancement of utilization of support personnel; decreased agency utilization; enhancement of recruitment and retention."

In plain English, that meant that its objective was to make maximum use of its staff RNs' clinical skills, to employ fewer agency nurses and to improve the recruitment and retention of staff nurses. Improvement would be measured by whether physicians admitted more patients or more patients chose on their own to come to West Paces; and whether there were fewer agency nurses and more satisfaction among patients, physicians and employees.

As in many hospitals today, at West Paces the nurse looked after all the needs of the patient to whom she was assigned. Many of her chores not only were routine ones such as feeding and dressing patients, checking blood pressures and other vital signs, but they also were not among those that the law dictated only a nurse could perform.

"Everything done for the patients—you did it," explained Lorri Parker, a young night nurse and team member. "If they needed a bath you did it. If they needed a Coke, you went down and got it, and on three-to-eleven shift you did transportation." It wasn't so much that she or others objected to the menial work. On the contrary, they were caregivers by inclination and took pride in making their patients feel good. But often there was too much to do in too little time. "It was very hard to organize your time," Parker explained. "These things just came up and you felt like you were always being pulled."

In the "C" step, the team summarized the overall situation, On a national level the nursing shortage had risen from 4.4 percent in 1983 to 11.3 percent in 1987. On the state level, the shortage was even greater, 13.8 percent; and at West Paces Ferry, greater still, with an 18.8 percent shortage, representing 65 unfilled positions. As at other hospitals, the slack was taken up for the most part by agency nurses.

Agency nurses posed problems. Explained Parker, "They're not familiar with your facility, policies and procedures. It can be okay if they're here for awhile or not afraid to ask questions. But usually they're basically here for their eight hours. If you have a problem, it's hard to track them down. The rest of us working here, we're going to be back tomorrow."

In the "U" step, the team undertook a detailed study of how nurses spent their time, asking them to keep a checklist of how many times they fed patients, set up meal trays and took vital signs. They discovered that a full 44 percent of the time nurses were doing things someone else with less training could do instead.

Who should that person be? The West Paces team was certainly not the first to recognize the problem. The American Medical Association had already developed parameters for a "registered care technologist." Nurses didn't like that idea, because it meant the RCT would be responsible to a physician who was seldom there. They didn't believe it fit in with the nursing hierarchy.

In the "S" step, the West Paces team recommended instead a nurses' helper, later to be known as a "general medical technician," who would attend a training program the team would help develop after settling on a job description.

Not long afterward, a course was developed in conjunction with an Atlanta career college. Taught by nurses, it was offered for the first time in 1988. Students spent four months in the classroom and two at the hospital as interns. Studies had shown that many nurses dropped out after discovering that they did not like nursing as well as they thought they would. The course would allow young people to explore nursing as a profession. "I thought six months would give me a start to see what it was like," said Kim Wendelboe, a twenty-year-old GMT on Lorri Parker's floor. After all, she noted, "I'd never been a patient."

Seventeen of the course's first thirty graduates went to work at West Paces. To accommodate them, the team redesigned the organizational structure. Each patient would have a case manager—a senior RN responsible for twelve patients. The case manager would supervise two other nurses, who divided the caseload in half. A GMT would work with the team. Thus, a single patient would now be attended by two nurses and a GMT.

Patients were not the only ones to benefit from the restructuring. There was an immediate 50-percent reduction in nonclinical work by RNs (although they still filled in when a GMT was not available). In July of 1989 the hospital spent $7,800 on agency nurses, compared to $11,000 a year earlier. That same month there were just six nursing vacancies, compared to nineteen some eight months earlier. These results were dutifully recorded in the second "C" stage. And in "A," the new system was extended from the first pilot nursing floor to other areas of the hospital.

Not everyone applauded the change. Some nurses missed being their patients' sole caregiver. The revised system meant yielding trust to the new GMTs. There was, Lorri Parker said, the idea that "no one can do it as well as I can."

She thought that physicians liked the system better because now it was easier to find the person in charge of their patients. "I don't think they understand why, but there aren't as many complaints as there used to be. They look for us rather than having to run around to find out who is this patient's nurse. They would call to ask a question or leave an order. If you didn't get there fast enough they'd hang up. Now there are two people they can reach."

The team did not plan to disband. Their survey had disclosed that nurses made many trips off the floor for a variety of reasons. They wanted to see if there were ways to reduce those trips. In addition, the team was interested in reducing the length of time it took to respond to call buttons.

The C-Section Story

West Paces was barely into its quality improvement campaign when Paul Batalden's group at headquarters began to push for physician involvement. Caldwell obediently invited twenty-five doctors affiliated with the hospital to a training course called Q131, a version of Q101 geared to physicians. Sixteen signed up and twelve made it through. It was held on two evenings and a Saturday from 8 A.M. to 2 P.M. to accommodate doctors' busy schedules.

Meanwhile, Lorraine Schiff, the hospital's manager of quality assurance, had been reviewing data, looking for areas to improve. One of the biggest issues in obstetrics was the high rate of cesarean sections. Feminists and other critics believed that doctors performed them almost routinely because they were easier than shepherding a woman through a difficult vaginal delivery—and more lucrative.

C-sections were so common that people tended to forget they were major surgery, involving an incision in the abdominal wall, with all the attendant risks. Atlanta had an active chapter of a womens' group dedicated to fighting C-sections.

The average C-section rate was one in four, both nationally and in Georgia. At 21 percent, West Paces' rate was below the average. But Grady Memorial Hospital, Atlanta's large public hospital where a lot of high-risk deliveries took place, had an even lower rate of 17 percent. Schiff and others in the obstetrics-gynecology department thought there might be room for improvement at West Paces. In addition, ob-gyn seemed like a good place to begin the quality effort: Not only had several of its physicians gone through the training, but it was a department with a lot of camaraderie and a tradition of teamwork. It was important that the department's first clinical team be successful. Other physicians would be watching.

One of the most enthusiastic practitioners to graduate from Q131 was a soft-spoken obstetrician, Alton V. Hallum Jr. Hallum was alarmed by the army of regulators stampeding through medicine. As he saw it, it was "a fight for the survival of the practice of medicine" against "Big Brother." He suspected that the new quality management offered a way out from under Big Brother.

He was very receptive when asked to participate in both the training and then on a team. "Given some background on what's happened in the business world, physicians now more than ever before realize we have to give of our time and effort to influence the quality of health care."

Hallum had another agenda. It seemed to him that people employed in medicine were working under intolerable amounts of stress. He suspected that the new quality management system gave people an outlet for change rather than allowing frustration to build to explosive levels. "If we don't give people ways of being successful, they're going to leave the hospital," he said. His own daughter, an

RN, was talking about that very possibility. Trying to raise a small child and work in such a stressful environment was proving too difficult.

Hallum became coleader of the C-section team, along with Schiff, herself an RN. Among the additional nine members were two other physicians and several nurses from Labor and Delivery. Because patients were seen for so many months in the physician's quarters, a nurse from Hallum's office was also on the team.

The FOCUS-PDCA training taught teams to frame their process improvement in positive terms as an "opportunity." The C-section team eventually formulated the following opportunity statement: "There is an opportunity to improve the clinical outcome and the satisfaction of our patients' birthing experience by better meeting the expectations outlined in their birthing plans. Vaginal delivery with minimal intervention is an integral part of most patients' birthing plan. Decreasing the number of cesarean sections and, thereby, increasing the number of patients who are able to deliver vaginally safely will improve our patient satisfaction. This will also decrease our patients' risk of morbidity and mortality."

The boundaries of the process were set: "From the first new OB visit to discharge from the hospital after delivery." The "owner" of the process was the physician.

In the "U" or data-collection step, a control chart applied to the monthly C-section rate disclosed that there was substantial variation in the process, from 15 to 26 percent of all births. The team also constructed a process-flow diagram and a cause-and-effect diagram on the decision to perform a cesarean section. In more than 40 percent of the cases, the cause was the baby's failure to progress in the birth canal. That was followed by breech births and fetal distress. In short, the top three causes were irregular, emergency medical situations. The fourth, however, was simply that the mother had previously had a C-section. That controversial practice accounted for 13 percent of C-section cases.

In the past, cesarean surgery had required a vertical incision that substantially weakened the abdominal wall to a point where it would not support a subsequent vaginal delivery. Surgical techniques had improved, however. Now commonplace was a much smaller and less invasive horizontal incision that left the abdominal muscle stronger, thereby substantially reducing the need for a repeat C-section.

The team probed deeper into data on repeat C-sections. It found that in 32 percent of the cases, the chief reason was once again "failure to progress." But in 27 percent of the cases, obstetricians were performing C-sections at the patient's request.

The team brainstormed to come up with reasons women might be requesting C-sections after already undergoing one. Never having experienced a vaginal delivery, perhaps they were frightened of the unknown. Or it could be that they were unaware of the risks of C-sections and didn't know that labor these days was managed differently from when they had their first C-section. It might be that their own mothers were counseling them, based on the old saw, "Once a C-section, always a C-section."

The answer to all this seemed to be more education. The team wrote a new opportunity statement: "The process of care can be improved for patients who have experienced a previous C-section by decreasing the incidence of repeat C-sections. This may be accomplished through education, communication and commitment of the OB team, which includes the patient, family, medical staff and nursing staff."

It would take some time to draft an educational plan and marshal the resources for its introduction. Whether there then would be a decrease in the C-section rate thanks to the team efforts would not, of course, be known for some months. Hallum nevertheless presented the team's story to a department meeting. "A doctor came up to me afterwards. He said, 'I see what you've done and appreciate what you've done. Is it really going to make a difference?' My answer: 'Even if it doesn't, which I think it will, if it gets everyone on board working as a team, it will have made a difference.' "

As for himself, he had been sensitized to look at systems rather than problems. One day in his office, Hallum realized he had little to do for twenty minutes, then was swamped for the next hour. When such things happened, instead of the usual "All right, who did it? Whose fault is it?" he and his partner, who also had been on the C-section team, were more apt to say "Something didn't go right. How can we change it?" Hallum asked his staff to begin collecting data on the patient flow: when patients signed in, when they were taken to the examining room, at what time he saw them and the time they were out the door. In that manner, they could see where in the process glitches occurred.

Not long after the team made its recommendations, Hallum found himself presiding over a repeat C-section. He charged the patient more than for a vaginal delivery and he didn't have to spend hours with her in labor. His team's work could mean fewer such cases. Nevertheless, he said, "Where I am in my practice, I want to give the best quality care in Atlanta or this hospital or anywhere else that gives me pride."

CHAPTER FOUR

Tri-Cities, Tennessee

Everyone can take part in a team. The aim of a team is to improve the input and the output of any stage. A team may well be composed of people from different staff areas. A team has a customer.

Everyone on a team has a chance to contribute ideas, plans, and figures; but anyone may expect to find some of his best ideas submerged by consensus of the team; he may have a chance on the later time around the cycle. A good team has a social memory.

At successive sessions, people may tear up what they did in the previous session and make a fresh start with clearer ideas. This is a sign of advancement.

—W. EDWARDS DEMING
Out of the Crisis

I. MOVING MOUNTAINS

As in newspapers around the country, foreign events dominated the front page of Tennessee's *Kingsport Times-News* on December 20, 1989. "U.S. Attacks Panama," declared the headline over the lead story. And in Romania, "Hundreds of Protesters Feared Dead in Government Crackdown."

Elsewhere in the paper, local news reflected events in a typical American community in the last month of the last year of the decade. There was crime. A bank robber decked out in camouflage clothing, his face smeared with shoe polish, had been nabbed after ordering tellers to put all their money in a brown paper bag. He made his getaway in a red Chevette. A sixty-nine-year-old grandmother was sentenced to fifty-six years in prison for her part in the abduction and beating death of a young Appalachian girl.

There were issues related to growth and the environment. The Kingsport Board of Mayor and Aldermen approved an annexation proposal over protests from several residents that the city's $1,950 fee for sewer hookups was too high. The board also approved a request to extend sewer service to a proposed outlet mall. At a public meeting in the library, people voiced their concern about a hazardous landfill proposed by the area's largest employer, the Eastman Chemicals Division of Eastman Kodak Company.

Also that week Kingsport was preparing for the holiday season. The Home Section offered recipes for Christmas treats such as honey candy and pumpkin cookies. Wine was an appropriate purchase: "Great California reds make gift-giving simple," proclaimed one ad. And for those who imbibed too much: "Holiday patrol scheduled." In sports, the East Tennessee State Buccaneers trounced the North Carolina State Wolfpack.

But, because it had become so commonplace, an event that didn't make the news that week was as important to the future of Kingsport as those that did: a three-day presentation at Tri-Cities State Technical Institute by twenty-two teams from local businesses, hospitals and public agencies operating under the rubric Quality First.

An orchestrated drive for quality embracing three municipalities and two counties, Quality First was an effort that more than any other was putting Kingsport and its sister cities, Johnson City and Bristol—known collectively as "Tri-Cities"—on the map.

That took some doing. The Tri-Cities region was located in the hills of eastern Tennessee, nudging the North Carolina border. It didn't matter whether you went to heaven or hell, these Tennesseeans quipped about local air service, "you had to change planes in Charlotte or Atlanta to get there." Despite being situated in what could scarcely be labeled a commercial hub, in three years Tri-Cities had gained a national reputation as a demonstration model for business, local government and an educational institution working in tandem to become a "community of excellence," one that put "quality first," based on the principles of W. Edwards Deming.

Kingsport was not the first community to seek such a transformation. Earlier, the city of Madison, Wisconsin, had pioneered the use of teams and statistical methods in municipal government under its mayor, F. Joseph Sensenbrenner. The achievements of its motor vehicle pool in collecting data on vehicle repairs, setting job priorities and establishing a schedule for preventive maintenance were widely documented. The effort was highly dependent on Sensenbrenner's patronage, however, and it bogged down when political power changed hands, but not before spreading to the private sector and to several Wisconsin state agencies through the efforts of the Madison Area Quality Improvement Network.

Established in 1984, the Philadelphia Area Council for Excellence (PACE), lodged in the regional chamber of commerce, launched teams from an assortment of companies that met in "roundtables" with consultants who acted as teachers and facilitators. By 1990, PACE had become a force for quality, with a twenty-two-member board composed of CEOs and senior managers, which hosted a continuing stream of seminars and nationally known speakers, including a yearly four-day Deming seminar. Project team training was done by Delaware County Community College; meanwhile, veterans of the roundtables had become the backbone of the organization. A monthly network meeting with a speaker regularly drew several hundred people, and there were "sub-users groups"—one that worked on just-in-time operations, another from hospitals and a third composed of total quality coordinators.

The Growth Opportunity Alliance of Greater Lawrence (GOAL) had also begun as a coalition of local business leaders, and it too had shifted its role, seeking to become a national resource organization for research, consulting and publications. In addition, each year it hosted a major quality conference. Held in 1989 for the first time in Boston, the three-day GOAL conference drew close to 1,000 people.

Although the Tri-Cities initiative came somewhat later to a more remote area, its instigators had ambitious goals. They were seeking a place to hatch a community-based approach to quality that would have universal application. A model, in other words, for community change.

The effort began in 1983 at a meeting hosted by the MIT Center for Advanced Engineering Study, whose director was Myron Tribus, a former Xerox vice president and assistant secretary of commerce in the Nixon Administration, who had enthusiastically embraced the Deming philosophy in the early '80s. The Center published Deming's books and marketed a video series based on his four-day seminar. But Tribus saw that there were limits to how much he could promote a Deming movement. "It was obvious that MIT was the wrong place to headquarter it," he explained later. "The things that you teach are so simple it seems stupid. It's not the sort of stuff that will make you a hero at MIT. Most of quality, in fact, is not teaching new things, it's teaching to forget—you have to unteach—teach people to forget ideas that they've known since childhood."

Tribus sought help not from from academia but from the National Society of Professional Engineers whose members dealt day in and day out with demands for quality in the workplace. The people he talked to were initially intrigued with establishing an organization like the Union of Japanese Scientists and Engineers, which continuously worked to improve and advance quality systems. At that meeting in 1983 were high-ranking executives from large corporations such as General Electric, Monsanto, U.S. Steel, Ford and General Motors. Representing Eastman Kodak was M. C. "Bud" Lunsford, manager of licensing and business development for Tennessee Eastman, who was also the Society's vice president for industry.

The group's conclusion on the prospects for an umbrella organization like the Japanese had was not a positive one, Lunsford said. In brief, it was "that it couldn't happen. There was so much fragmentation already between professional and technical societies. Everybody thought they owned a piece of quality. Most companies thought they'd already done it. To start up a new society just wasn't something that was doable here at that point."

But the meeting was not a total loss. A seed had been planted. Dr. Deming frequently pointed out that Japan had no resources of its own—that it was, more or less, in Lunsford's words, "a rock in the middle of the ocean with nothing but people." A comparison could be drawn between Japan and many American communities just pulling out of a recession, communities short on resources and jobs but long on human potential. Many technical people who worked for large corporations with far-flung operations made their home in such communities. There they belonged to local chapters of organizations like the National Society of Professional Engineers, the Institute of Electrical and Electronics Engineers, the Institute of Industrial Engineers, the American Society for Quality Control, the American Society of Mechanical Engineers and the American Statistical Association. Perhaps the chapters could form local quality councils to act as technical advisers and become the catalyst for change. In short, Lunsford said, he and the others reasoned that "even though we might not be able to do something nationally, we can, community by community, get this thing started."

There were limits, however, to what they could do on their own, with no political clout. They would need to persuade local government and business to participate. Both, of course, had reason to do so. Municipalities needed to increase their tax base, business needed to become more competitive. And everyone wanted to see more jobs created.

Lunsford knew of one such community where it might work—his own. Kingsport was the home of Tennessee Eastman's huge chemical plant. With 11,000 employees, it was Kingsport's largest employer. In addition to the Eastman, as locals called it, Kodak operated the adjacent Holston Army Ammunition Plant for the U.S. government. Kingsport also was home to Mead Paper and Arcata Graphics, a nationally known book manufacturer. Kingsport had so many chemists, physicists and engineers living in the area that it supported healthy chapters of some fifteen technical societies.

Kingsport was an unusual community in several other respects as well. Its founders in 1917 were progressive railroad entrepreneurs who had sought the help of outside experts in designing the town and its government. Thanks to a sensible planner from Cambridge, Massachusetts, industry occupied the plain along the north fork of the Holston River, while residences sat on higher ground. A commercial strip separated the two. The city charter giving Kingsport the first city manager government in Tennessee was drafted by the Rockefeller Foundation. And education experts from Columbia University in New York advised on the education system. Thus, Kingsport had a tradition of seeking outside help from experts and a history of professionalism in government.

Thanks to the concentration of industry, Kingsport also had a large middle class and more jobs than people—rarities in the Appalachian Mountains. Its political system was fairly stable; it had amenities such as a symphony, a fine arts center, a baseball team (the Kingsport Mets) and a 3,000-acre nature preserve and park that housed an observatory and planetarium. Eastman employees took an active role in the community. It was said that "when Tennessee Eastman talks, everybody listens." That could be good or bad, but it was a fact of life.

Kingsport proper had a population of about 38,000, but it was part of a metropolitan area with close to a quarter of a million people. Next door was Johnson City, with 44,000 people, and Bristol, Tennessee, with 23,000. Bristol was actually two cities, divided by the state line. Bristol, Virginia, had some 25,000 residents.

In the late 1970s, the Rochester-based Eastman Kodak and its divisions had embarked on the quality journey that eventually would bring the Tennessee Eastman division into the Deming camp. The idea of using their expertise appealed to its executives. Many considered Kingsport their permanent home. They and their families were involved in many ways with many causes. Why not quality?

In addition to Lunsford, another who felt inspired by the Deming approach was a city councilman from Eastman named John Douglas, who began to indoctrinate the city manager, Jim Zumwalt. Not that he needed to. Zumwalt, a philosophy major with a graduate degree in public administration from the Kennedy School at Harvard, had previously been the city manager of Boca Raton, Florida. He believed in empowering workers to make changes, and early on he attended a four-day Deming seminar at Ford. It was an added advantage that the Kingsport mayor at the time was an engineer, as would be his successor.

When the president of the Kingsport Chamber of Commerce, W. E. Ring III, heard about what was going on, he too was inclined to be helpful. Ring was the third-generation president of a foundry his grandfather had started back in 1927. With the decline of the steel industry in the 1980s, the foundry lost its biggest customers. So steep and so sudden was the foundry's decline, Ring said much later, "We were dead and didn't know it." The downturn in steel was also disastrous for the coal industry, and the companies that depended on it, of which there were many in that section of Tennessee. There were a number of other, smaller companies that hadn't recovered from the recession or were feeling the pinch of foreign competition.

Quality First also addressed another goal of the chamber, to attract new industry to the area. What had happened to steel forced Kingsport city fathers to acknowledge how dangerously dependent they were on a few large employers. Until the early 1980s, it had been unthinkable that a plant as old and stable as Tennessee Eastman could go out of business. It had been there since 1920, when it was built to produce methanol—wood alcohol—for Kodak's photographic business. Now it manufactured a variety of chemicals, fibers and plastics used for everything from steering wheels to toothbrushes. But it could go under, and if it did, Kingsport would be a ghost town like Gary and Youngstown, where the steel mills closed down. The city had pledged $3.5 million to develop industrial sites for new industry. Quality First could only bolster that effort.

Ring organized a committee of the Chamber of Commerce, including people from manufacturing plants, banks and hospitals as well as car dealers and even a restaurant to support Quality First. Another resource fell into place.

Meanwhile, back at MIT, the quest for a community model had led Myron Tribus to a training project based in Jackson, Michigan, called Transformation of American Industry. Its acronym had an Oriental sound: "TAI."

TAI had been hatched in 1984 by Carole Schwinn, an assistant to the president of Jackson Community College, her husband David (an alumnus of Ford Motor Company's quality office), and by Michael Cleary, a professor of management science at Wright State University in Dayton, Ohio. It grew from Carole Schwinn's efforts several years earlier to develop a training program for local businesses, many of which were suppliers to the auto industry. "The auto industry was in such deep trouble that our community was in deep trouble," Carole Schwinn said. Jackson had a 17 percent unemployment rate. And the big carmakers were issuing quality mandates to their suppliers. In her conversations with the businesses in Jackson, she said, "Everybody talked about quality and SPC (statistical process control). Everybody had a letter from a GM or Ford that said 'You do quality or you die.' " For herself, this quality business was all new. She had never heard of SPC. But her job at the college was to foster links with local business, finding ways for the college to help with their needs. And what they said they needed was quality.

She contacted Cleary, who contacted David Schwinn, then at Ford. The trio developed a Deming-based training course that would be appropriate for Jackson and other community colleges, and they sought support from sponsors that eventually included Ford, GM, TRW, Eaton Corporation, the Michigan Department of Education, the Iowa Productivity Consortium and the American Association of Community and Junior Colleges.

Learning of their efforts, Tribus enlisted the Schwinns to help with Quality First planning and training in Kingsport. The local sponsor would be Tri-Cities State Technical College. Tribus realized that technical or community colleges were actually well suited to the training role because of the allegiance they felt to the community, unlike larger institutions such as MIT that had a more diverse student body and more emphasis on scholarship.

On May 14, 1986, the coalition of supporters staged its kickoff dinner at a local country club, with Myron Tribus there to whip up enthusiasm. Said Lunsford, "Myron has a way of really making people go out and want to do something and we had something for them to do right there." The companies were asked to sign up for the first round of training. Some had agreed in advance to do so. "Don't try to start this program cold," Tribus would caution in a "template" or pattern he presented the following year.

Nineteen teams began training on September 8, 1986. Tennessee Eastman sent three. And the city of Kingsport sent four, from the water department, custodial department, fleet maintenance and street maintenance. There was one from Tri-Cities State Tech itself. The others were from Kingsport Foundry and Manufacturing Corporation, Strahan Ink and Lacquer Corporation, Arcada Graphics, AFG Industries, Unisys Corporation, Holston Defense Corporation, United Intermountain Telephone Company, Hoover Harrison Associates, Holston Valley Hospital, Looney Chevrolet and First American National Bank.

The Tri-Cities Tech dean of instruction, meanwhile, had tapped a retired U.S. Marine sergeant and coal miner's son with an engineering degree to head Quality First. Engineering instructor Dick Hale had just stepped down as president of the faculty when he was asked to take over.

"What's my job?" he wanted to know. He spoke with a mountaineer's twang.

"I don't know," replied the dean. She invited him to review some books and videos. That was the beginning of his education. Hale sat through the training given by the Schwinns, attended the first of several Deming seminars and sought in other ways to educate himself. Shortly thereafter, he was in the classroom, training the third round of teams.

From the beginning, the program's leaders realized the first teams had to show dramatic results to convince their employers and other companies that the quality effort was worthwhile. Even though the training would cost just $2,000 for a team of five to seven people, small companies could ill afford to waste money or the time of their limited work force. Political support, too, depended on results.

Politicians, as Lunsford put it, were "risk-averse." But the course developed by the Schwinns was "learn-do"—the teams focused on an actual work process in need of improvement.

Top management, explained Lunsford, had "to understand there's something in it for them. You stroke them by having them send people and those people have successes. And the way they measure those successes initially is per dollars on the bottom line. 'Can I tell my boss I paid $2,000 and got $20,000 back?' If it looks that way then he can send another team in. And if he gets that two or three times, then what he can start doing is start building facilitators in-house and move it across the whole organization."

Once there were successes, publicity would be critical to spreading the word. It was important to create an air of excitement, to get leaders talking about what was going on. Said Lunsford, "We felt like you couldn't make it a way of life if the business execs came in and their industrial relations people told them this is the way to manage the company, and then when they went out with the good old boys on the golf course or the club in the evenings, business was something different. So we felt like you had to attack the whole culture. You had to have them in the off-time, or when they were in those back-rooms chatting with each other, the things they needed to be talking about were: 'How do we improve the way we do things? How do we empower people to do more for the company?' "

The technical experts in the community were especially valuable in helping companies choose projects and teams to focus on rapid improvements. The Japanese had an analogy for beginning with easy projects that yielded big results. They called it picking "the low-hanging fruit." There was nothing particularly wrong with that, as long as people realized that it didn't stop there. Eventually they would be forced to work on more difficult processes to continually improve. Here in the backwoods of Tennessee, the equivalent tactic was called "killing the fat rabbit first."

Soon the local papers blossomed with news of slain "fat rabbits"—reports of big money savings and testimonials from business and community leaders. In nine months, sixteen Quality First teams from businesses, service groups and the Tri-Cities governments were said to have saved $3.2 million.

What would become the city of Kingsport's best known team, its bathroom cleaners, put a halt to disappearing rolls of toilet paper and switched to more efficient cleaning products, among other reforms.

City manager Zumwalt boasted that the subsequent savings of some $30,000 was enough to pay for all the money he'd spent on training.

A team from AFG Industries, a glass company, racked up $100,000 from improvements in its inventory system. The accomplishments of Bill Ring's foundry were particularly impressive: increased market penetration of 50 percent, for added revenues of $600,000; scrap levels cut in half, for savings of $100,000; savings of $100 per casting in cleaning time.

Bill's son Drew, the operations manager and a member of the first team, praised the hands-on approach to learning the improvement process. "The training wouldn't have worked as well if we hadn't been working a project at the same time."

Said Lunsford, "With success stories like that, we got the bank, the hospital—those folks have just kept coming back with team after team, and most of them have started their own programs now to get it in-house. . . . I don't think you could find a company in the area that hasn't been touched by it."

By 1989 the savings were up to $20 million. But there were team members who realized the major accomplishments were not measured in dollars. "Sure we saved a lot of money," one AFG team member told the *Kingsport Times-News* as early as 1987. "But the most valuable thing was the learning process. We've already seen other areas where we can apply the same techniques." Indeed, AFG would train a dozen or so teams in the first three years of Quality First.

Although there were exceptions, most of the teams that went through training in the first two years were composed of employees, not managers. By then, however, the program was so popular that Quality First coordinator Dick Hale was in a position to pressure a new company to form a quality steering committee as its first team. "Once I've done that, the other teams just fall right in."

That was always the ideal approach, of course, but it hadn't always been possible. Years after taking the job, Dick Hale would have a discussion with Deming on this point. Deming, of course, was firm that top management had to be committed to the transformation as a prerequisite for employee efforts.

Recounted Hale, "He kept saying 'Top management down, top management down.' And of course that is the optimum way. . . .

"I said, 'Dr. Deming, it's like this. If I waited to have management teams come in first, starting from the top management down, I would still be sitting there waiting to start training. What we did was, we took some lower-level people and turned out successful projects. And then we were able to go bottom up.' " Deming, Hale said, told him he understood.

Specifically for managers, however, Quality First brought in consultant Brian Joiner, who had Deming's endorsement to conduct a four-day seminar entitled "Dr. Deming's Fundamental Message for American Managers." Joiner's associate, Peter Scholtes, whose textbook on team training was a reference for the course, also came to Tri-Cities for a one-day workshop on "Performance Appraisals—New Directions." Scholtes was waging a one-man campaign against the use of merit ratings, one of Dr. Deming's "Seven Deadly Diseases." Also, from time to time, Tennessee Eastman experts offered courses in statistical quality control.

In the beginning, Hale had set aside an afternoon a week to telephone companies that had shown an interest in Quality First. "We have never door-knocked. I will not door-knock—call a company and tell them about the program. . . . If they don't have enough concern about the quality issue to at least call and ask what the program is, I'd be wasting my time."

As the course grew in popularity, he found himself doing less promotion. Moreover, so many teams came from companies that had sent others that technical advisers no longer needed to work with them to select members and projects. A repeat company now knew enough to handle that alone. In the case of a new company, Hale would meet with the management to choose one of two procedures. The company could select a team first, whose members brainstormed to come up with a project. That worked best when teams were composed of managers from small companies because it broke down barriers and educated them in the problem-solving process. Or management could first select the improvement project, and then the employees best suited to work on it. No team was allowed to work on something that didn't have management's prior approval. And no team's recommendations could be neglected. Management didn't necessarily have to adopt them, but they had to agree in advance to respond within 72 hours.

The teams trained over a period of three months, attending class one day every other week and working within their companies on the off weeks. Each class consisted of five teams. Although teams from different companies seemed to benefit from sharing their experiences, there was no rule that said several couldn't be from the same company. That had the advantage of mixing internal customers and suppliers. Teams drawn from different departments could see how their operations related to others.

On the other hand, different companies enjoyed getting to know each other. At one point Claudia Leonard, general manager of a company that made plastic caps, considered doing in-house training but thought better of it. "I feel that you lose so much when you don't listen to the other companies."

She herself went through a session with teams from glass and steel companies. "Many people work for the same company for years and years. They're in tune just to what that company does, in terms of policies and procedures. And it's nice to hear how other people handle things."

There were lessons to be learned. Drew Ring's group saw a team from a paint company fail because a vice president couldn't yield control. "Everybody knew it was going to happen." On the two days the vice president wasn't there, "the team ran great." On his return, however, he told team members what they could and couldn't do. "And they just sat there and did nothing." At "graduation"—the final presentations—"he congratulated everybody else and said he didn't know why his team couldn't do better."

Quality First could accommodate twenty-five teams in each three-month session. Hale did most of the instruction, using the TAI instruction model that came with a handbook and videos, with some assistance from other faculty and Tennessee Eastman professionals.

At the close of each classroom session, the teams signed a contract covering what they planned to do in the off week back at their work site. When the class met again, they gave a ten-minute update on their activities. This produced a little healthy competition. Explained Hale, "All the people have pride in their organization. So I don't have to drive the team. One team gets up. 'We've done this and this and this and this.' The other teams, 'We haven't done it yet. We better get ourselves in gear. They're going to show us up.' That's what drives it."

The finale for the teams was a public presentation, like the one held that week before Christmas of 1989 in the Tri-Cities Tech auditorium. The teams had begun at 9 A.M. on Monday, December 18, with a presentation from Line Power Corporation, a firm that designed and built power supplies, transformers and other specialized electrical equipment. They continued through Wednesday morning, with reports from five hospital teams. About half the twenty-two companies making presentations were involved in heavy to light industry, including a foundry, a manufacturer of plastic bottle caps and another that made metal folding chairs.

On the service end, in addition to the hospitals, there were also teams from both Johnson City and Kingsport, as well as from another community college and the Sullivan County School Board.

The school board team, composed of the board chairman, an assistant superintendent and three other members of management, tackled its use of substitute teachers—a sore point with principals who had trouble getting substitutes, and with the substitutes themselves, whose complaints included low pay, among others.

A team from MECO Corporation addressed paint defects on one of its products, metal folding chairs. The Bristol Regional Rehabilitation Center looked at ways to increase sales and reduce losses in its food service department. Holston Valley Hospital and Medical Center focused on its discharge process. And David Austin, an electrician from the city of Kingsport, presented an update from a maintenance team that had created a preventive maintenance process for its heating, ventilation and air conditioning systems.

Working with such small- to average-sized companies like these was "our goal here," said Dick Hale. "That is our mission. They can turn around so quick. A manager and the training can get things to happen!"

By the end of the decade, Tri-Cities' Quality First had a constant stream of visitors from other communities. The college changed its name to Northeast State Technical Community College. Hale was working with some neighboring towns to set up their own versions, and he had also paid a visit to West Palm Beach, where an effort was underway. David and Carole Schwinn, meanwhile, had moved on to other communities, including Erie, Pennsylvania, where the chamber of commerce established an excellence council and invited them to conduct team training. After several rounds the couple trained eight people to take over. The excellence council also oversaw the formation of twenty-two committees on virtually every aspect of community life, from social services and sports to industry and the environment, all engaged in discussing what quality meant. The mayor and the county executive jointly proclaimed the 1990s a "decade of excellence."

The Schwinns were heartened by the example of Erie. "We never expected to see it happen. We used to wonder if you didn't have an Eastman Kodak like Kingsport, could you make things happen?" Erie seemed to suggest that the answer was yes.

II. SMALL COMPANIES, BIG CHANGES

For most of its history, quality had not been an issue for the family-owned Kingsport Foundry & Manufacturing Corporation, which could make anything from a coke oven door to an elbow joint the size of a bathroom. The foundry was, in practice, a job shop, often casting one-of-a-kind items that weighed as little as a few ounces to as much as 40,000 pounds, using sand molds that were destroyed afterward. When producing huge castings, it was important "to get it right the first time," said Drew Ring, the great-grandson of the founder. "You can't afford to make it twice."

Wiley Everett Ring established the foundry in 1927 with three other men, principally to make castings for paper and chemical plants. The founder, his grandson would later say, was "very, very independent." So opposed was he to government intervention in business that during World War II he refused to run a plant for the government and almost went to jail as a consequence. Shortly after the war, he turned down a request from Russians who sought coal cleaning equipment, because they were Communists. Not only was he his own man, he was an autocrat as well. So much so, Bill Ring recalled, that "if you wanted to buy a certain size piece of coal equipment and they wanted you to have another size, they wouldn't sell you what you wanted, they'd sell you what they thought you needed."

Wiley Everett Jr. took over in 1945 when his father died and continued to expand the company. In 1958, W. E. Ring III, called Bill, joined his father. He had degrees from Virginia Tech in mechanical and industrial engineering.

Foundry work was like no other—dirty and physically taxing, hot in summer and cold in winter. Touring a foundry was like stepping into the nineteenth century. Filled with the steady roar of a powerful ventilation system that sucked dust from the air, the building was a long cavern, with a 35-foot-high pitched ceiling. Dust-laden beams of light filtered weakly through soot-blackened windows. The cement floor was covered in areas with two inches of sand, to keep molten metal from spattering when it dripped. Flames leapt from drums where workers burned wood for added heat.

The workers who did best in this environment were country boys who already had some job experience—in timbering, perhaps, or construction or mining. Turning out one-of-a-kind products appealed to their individualism. They were not automatons, manning a station on an assembly line.

In the days of Wiley Everett Sr., and well into the 1950s, foundry workers were artisans, practicing a trade they might well have learned from their fathers. "They could make anything with a mold," said Bill Ring. But technological advances changed that. Automated equipment required greater mechanical skills. And the materials had changed. Where once the foundry had used sand mixed with clay to form a natural bond, and a worker could check its texture by running his hands through it, now various chemical binding agents were employed. Unlike the earlier molds, these required no baking, thus speeding up the job, but the mix of ingredients was critical.

The quality of the final product, in fact, depended in large measure on the mix of sands used in the mold. All sand was not created equal. One variety had round grains, another angular. And each had different properties. The round sand required less chemical binder because of its smaller surface area, and was thus cheaper to use and produced less gas when heated, causing less damage to castings. The angular sand packed tighter and gave a stronger mold. The mix of new to reclaimed sand also affected the characteristics of the final product. Moreover, a 15-pound casting required a mix different from one that weighed 300 pounds.

The period from 1962 to 1981 was one not only of growing technical sophistication, but also of steady expansion. Several major chemical companies closed their in-house foundries and Kingsport got their work. Most of the foundry's other customers were steel or steel-related industries. Almost certainly unlike his grandfather, Bill Ring had no compunction about taking a helping hand from the government in the form of a $150,000 SBA loan to purchase a new coke furnace, or cupola, to increase manufacturing capacity.

As a manager, Ring wasn't the autocrat his grandfather was, but he was by no means democratic. He reviewed all the data and made all the decisions. He would later characterize his style as "management by conflict," which was taught in the early '50s by Virginia Tech professors, many of whom hailed from the auto industry. In their view, not only was conflict not bad, it tended to sharpen issues and bring out the best in people.

Ring's father had managed in yet another way, one that was more oriented toward consensus and committees. But "even with his committees, workers were not given information," said Bill Ring. "Top management was very secretive." In conflict management, people needed information to have ideas. But decisions were still Ring's province. "In the '60s and '70s," he said, looking back on it, "we gave them the information, but we wouldn't let them make the decisions. That was the stupid part."

So it was that for years all data was funneled upward to Ring for action. What that meant, son Drew said, was that when his father signed off on the temperature reports of the sand coming off the line, "it wasn't timely; it wasn't accurate and the people thought that if he looked at it and approved it, they didn't have to look at it in between."

"What we did," Bill Ring reflected, "was, we took away the pride of the workman. He didn't have that real high degree of skill. A lot of times he didn't even know what he was producing and he didn't want to know. So we lowered our standards."

Ring was aware that quality was slipping. In the late 1960s he called on the Arthur G. McKee Company in Cleveland, for which his grandfather had worked before creating the foundry. McKee was seeking to replace ammonia distillation towers his grandfather had cast for them in 1927 and that were still in use. By then, Bill Ring said, "we weren't making castings that would last thirty-five years."

Nevertheless, sales were healthy and Ring thought "we were doing a good job." Employees seemed reasonably content. Although Kingsport workers belonged to the United Steelworkers, there had never been a strike.

In 1982, the year the steel industry collapsed, Kingsport had profits of about half a million on $7 million gross. The next year, seven of its ten customers, in Ring's words, "for all practical purposes ceased to exist." The company lost a quarter of a million dollars in 1983. Even so, Ring viewed the situation as a temporary recession that could be dealt with simply by retrenching slightly and abolishing some jobs.

The following year the company recovered slightly, but still lost money. In 1985, with losses of close to $600,000, Ring said, "we recognized we weren't going to recover." In just four years, sales had slipped from $7 million to $3.5 million. The work force had shrunk from 160 to 75. Kingsport, of course, was not alone in its suffering. Beset with the same problems, two-thirds of the foundries in the area closed down.

The once harmonious relationships at Kingsport Foundry became fractious. Recriminations flew, said Ring. " 'Hey, it's your fault, not mine.' 'Hey, it's yours. You didn't hold it up. You didn't do what I asked you to do.' Plant workers said, 'Hey, you didn't give us the tools to work with. You didn't really train us. It's your fault.' "

The workers blamed management for the cutbacks, and Ring privately wondered if they were right. He began to question his own ability to manage.

In 1985, the foundry asked for and got a 12-percent wage cut from the union, after opening its books to reveal how truly desperate the situation was. It was clear that if the foundry were to recover, it urgently needed new markets. Steel did not look like it was going to make a comeback. "Our steel mills were obsolete. Our engineers were obsolete. They had never really designed and built a big huge state-of-the-art steel mill." There was fierce competition from Japan and West Germany. Kingsport lost a coke oven job in Cleveland to a Japanese company that charged 30 percent less than their production cost would have been.

Adding a sales force was clearly a requirement. None had been necessary when the company worked steadily year after year for the same large corporations. In addition, new technology could help increase productivity. But customers were insisting on lower levels of defects—less sand, slag and internal gas voids in the finished product—plus conformity to their specifications and superior surface finishes.

It was understandable, then, that in 1985 the words "Quality First" struck a responsive chord in Bill Ring. He had everything to gain and nothing to lose. He enrolled five of his managers in the initial training, among them his two sons, Drew and Victor, both of whom had followed his footsteps to Virginia Tech to earn engineering degrees. Drew was the manufacturing engineer and Victor the foundry engineer as well as its purchasing agent.

Such people were difficult to spare. Unlike larger companies,

Kingsport Foundry had no real staff. A person in the front office generally performed multiple duties. The personnel manager, for example, was also the office manager. There was no engineering department, no maintenance department, simply people in charge—a half dozen managers, and eight superintendents out in the shop.

The first team concentrated its efforts on reducing defects in castings for one of its major customers. Through a variety of improvements, the reject rate was cut from 13 to 5.7 percent. So urgent was the foundry's need for quality, however, that Ring felt he needed to move faster than the training permitted. On returning to work, the five managers were asked to form teams and teach employees the problem-solving process. Over the next three years, there were upwards of fifty teams.

A small company like the foundry could ill afford the loss of time required by team projects. "As it was," Drew said, "we had to work off-hours—in the morning at 7:00, 5:00 in the afternoon and evenings." So intense was the effort that after the initial gains, managers yielded briefly to the temptation to let up. Workers got the message and also backslid. And the company discovered, Drew said, that "Left alone, things go back pretty much the way they were before. . . ."

It was not enough merely to complete the Plan-Do-Check-Act Cycle they had been taught in Quality First training. "Once you check and act, you can't leave it alone. You've got to come back and check about once a week," Drew said. And that meant "You've got to find somebody who has the time to check and follow up, because you find there's a thousand things that you got to do, and you do six hundred, and you hope it's the four hundred don't eat your lunch." One way or another they made time.

But there was more to the quality transformation than forming teams. "We had to change how our workers thought," said Bill Ring. "They had been dictated to for so long." In the past, for example, if something went wrong in the mold area, it was customary to transmit the information to the lab, which analyzed the problem and reported to Ring, who made a decision and relayed it back. The whole thing could take a week. "In all that time, we may have scrapped twenty castings. The action time and what you had to do was too far removed. So therefore, we had to move it back out onto the floor. The man in action, he's got to see the same results that we would see, and he's going to have to have the same basic information we would have to make a decision.

"But *he's* going to have to make it."

That posed another problem. Ring discovered that as many as 20 percent of his employees were functionally illiterate. "Now we moved into the process where the men on the floor are having to control everything, but 20 percent of them couldn't read. . . . We're getting high school graduates who can't effectively function in a Deming work environment."

In time, that would become the company's biggest problem. Ring's first thought was to make literacy training available. But he discovered employees were embarrassed to attend adult education classes. After learning that some companies had success with instructional computer programs, management budgeted in pilot funds for 1990. Computers allowed people to work on individual programs in private. It was imperative to bring workers up to speed, but also not to damage their pride.

Said Ring, "They've got to be able to understand the basic technical areas and limits of this process, or they can't make the decisions. Then they've got to be able to communicate those decisions back through the processes, so everybody knows. It's a great big team now."

As the foundry began to work on employee development issues, it became clear that Quality First had profound implications for the entire community. Ring found himself becoming involved in broader issues such as literacy and health care.

Although he described with enthusiasm what Quality First had done at the outset for Kingsport Foundry, "painful" was a word that recurred frequently. "We're not going to get there for another five years; this is not a quick process. It is a long growth success process that at times can be painful. . . ."

The hardest part for him personally, he said, was "to relinquish the decision-making process, knowing that the person who is going to do it is going to make a mistake, and is not going to learn unless he makes a mistake."

That the foundry was a family business made it that much harder for him. "It's much more difficult if it's a son . . . you want him to be so much better and not make the mistakes you made. But then you realize if he doesn't make mistakes, he's not going to be any better than you were."

There were casualties along the way. Two of his supervisors were unable to adjust to the expanded role of the work force. Ring eventually eased one into retirement and phased the other into a consultant status.

If the transformation cost several people their jobs, it preserved far more. The condition of the ailing foundry improved dramatically. By 1989, the company was earning a profit of $100,000 a month on sales of $10 million a year. It had seven major new customers to replace the seven it lost—primarily in the power-generation and air-compressor industries. Scrap levels had dropped from over 14 percent to just below 9 percent. Employment, which had fallen to 75, was back up to 180.

But there were rewards that went beyond dollars and cents. The company decided it made sense, for example, for workers in some cases to visit customers to learn firsthand of quality issues. Ring was not prepared, however, for just how much impact such visits could have.

"We've taken teams as far away as Chicago—a five-person team, a four-person team, to say 'Hey, we're having a problem on this General Electric casting; we're having a problem on this air-compressor casting. Let's go into their plant and see exactly what will they want us to do.' We take those teams in and then they begin to see . . . 'Hey, we're supplying only one casting. They put thirty castings together to make an assembly. And here, if they've got one little problem with our casting, look what it does to everything else.'

"You'd be totally amazed at how these people, when they come back, and then they get in our plant, the effect it can have, the ripple effect throughout the entire work force of 'Hey, here's what we really do for this company up there. It goes into an air compressor like you see on the road. Every time you pass by just look at it. We make that thing.' "

In other words, one visit to a customer could generate an enormous amount of pride in the work force. And, Ring said, "I don't think you can have a work force, without pride . . . If you don't have that, I don't think you'll have a viable work force very long.

"It's exciting to begin to see it move and turn. It's hard to describe really the satisfaction you get from that . . . the camaraderie that you build in all the work force . . . you come through a period like we come through, you either got to come out of it united or you don't come out at all."

* * *

On the same day during that pre-Christmas week of 1989 that a team from the Kingsport Foundry & Manufacturing Corporation presented yet another project in its continuing battle with sand, a company called Cap Snap Company took the podium to present its plans to knock down a wall and free the flow of supplies. Like the foundry, Cap Snap was a small Kingsport manufacturer. But there the resemblance ended.

Whereas the foundry made weighty one-of-a-kind, labor-intensive products, Cap Snap's automated injection machines spit out 3.5 million colored plastic container tops each day.

Whereas the foundry in 1985 found itself in financial peril, Cap Snap occupied a secure niche in its industry, with a 15 to 20 percent yearly growth in sales.

And whereas the foundry was an indigenous family-run company, Cap Snap was owned by California investors. Built in 1977, its Kingsport plant was one of three.

But Cap Snap general manager Claudia Leonard—who was, as it happened, the granddaughter of the snapping cap's inventor—was as enthusiastic about Quality First in her way as Bill Ring was in his. It was the words "continual improvement" that really snagged her. For Cap Snap, the program represented a way to stay above a pack of competitors who would have loved to dislodge the little company from its enviable roost.

In the 1960s, Claudia's grandfather, George Faulstich, owned a California company that sold spring water in five-gallon jugs with cork stoppers. He invented the cap with a pull-off tab to replace the corks, and situated two injection molders in his water company. Soon other companies wanted the caps, and in 1965 he incorporated Cap Snap and established a factory in Menlo Park.

From a single blue cap, the product line expanded into more than a dozen sizes in twenty-two different colors, including orange, purple and pink. Some of the caps had paper labels; others were embossed; still others had names inked on. Some had foil inner seals; others didn't.

As it grew into a nationwide business, Cap Snap sought a site for a new plant closer to its midwestern customers. Tennessee Eastman, one of its suppliers, suggested Kingsport, which was centrally located near major highways. The original plant was 20,000 square feet. By 1989, it had grown into an 86,000-square-foot facility. After a New York plant was added in 1986, Cap Snap was within a day's drive of all continental U.S. customers. But it also had customers in Europe, South America and Asia.

In time Cap Snap led the competition, with $20 million in sales. That was good news, of course, but it created a new set of pressures. Said Claudia Leonard, "We had been the underdog and all of a sudden we emerged as the top dog, the largest manufacturer of this type of cap for the water and dairy industry. Now we had people on our tails. To keep that edge we needed something to help us."

Part of keeping that edge meant continually modifying the design of the cap, to hold onto the patent. The changes didn't have to be major. A switch from a tab with round edges to one whose square edges were easier to grip was sufficient. But such modifications were critical to staying ahead.

In addition, Cap Snap needed to stay abreast of changes in the packaging industry, which was in constant flux. Environmental pressures to recycle plastic, for example, meant that labels currently made of paper soon needed to be made of a plastic that could be easily reprocessed along with the caps themselves.

Leonard saw in Quality First "something to help us."

She enrolled a Cap Snap team in the second round of training. It tackled downtime on a color-adding machine, coming up with a new procedure that saved $30,000.

"I was impressed," she said. She could see not only financial benefits, but intangible ones as well. What happened when decisions were based on data, for example, was that "it takes people from being right or being wrong with their opinions . . . and yet you still let the people shine when they identify the problems and the improvements." As a former teacher, Leonard was sensitive to the way management could have its "pets." Teamwork took favoritism out of the workplace. "This way everyone can get the recognition when they work on something that's successful."

She asked that first team for its recommendations. "They said 'Pick another team.' Instead, she told them to do so, asking only that they come up with a mix of people by sex, departments and rank. She asked to be on that second team. "I thought it was important that I understood." Her team included machine operators and shift supervisors. With her there, the meetings were sometimes awkward. She found it necessary to limit her participation, because it seemed to intimidate the others. Her team worked on reducing waste on the printing machines, where caps had a tendency to fall off the pegs that were supposed to hold them firmly in place. The team came up with machine modifications.

Cap Snap also dispatched department managers to Brian Joiner's four-day Deming seminar and they restructured themselves into a management quality team, with Leonard shifting more and more into the role of a facilitator. The management team began to meet weekly to wrestle with the new philosophy, discussing the Fourteen Points and how they applied to Cap Snap. In the small meeting room where their sessions, and those of other teams, took place, evidence of their brainstorming covered the walls. They were merciless in their self-assessment of Cap Snap culture and themselves as managers. One list compared where they were now with another of where they wanted to be. Now, for example, the company culture was character-ized by "revenge" and "running rampant." What they wanted was one where there were "no repercussions" and "people asking ques-tions if they don't understand." The "now" list on "pride of work-manship" was very long: "some lacking;" "put in eight hours;" "recognition missing;" "don't understand end use;" "put up barri-ers;" "not enough training;" "not enough positive feedback."

Such sessions broke down barriers among the managers them-selves. People felt free to tell Leonard, for example, that she needed to exercise less control. "That's the hard part of management—to let go," she reflected. But she saw pronounced changes in other manag-ers and believed that she herself was asking more questions and downloading more.

Meanwhile, teams continued in Quality First. A team developed an absenteeism policy where one had barely existed before. Among the changes was more cross-training so people could fill in for each other.

Training for new employees was also increased. Whereas once employees learned their jobs from the shift supervisors, now the training was assigned to people in quality assurance, a department whose role was gradually evolving from inspection to training to ensure consistency and reduce variation.

The training itself was redesigned to be both oral and visual, "because people learn in different ways," said Leonard. "You can't blame an individual for not understanding if you haven't communicated to them in the way they get information." And Cap Snap enlisted the aid of Tennessee Eastman to train in-house facilitators for the teams.

The sales representatives took it upon themselves to make videotapes of customers' production lines so workers could see their caps in use.

Cap Snap had the luxury of proceeding at a less pressured pace than failing companies such as the Kingsport Foundry. "If it takes five or six or seven years to get everyone trained and going, it's fine," Leonard said. "It doesn't have to be perfect."

III. QUALITY STORIES

Holston Valley Hospital

Calling themselves "Deming's Dynamic Dischargers," a team from Holston Valley Hospital, a 657-bed facility that was Kingsport's third largest employer, was assembled from nursing, patient registration and patient transport to look at the discharge process, which patients had complained was too slow. A survey of patients disclosed that in two consecutive months, 12 and 14 percent answered "no" to the question "Were you discharged promptly when you were ready to go?"

Their project was described as follows: "Improve/expedite patient discharge. This will be from the time the physician writes the discharge order until the patient exits the hospital as a discharged patient."

In its data collection phase, the team flowcharted the discharge process and quickly saw that there was a bottleneck when a patient was not registered as having what was called a "courtesy discharge," which meant that all payment arrangements had been made. In the absence of a courtesy discharge, the patient had to stop at the accounting office on leaving. In fact, often the arrangements had been made but not communicated to the nursing floor, so that the patient was being needlessly directed to the accounting office. This delayed the discharge and also wasted time for the accounting and transport staffs. The team came up with a computer entry for the discharge information.

The primary cause of delays, though, was a hospital policy that dictated that each discharged patient be escorted by a hospital worker to a waiting vehicle. This took place even though that same patient might have been navigating hospital corridors under his or her own steam for days. Reported the team, "We did this because it has 'always been that way' and everyone assumed it was 'law.' " Hospital lawyers advised to the contrary, however, as did a Medicare/Medicaid specialist. A new procedure was instituted for determining when a patient required an escort.

"Initially, it was thought that Central Transport was the prime culprit in lengthy delays in discharge," the team confessed. It was true that there had been delays because wheelchairs were not always available when the discharge order came down. Allowing patients to walk out unaided freed up both people and equipment.

A survey of 1,259 discharges in the month following the new procedure showed that 33 percent of patients were walking out unassisted. "This saves at least twenty minutes per patient of transport time, and based on this information we will experience an estimated cost savings of $8,985 a year," the team reported.

In summary, said the team, "The process works. Changes have begun with process improvement. The barriers between the various areas dealing with patient discharge are coming down. The team's purpose is to improve the process constantly and we plan to that end."

MECO Corporation

MECO Corporation, a Greeneville, Tennessee, manufacturer of barbecue grills and metal folding furniture, assigned its seven-person team to find ways of reducing paint defects on metal folding chairs.

Looking at six months' worth of data, the team found that paint defects fell into three major categories, but that one—hook marks—accounted for 68 percent.

Suspended from two hooks, the chairs traversed a moving line through a five-stage washing process, a drying oven and painting, then on to inspection. Those that passed were baked, then inspected again. If they failed at that point, they were stripped and they began the process over again. The team believed that faulty hooks, weakened by high temperatures, were the culprit, allowing chairs to slip off. Data collected over a six-week period showed that the team was correct. Some 1,629 dropped off in the oven, in overhead netting or in the paint booths, while another 6,459 were hanging by one hook, allowing them to bump into chairs ahead and behind, increasing by 50 percent the chance that those would be damaged. In a twenty-two-week period, 21,791 chairs required stripping and repainting. That was just 6.69 percent of the total, but it cost nearly $40,000.

As a result of the team's recommendations, the plant ordered a stronger hook. The purchase of a new oven with temperature controls and a water supressant system to extinguish fires would hold temperatures to 800 degrees, and further minimize damage to hooks. After these changes the line was monitored. There were just 477 rejects, compared to 3,789 for a similar prior period. The team projected annual cost savings of $112,408.

The team credited Quality First with teaching them about the tools now being used to improve other processes at MECO as well as with improving communication between team members and production personnel, "the heroes in this plant."

Sullivan County Board of Education

When an upper-echelon team from the Sullivan County School Board held a brainstorming session for project selection, fully thirteen possibilities popped up on the list. Among them were substitute teachers, budget, implementation of technology, discipline policy, middle-school athletics and student and parent apathy.

The board chose the substitute teacher issue, a frequent source of complaints from both principals, who had trouble getting substitutes when they needed them, and from substitute teachers, who thought their pay of $30 or less a day was too low. There was a general consensus on the team that the process of recruiting and assigning substitute teachers could use improvement. A subsequent survey of principals showed that eighteen of thirty agreed.

The team brainstormed again to draw up a list of problems with the existing process. Pay and availability of substitutes were clearly two issues. The others were their training and evaluation. In addition, the team was interested in the amount of teacher absenteeism that made substitutes necessary in the first place.

In gathering data, the team discovered that there were peak months for substitutes. During the 1988–89 school year, for example, they were in demand nearly twice as much in May, when teachers tended to use their accumulated days off, as in September. The second highest month was April.

Reviewing availability, the team examined work records and discovered that many substitutes worked only a few days, while others worked many days.

The team decided to survey principals on various aspects of the substitute issue. Duplication of calls popped up as a major problem. Because principals all worked from the same lists, they often called the same people. Eighty-seven of the respondents were required to call more than one substitute at least some of the time, usually with only hours to go before school started. Fourteen of the respondents thought substitutes should get more pay. Not unexpectedly, a survey of substitutes elicited agreement on that point as well.

The team made five major recommendations: that substitutes' maximum salary increase to $35 a day; that the calling process be centralized to prevent duplication of calls and spread the work to more substitutes; that the process be computerized; that lists be updated frequently; and that the board look into reducing teacher absenteeism, perhaps by paying teachers not to take personal days.

Cap Snap Company

Cap Snap had grown so rapidly since moving to Kingsport that space was a real problem. At one point in the decorating room, where caps were labeled, there had been five labeling machines; now there were ten, and thanks to crowding they no longer lined up with the bays through which a forklift delivered the stock on pallets.

"Lack of space in the decorating room" was the project selected by Cap Snap's fourth team, composed of a printer operator, forklift operator, two shift foremen, a billing clerk and an electrician. In time the project was redefined more precisely as "excessive rework in the decorating room." Data collected on the ten machines showed that a stock change took 1.6 minutes on the machines that lined up with the bays; on those that were behind the wall, however, the stock change took 5.7 minutes because of pallets on the other machines that had to be moved out of the way of the forklift. The team recommended removing the wall, a change it estimated would save $1,500 a year on rework.

Management endorsed the team's recommendation and assigned it the task of overseeing the demolition of the wall and the construction of a more open structure to take its place.

CHAPTER FIVE

The United States Navy

Management in authority will take pride in their adoption of the new philosophy and in their new responsibilities. They will have courage to break with tradition, even to the point of exile among their peers.

—W. EDWARDS DEMING
Out of the Crisis

The real heroes in making Total Quality Management work were the depot commanders who took it up and believed in it and practiced it at substantial risk.

—FORMER ADMIRAL JOHN KIRKPATRICK
March 1990 interview

I. GETTING UNDERWAY

The news that Col. Jerald B. Gartman was coming back, this time as commanding officer, was no cause for celebration at the Naval Aviation Depot at Cherry Point, North Carolina, back in 1986. Gartman was remembered only too well as an exacting production officer from 1980 to 1982, a man with a temper who constantly rode herd on managers and workers to get the work out on time. The son of a Missouri farmer, he held degrees in industrial engineering and systems management, but academia had not smoothed the rough edges of his personality. Gartman was both open and blunt. He had a chestful of combat ribbons from Vietnam, where he had been shot down a half dozen times, and he ran his command like a battle post.

Cherry Point was one of six naval aviation depots that repaired, overhauled and modified military aircraft, and it was the only one run by Marines. The Navy high command had let it be known they weren't happy with the record of the depots, and for good reason. Between 1981 and 1984 they lost $300 million. By 1986, the financial situation had improved but a voluminous report for the Navy by a team of consultants had been highly critical of the way the depots were run, and the brass were looking for ways to cut them down to size.

So when Cherry Point got the news that Gartman was taking over, no doubt with a license to kill, the reaction—this being the Marines and all—was, as Jack Adams would later recall, "Oh, shit." Explained Adams, who would become Gartman's point man on quality, "He could be an absolute madman when he wanted to. And everybody was saying 'He's going to destroy us.'"

But this was not the same Jerry Gartman who had left in 1982. This was a Jerry Gartman who had been to a W. Edwards Deming seminar and now talked about how to increase productivity by focusing on quality. In short, Gartman had left as a Theory X kind of manager and come back, Adams said, "with *Out of the Crisis* in his hand. He wanted this thing done." This thing was "TQM"—Total Quality Management, the military's name for its quality drive, based on the Deming method, though Dr. Deming himself never used the term.

The CO had not turned into a teddy bear, of course. Even four years later, as a self-described TQM zealot, Gartman would still maintain he was motivated only by his desire for results. "If I could use whips and chains and get better results, I would do it."

Adams discovered that his boss had not lost his iron will as soon as Gartman selected him to be TQM coordinator. "No, thank you," Adams said, thinking with apprehension of the workplace politics involved.

"I'm not asking you to volunteer," Gartman told him.

The chain of circumstances that resulted in the conversion of Jerald B. Gartman could be traced back to 1981, when a young research psychologist named Laurie Broedling from a military think tank called the Navy Personnel Research and Development Center heard Deming speak at a conference in San Diego. She was the leader at that time of a team studying organizational improvement.

NPRDC was an applied research center whose mission was to find better ways to attract, select, train and deploy naval personnel. Back in 1981, Broedling was working on productivity improvement in onshore support systems, as opposed to the fighting forces aboard ships and planes—a distinction often made when speaking of naval operations. So it was that she happened to attend a conference at the Kona Kai Club on labor relations and on the quality of work life that featured W. Edwards Deming.

Broedling expected Deming to speak about the use of statistical sampling, which he had pioneered at the U.S. Census Bureau, a topic of some interest to her because she frequently dealt with surveys. Instead, she heard an abbreviated version of his revolutionary-sounding philosophy. She would later recall its effect. "I was mesmerized . . . I guess the eureka part of it was that it brought together a lot of things that had bothered me for a long time." One was Deming's opposition to performance appraisals, which seemed to work to no one's satisfaction in the federal government no matter how much they were redesigned or modified. NPRDC was constantly asked to come up with a better way to rate people. According to Deming, there was no better way to destroy people than to rate them.

At Laurie's urging, the next NPRDC researcher to hear Deming was Steve Dockstader, who attended a two-day seminar in Boston. He and his wife, Linda M. Doherty, who was also a psychologist at NPRDC, had previously heard him on the NBC special "If Japan Can . . . Why Can't We?" The program was advertised while they were on a car trip with their children. That night they pulled into a motel and parked themselves in front of the TV to watch. That program emphasized Deming's statistical contributions, and like Broedling Dockstader fully expected to learn about statistical quality control at the Boston seminar. And like Broedling he was surprised. "What I heard about was management instead."

Over the next decade, NPRDC served as an incubator for application of the Deming method to the public sector, which came to be known as Total Quality Management (TQM).

Meanwhile, Broedling and other quality advocates lobbied the Navy at ever higher levels to become involved with quality methods. In the late 1980s, with a former GM executive, Robert Costello, in charge of acquisitions, the Department of Defense as a whole lurched fitfully in that direction. On March 30, 1988, then Secretary of Defense Frank Carlucci issued a memo pledging that he was "giving top priority to the DoD Total Quality Management effort as the vehicle for attaining continuous quality improvement in our operations" in order to meet presidential productivity objectives.

Within DoD, the Navy continued in the lead, and within the Navy, the Naval Air Systems Command (NAVAIR), which oversaw depots like that at Cherry Point, was out in front. By 1989, an estimated 21 percent of the NAVAIR work force was involved in formal process improvement efforts. NAVAIR had sent 2,000 people to four-day Deming seminars.

By 1990, the Navy had a Secretary firmly committed to quality in the person of H. Lawrence Garrett III, and an equally committed Under Secretary, J. Daniel Howard, who had attended a Deming seminar and now sermonized on quality. Perhaps most telling about the changes taking place was Broedling's elevation to the status of TQM expert-in-residence at the Pentagon. Her appointment as a Deputy Under Secretary of Defense was announced on February 13, with a release that quoted W. Edwards Deming: "The appointment of Dr. Laurie Broedling to teach management principles for optimization at the DoD is the right start, I believe, toward accomplishment of the responsibilities of government for cooperation with industry and education."

As the 1990s dawned, the Navy—along with the other services— had an unprecedented financial crisis on hand. Spurred by the Cold War meltdown, the Congress and jaded taxpayers, irate about $999 pliers and $436 hammers, were pressing for huge reductions in military expenditures. It was sometimes said that the federal government lacked an incentive to make quality improvements. No more. Observed Under Secretary Howard, "We have a sense of urgency. If any private-sector company was faced with a drop in their bottom line of the sort that we are anticipating over the next five years, they would declare bankruptcy tomorrow and walk away. What we are looking at in the most rosy of scenarios would amount to catastrophic failure in the private sector.

"If we're going to maintain a viable maritime force over the next decade, we have to find a way out of the crisis, and one of those ways is through quality-focused management and streamlining every efficiency we can get from everywhere, because we're not going to get any more money. We're going to get a hell of a lot less. . . . Ten years from today there's no way we can predict where our budget's going to be, except we can be absolutely sure we're going to be a smaller organization than we are now, with an undiminished mission, and that is to protect the national interest of this country."

In the early 1980s, the future didn't look bright for a Deming-style initiative in the Navy. NPRDC's first feasibility study concluded that the approach would be next to impossible, owing primarily to the great mobility of management, a "deadly disease," according to Deming. Mobility was built into the military system. On average, the military shore command and the membership of all the fighting forces changed posts every two or three years in a giant game of musical chairs. Moreover, commanding officers sought to distinguish themselves during each tour of duty by introducing new programs or reforms. That was how they worked their way up the promotional ladder. "In order to get a good fitness report, they need to have done something on their watch that is theirs, that they can be identified with," explained NPRDC's Linda Doherty. They were not particularly interested in carrying on the programs of their predecessors. Indeed, they could show rapid improvement by cutting those programs—and the attendant costs. Thus mobility and the performance appraisal system were fused.

Mobility was most pronounced in headquarters, where admirals and political appointees tended to come and go even more frequently than below. Above all, TQM demanded continuity—but the system wasn't designed to provide it. Nor was there a constituency for slowing the constant movement. In trying to superimpose the Deming philosophy over current practices, no one questioned the current practices. Said Dockstader, "No one saw it as a paradigm shift. . . . that maybe you didn't need to move people."

In addition to mobility, there were other military characteristics that the research psychologists viewed as impediments. The Navy drew action-oriented people—folks who tended to jump from the "Plan" step to the "Act" step in the Deming cycle, leaving out the interim "Do" and "Check" or study stages. No "quick fix," TQM took time and patience to organize teams that would study processes and produce recommendations for action. It was understandable that military people would have a problem with that. In the heat of battle, you didn't form a team to study the appropriate moment to fire a torpedo.

In the early 1980s when the NPRDC people were discovering Deming, so too were some naval installations, among them the North Island naval aviation depot just across the mouth of the bay from Point Loma, where NPRDC was situated. Eventually the two connected. For NPRDC it was an ideal test site. Both the commanding officer, Phillip Monroe, and Bill Cooper, head of production, were eager to get started. Moreover, they thought they could get support from their boss, a rear admiral named John Kirkpatrick, who had previously been the commanding officer of North Island and now was in charge of all the naval aviation depots. Kirkpatrick was eager to see some changes that would stem financial losses. Monroe and Cooper seized the opportunity to tell him about their plan for a pilot project using the Deming method.

Kirkpatrick listened with interest to a briefing by NPRDC. While the depots were not in business to make a profit, their goal was to break even, not go broke, as they appeared to be doing. Trying TQM there would not be a great departure from doing it in private industry. The depots operated in certain respects like any business— bidding on jobs, buying parts and other supplies and paying wages. Their customers were primarily other Navy air operations, but they also did work for the Army and the Air Force.

Unlike private industry, however, the depots' prices were ultimately set by the Comptroller of the Navy, through a complicated process based on the number of man-hours, or norms, and the cost per man-hour, or rates. The financial problems of the early '80s arose because the norms and rates had been set too low. It was all part of a productivity drive. "The Comptroller of the Navy wasn't crazy," Kirkpatrick explained. "He thought there was inefficiency in the process, and that by cutting the rates and norms, he could force them to become more productive and efficient. But they didn't know how to become more productive and efficient. So they just lost money."

Not that the people in charge of the depots didn't try to save. They cut travel, property maintenance, training and other so-called frills in their budgets.

Previous efforts to increase productivity in other ways had not been successful. Quality circles had popped up like mushrooms throughout the Department of Defense, including the depots. By 1984, there were 2,000 circles in DoD, but they didn't seem to be working well. NPRDC would eventually study 500 of them, concluding in an April 1989 report that "even though the quality circles operate in accordance with accepted procedures, meet regularly, are run democratically and generally follow guidelines set forth in training," management by and large ignored their suggestions. That, in time, was the kiss of death. The Pearl Harbor Naval Shipyard, for example, had eagerly chartered quality circles. In 1980 there were roughly thirty; by 1984 there were two. "While management showed support for quality circles in terms of money, facilitators, training and member time, they were less supportive of solution implementation, personnel development and recognition," said the NPRDC report. In addition, the quality circles did not have firm procedures for measuring quality, and therefore didn't have cost-benefit ratios that could later be translated into cost savings, a major way to capture management attention.

Appointed to his post in August of 1984, Kirkpatrick was certainly disturbed by the $100 million-a-year losses, but he was far more upset at the way quality was going downhill. Inspections routinely turned up an across-the-board defect rate of 3 to 4 percent. As a former fleet maintenance officer, he had personal experience with the depots' shortcomings. He would never forget the leaky engine that made it all the way from the Jacksonville, Florida, depot to the Diego Garcia base on an island in the Indian Ocean. The oil leaks became apparent as the crew removed the engine from its pressurized container and tested it down in the engine shop. That meant a plane that couldn't fly, which stood out like an ink blot on the daily readiness reports. Kirkpatrick did not think the defective engine had been knowingly shipped, but he was convinced someone must have realized it was marginal. A subsequent audit of the Jacksonville shop turned up cloudy technical instructions and stiff pressure on workers to meet schedules, putting quantity ahead of quality.

As a result of the bad publicity the depots were getting, "morale was lower than a snake's belly," the admiral said.

When Steve Dockstader and the people from North Island briefed him on their plans for a trial of the Deming method, Kirkpatrick was hooked almost immediately. "It was so simple. It made so much sense. I said why don't we do it everywhere?" Dockstader discussed the mobility issue as a roadblock. "That's unsatisfactory," Kirkpatrick said. "We just have to figure out how to do it." Eventually he would decide mobility was less a hindrance than some people thought. Even though people moved around, they stayed within the Navy—the same corporation, it could be said. Not like in private industry, where people really jumped ship. But the "on my watch" syndrome—the desire to leave one's mark as a CO by doing something distinctive—was clearly disruptive. Kirkpatrick subsequently supported a change wherein the commanding officer of a depot would first serve one notch below as executive officer, giving him a four-year tenure on average.

He also told the NPRDC psychologists that they would have to do more than study and document results; they would have to come up with a workable scheme and do the training. This was a new role for them and it took some persuasion on his part to get them to accept it. For their part, the NPRDC people knew enough to tell Kirkpatrick one thing: He would have to head the TQM push.

In January of 1985 Kirkpatrick announced to the depots that quality was a top priority. He began to dispatch large numbers of high-ranking officers and civilians to the four-day Deming seminars, sponsoring two himself in San Diego and Jacksonville. At that time, no one knew quite what to call what was then being referred to as "Statistical Process Control" or "that Deming stuff." There was consensus that it needed a name, that people needed to be "talking the same language," Kirkpatrick said. The Japanese called it "Total Quality Control." The first two words sounded okay, but no one liked the word "control." Not only did it sound sort of Machiavellian, but it had an inappropriate connotation. The military talked about "command and control" in connection with weapons systems. At a meeting that summer Steve Dockstader remembered one member of the group from Kirkpatrick's staff, a behavioral psychologist named Nancy Warren, saying as they kicked ideas around, "What we're talking about is managing quality. Why don't we call it 'Total Quality Management.' "

Thus history was made.

The naval air depots, until then known as naval air rework facilities, also got a name change after Kirkpatrick heard Deming inveigh against waste and rework. If they were going to follow Deming, it no longer seemed appropriate to designate them "rework" facilities.

That summer, Dockstader outlined a two-phase approach for the application of TQM, a sequence he believed addressed two existing conditions: mobility of management and an action-oriented demand for results.

Deming often talked about the need to develop a "critical mass" of people who understood his philosophy and spoke the same language of quality. In Phase One, that critical mass would be formed from the top down, along Navy hierarchical lines, and those involved would announce and define the new quality philosophy. Management teams called "Quality Management Boards" (QMBs) would take charge of changes in the system and direct the activities of process action teams (PATs). The teams would deal with tough problems that would yield some immediate results, to show that TQM worked. This would help disarm the skeptics.

In Phase Two, management would address such systemic issues as forging a new relationship with suppliers, doing away with the performance appraisal system and introducing the "voice of the customer" into all operations. Perhaps issues would emerge from Phase One, such as a surplus of workers, or excessive layers of managers. Those would be addressed in Phase Two as well.

The modus operandi was to export whatever worked at North Island to the other depots, a kind of "rolling implementation plan."

As Kirkpatrick and others watched with interest, by summer of 1986 North Island was generating success stories involving team efforts. NPRDC researchers examined them under a microscope, documenting not only what worked but what didn't. One clear-cut victory, for example, took place in the shop that removed old metal plate from aircraft components and applied a new coat. The part to be plated was attached to an anode submerged in a plating solution. A current passed through the anode, causing a chemical reaction that resulted in deposits of metal molecules on the surface of the part. For the process to work, the anodes had to be free of lead salts that built up over a period of time. A clogged anode contributed to underplating, uneven plating and thin plating.

At the time a team was organized to examine this process, the anodes were being dismantled and taken to another shop for sandblasting if they no longer functioned properly, about every six months. The affected tank would be down for as long as a week or more. Four feet long and made of lead, the anodes were difficult to remove. Often they were so corroded they couldn't stand up to the sandblasting and had to be replaced—at a cost of $300 apiece.

Checking elsewhere in the country, the team learned North Island was not alone in having no regular cleaning schedule. Experimenting in stages, the team eventually came up with a procedure in which anodes were soaked every six weeks in a cleaner over a weekend, then spray-rinsed with an air-water spray cleaner located in the plating shop. Not only did this remove the lead salts without damaging the anode, it minimized downtime for the whole tank.

While praising the team for its commonsense approach and participative decision making, the researchers noted that members resisted the use of systematic data collection in favor of using their expertise and relying on day-to-day experiences. Because they collected no baseline data—such as, for example, the conduction of anodes relative to their age, tank downtime and quality of plating—it wasn't possible to translate the gains into cost savings, which could have dramatized the success of the project to others outside the plating shop.

Reluctance to gather and analyze data was a failing in other case reports as well. A joint team from the grinding and plating unit clarified and standardized certain procedures that everyone knew were causing variation. But once again, the process was not thoroughly documented. "In fairness to the artisans in plating," the researchers remarked, however, "they are not strongly encouraged by managers to use data to investigate issues and make decisions."

Having North Island so conveniently under its microscope, NPRDC was able to continually refine its training model. Meanwhile, Admiral Kirkpatrick took the show on the road, lobbying for quality at the other naval air supply depots under his command, which were proceeding at a somewhat uneven pace. In some, he recalled, "they treated me like I was from outer space. They were incensed at the implication that they were not doing quality. But my role was to keep pressing the commanding officers. As I continually talked about it and asked about it, people began to realize, 'This is real. This crazy guy is not going to go away.' "

Also in 1985, the Navy comptroller had revised depot prices to stanch the losses. But they were still expected to lose more than $50 million. Kirkpatrick stunned everyone by predicting they would make money—and indeed they did. To be sure, it was just $2.3 million on a budget of about $2 billion for the entire Naval Aviation Logistic Center, but they also liquidated some $20 million in debts. It was too early to credit the fledgling TQM movement for the gains; perhaps, Kirkpatrick said, it was merely the Hawthorne effect—that when the spotlight was focused on long-ignored issues, they tended to right themselves, at least for the short term.

He predicted another profit of $55 million in 1986. "I was wrong. We made $125 million in 1986." These savings, however, immediately generated additional cost reductions from above.

As a new round of penny-pinching took effect in 1986, other events made that a tumultuous year. In January the secretary released a report from the consulting firm of Coopers & Lybrand that accused the depots of mismanagement and waste, and recommended 104 ways to deal with it, such as an inventory control system, computerization and a job-by-job analysis aimed at cutting those that were superfluous. The consultants felt the depots could increase productivity by cutting their work force of 24,000 by as much as 15 percent, with no ill effects.

Although Kirkpatrick had discussed TQM at length with the consultants, arguing that it would result in more work for less money, and could be accompanied by a natural attrition of the work force, the final report contained no mention of TQM. Kirkpatrick was exasperated. He agreed with many of its findings about where problems existed, but he thought the solutions were by and large the same bankrupt methods used in the past to make workers pay for management's shortcomings. This was especially true of the proposed layoffs. "I've got to tell 4,800 people 'You're going to improve productivity *and* you're going to lose your jobs?' " he protested. The consultants wanted a 15 percent cut in the work force? "I'd be as well off to have people line up and count off by sixes and lay off every sixth man. It would be just about as effective and it would cost less." The consultants had also written themselves into the plans for the future.

The Assistant Secretary of the Navy over Kirkpatrick's command, Everett Pyatt, also had ideas for increasing productivity. Earlier, he had mandated competitive contracts at the Navy shipyards, and now he wanted the depots to compete as well, not only with private contractors but also among themselves.

Until then, the work of the depots was more or less guaranteed. They did the major scheduled overhauls known as "depot-level maintenance," along with repairs, while major modifications generally were handled by the prime contractors—the people who had built the aircraft. The maintenance contract was usually divided between two sites, one on the East Coast, the other on the West. This protected the Navy's security, were problems to develop in one area, and it also cut down on transportation expenses. Even so, there was some competition between the depots. Each wanted as much work as it could get, and each had a constituency whose congressional watchdogs maintained a vigilant attitude. But that was not the same as going head-to-head.

Kirkpatrick was appalled. TQM was just getting underway. The depots needed to communicate and cooperate, not compete among themselves. "We had worked hard at building a corporate sense of trust. I could see no better way of destroying it." But he had no choice. It was also his task to select the first competitive jobs. He decided to put the troops to a real test.

It had been widely assumed that old, familiar equipment would be chosen for the contract competition. Kirkpatrick selected the most modern instead, the maintenance contract on the F–14 Navy fighter jet. The Norfolk and North Island depots, which had been doing the work, would bid against each other; the winner would bid against private contractors.

What Kirkpatrick feared did in fact happen. "It was terrible. All communication ceased." But when the bids came in, although different, they were so close financially that Kirkpatrick successfully argued that the Navy's final bid would be stronger if the two depots worked on it as a team. At that point they hired Coopers and Lybrand to assist.

They needed all the help they could get. "We didn't even know how to prepare a bid." Bidding against Grumman Aerospace Corporation and LTV Aerospace & Defense Company, the depots won in a scrupulously administered competition. Next, the Jacksonville and Alameda depots went after the contract to do major modifications on the P–3, a four-engine patrol aircraft used in submarine warfare. They won that one as well.

Even though he believed, as Dr. Deming said, that such competition was unhealthy in the long term, Kirkpatrick privately congratulated himself when the depots won the contracts. "The fact of TQM, I am certain, enabled them to win—the teams, the analytic tools. Without having been exposed to those, they would never have succeeded." He knew, however, that despite the evidence, some of the Navy hierarchy, all the way up to the secretary's office, still did not believe TQM was a route to greater productivity.

Elsewhere in those years little quality oases bloomed in places where the commanding officer had become a champion of TQM. At the Pearl Harbor naval shipyard, Captain Robert Traister launched a Deming-based effort to counter high costs, shrinking budgets and rework that consumed 15 percent of the shipyard's time and money. A May 1988 article in the *Journal of Ship Production* documented the Pearl Harbor effort: "If our experience is typical of the eight public shipyards that employ approximately 60,000 people, this means that the equivalent of 9,000 or more people (that is, the equivalent of another shipyard) are doing nothing but rework full-time," it noted. The quality circle program was revitalized with the management support that had been lacking in the past, and the shipyard launched a massive training program for managers and teams in problem-solving tools and techniques.

In 1987, the Fleet Accounting and Disbursing Center–Pacific (FAADC–PAC), the Navy's principal accounting operation on the West Coast, sought the help of NPRDC after Captain Keith Nyenhuis took over. Nyenhuis had seen his former organization, the Naval Supply Center, struggle with TQM, experiencing a painful false start that emphasized only Statistical Process Control (SPC). With a command of his own, he realized reform had to begin with senior management.

FAADC–PAC cut paychecks, paid vendors and provided other financial services to some 700 "activities" in ships, squadrons, bases, airstations and other units. Recently reorganized and expanded, the office was lagging far behind in some payments and had a poor reputation with its "customers." Executive director Linell K. Fridella summarized the situation this way: "Our work force grew, our activities grew, and our problems grew as well."

Nyenhuis asked his managers whether they had ever sought the opinion of customers on their service. "The answer was 'Absolutely not. Why should I ever do that? In the past all they've given me is a bunch of grief.' I decided to take the department owners on the road—to meet the customers."

He scheduled four such meetings, opening each one with the announcement that FAADC–PAC was not happy with its track record and wanted to work with them to improve performance. "It was a bloody time in this organization's history. It was not fun—to have our customers telling us what we were doing wrong." The meetings produced a list of 125 action items, and the agency went to work with the help of some ten teams under TQM coordinator Pat Jordan. Like the supply depots, FAADC–PAC used the NPRDC model with quality management boards and project action teams.

Six months later, the managers went out again to meet the customers. This time there were only thirty or so action items. Many of the improvements had resulted from increased communication between the people in information systems and the work force, so that computer programs were tailored to their needs. By the third meeting with customers, so few irritations remained that most discussion centered on changes in the works. "There was an entirely different attitude out there than there was two years ago," said Nyenhuis.

One team wondered whether there could be some way to thin the 225 computerized expenditure reports that arrived weekly and monthly in multiple copies—typically thirty-two on paper and sixteen on microfiche. Law required that the copies be stored for two years. Thick reports filled whole rooms, limiting space available to people. And the bill from the data processor was $9.5 million a year. The team surveyed users to see how many copies of the reports they actually needed. They concluded that the number often could be cut by a quarter, or that microfiche could be substituted for paper, taking up much less space. The implications of that team's study were enormous, not only for FAADC–PAC but for other military units awash in paper.

Such quality efforts were likely to fade if not institutionalized with support from the top. Indeed, a change of command at North Island had temporarily eroded the depot's gains. And things slowed at FAADC–PAC when Nyenhuis left. Meanwhile, things were also stalled at the top. Even though booster John Kirkpatrick had moved up the chain of command at NAVAIR and was trying to rally support in Washington to the quality cause, there were limits to what he could do. But other forces were at work.

In 1987, Robert Costello, who had been head of purchasing at General Motors and involved with the Toyota joint venture that produced Chevy Novas, was appointed Assistant Secretary of Defense for Production and Logistics—a job that put him in close contact with defense industries. On a scouting trip to North Island, Costello met Broedling. He was "wildly enthusiastic" about what he had seen, she said. "He decided if people in San Diego could do it, it could be done." And when he became Under Secretary for Acquisition in late 1987, he was in a position to make things happen.

And happen they did. Secretary of Defense Frank Carlucci declared the following March that TQM had already "achieved reduced costs and increased efficiency and effectiveness in several DoD components. We now need to expand the TQM effort throughout DoD. The ultimate goal is the satisfied quality-equipped, quality-supported soldier, sailor, airman and marine."

Whereas before, Kirkpatrick and the depot commanders had been out front on the quality, quietly supported by the commander of

NAVAIR, then Admiral Joe Wilkinson, now TQM "was the thing to do," Kirkpatrick said.

In May, Costello sponsored a four-day Deming seminar for the military, which attracted a number of high-level admirals, generals and political appointees. And in August, Broedling helped put together a three-hour briefing for fifty top-level people at the Pentagon, which Carlucci opened with the statement that TQM was "the most important thing we can do for our war-fighting capability."

What impressed Broedling about the briefing was that "no one ever seemed to remember being together on any topic relating to leadership. The mere fact that it happened made quite an impression." Among those people in attendance that day was H. Lawrence Garrett III, then Under Secretary of the Navy. Afterward, he asked Laurie Broedling to be his technical adviser on TQM. "He said, in typical tongue-in-cheek humor, 'Well, I guess I have to do this.' " He wanted to know how.

It was an astonishing leap upward. As Broedling's colleague Linda Doherty summed it up, NPRDC was "a little tiny spec in the Navy. Usually if we were dealing at some high level, it meant something bad happened." Not this time.

Garrett had served in the Navy as a machinist mate, a naval flight officer and—after earning a degree from the San Diego School of Law—a legal adviser to the submarine commander of the U.S. Fleet. He also held an undergraduate degree in business management.

To him, TQM was nothing new. "This is what I've been doing for twenty years wherever I go," he reflected some months later. He believed, as Deming said, that people "do want to do a better job and often you find it's the system that's impeding them." Moreover, it seemed to him that quality methods were working both in private industry and in the naval air systems command. "So why take issue with it?"

Garrett assembled an executive steering group of the top twenty military men and civilians in the Navy. (In keeping with the DoD penchant for acronyms, it was known as DON-TQM-ESG.) Garrett knew that there was a tendency among these high-level officeholders to send surrogates to such meetings. The next thing you knew you had a lieutenant sitting in the admiral's seat. As an indication of how important he viewed this group, he ruled that members were forbidden to send substitutes. If they were absent, their seat remained empty. He figured if he could be there, "so can they."

Once again, the people in the group had never before come to-gether routinely for reasons pertaining to broad leadership issues. Broedling was assigned to develop a TQM education plan for their approval. It included videos, reading materials, speakers and other presentations. She also persuaded Dr. Deming to speak to the group for two hours on their leadership responsibilities for quality. After-ward there was lunch with Garrett, who, in a promotion that boded well for TQM, had become Secretary of the Navy.

Nowhere was there more mobility in the service than at the top. By 1989, with a change of administrations, both Carlucci and Cos-tello were gone. But in another piece of what Broedling termed "incredibly good luck," Costello was succeeded by John Betti, who had been at Ford Motor Company since 1962 in a variety of posi-tions, the last as executive vice president for diversified products operations. His work had brought him into contact with Deming, Ford's chief consultant since 1983, and he was a quality booster. Betti tapped Broedling to become his Deputy Under Secretary for TQM.

Meanwhile, back at the Navy, a career foreign service officer, J. Daniel Howard, who had been Assistant Secretary of Defense for Public Affairs under Carlucci, was appointed to Garrett's old job as Under Secretary. Garrett asked him to head up the TQM drive.

Howard took his mission very seriously. He had spent most of the decade of the 1970s in Japan, when the country was emerging as a formidable economic power. He had attended meetings of the Japan Productivity Center, run by the Kei-dan-ren, the Japanese equivalent of the National Association of Manufacturers in the United States, where from time to time the Japanese would make a reference "ac-cording to Dr. Deming."

"I didn't know who in the hell Dr. Deming was. . . . It would come up again and again." He eventually learned more about the man and his method, and the effect it had had in Japan, but "I didn't really understand . . ."

Howard enrolled in a four-day Deming seminar in early 1990. Few people have that experience without a series of intense reactions, sometimes negative. In Howard's case, he said, it was "the most phenomenal educational experience I've had as an adult." All sorts of "light bulbs went on."

He said he suddenly understood why, for example, some twenty years earlier in Japan with the U.S. Information Service, he had experienced such a difficult time in building attendance at cultural programs designed to win friends and influence among the Japanese. The failure to draw all the people who had been targeted had troubled him for years.

Using computers, his dedicated staff had assembled a list of 1,800 prominent Japanese and designed a series of lecture discussion programs that would interest them.

Over a period of several years, some 70 percent of the target audience attended at least one program. But Howard wanted the remaining 30 percent. He told his staff, "These are important people. We ought to be getting them in here. We must be doing something wrong. . . . I insisted my staff design programs to appeal to their interest." His staff did so, coming up with specialized events for the 30 percent, and studiously consulting quarterly printouts on attendance for the results. While the center did succeed in attracting a handful of the holdouts, someone suddenly noticed that repeat attendance at the mainline programs was falling off.

Howard was frustrated. "I never knew what was wrong. All I knew, my staff was exhausted; they were practically in revolt. So I gave up in despair." He never understood what he regarded as a failure. "I did the things I thought you were supposed to do. I had a good staff. I had excellent rapport with them. I provided strong leadership, a great sense of direction. We all worked like hell. I think if they'd had the stamina and I had had the stamina to keep it up, I'd have driven them straight down the sewer . . ."

The bulb that shed light on that experience, Howard said, was Dr. Deming's funnel demonstration—designed to show the ill effects of "tampering."

In that demonstration, Deming dropped a marble fifty times through a funnel, marking the points where it came to rest. The object was to cluster the points. But the more he moved the funnel to assure the marble would drop closer to its last point, the more the distances between points increased. The best results were achieved by holding the funnel in the same position. The point Dr. Deming made was that "tampering"—well-meaning but uninformed adjustments—merely increased variation, producing worse results, not better.

Howard realized that twenty years ago he had been guilty of tampering.

Again "the light bulbs went on," he said, when he heard Deming lambast performance ratings as arbitrary and devastating to morale. In agreement, Howard rose to his feet to deplore the government's system as "bankrupt" and to declare his commitment to change it.

After the Deming seminar, he visited the naval aviation depot at Cherry Point, which had become a leading proponent of TQM, and he spent two days at NPRDC in a seminar with Linda Doherty, Steve Dockstader and others to bring him up to speed. Afterward, he lectured the executive steering group on the urgency of the mission at hand and on his vision and expectations.

As Howard saw it, his immediate tasks were to bring some coherence to the TQM effort through education and leadership from the top and to chip away at the barriers between commands that threatened to lead to "total savagery" in the period of cost-cutting ahead.

Although TQM had been announced two years earlier, the department had made no concerted top-down effort to educate the troops. Outside consultants—"Beltway Bandits," some called them—were marketing TQM and many Navy units were buying their programs. Howard described the following scenario: "After a one- or two-day awareness workshop of some kind, run by somebody someplace, they came back as the TQM expert and begin to immediately implement it. . . . They will try something, and they will work at it for awhile, and they will put pressure on their employees to make it work and they will do the same damn kind of sloganeering that we've done so many times in the past: 'Cut costs, work harder.' And at the end of the second or third quarter, they will report cost savings. The comptroller will come in and say, 'You did a good job. We're going to take that money away from you. Go on and do more.' And the employees, they're no dummies, they figure the more they save, the more's going to be taken away from them, the harder they're going to have to work. You get a slowdown. It's happened a million times before."

Unless something were done to intervene, he said, "We will really forever have blocked any opportunity to make any real change in the system wherever that has taken place. We will generate our own roadblocks."

He also foresaw that long-standing competition between various branches of the Navy could erupt into total warfare as programs got cut. "We don't see ourselves in the Department of the Navy as a system. We see ourselves as platform sponsors of submarines, or of naval aviation, or of surface warfare or of the Marine Corps." The way it was set up, if one branch wanted a new weapons system and funds were short, the "only one way to get the system, somebody has to lose. So your planning has as an adjunct the catastrophic failure of somebody else. Their program has to go belly up for yours to succeed." In the short run, he said, the challenge was to make sure "the barriers don't become any higher. Over the long term I think we have to have fundamental change in the system."

The changes had to take place in Navy headquarters, with people working together. "I couldn't work this by myself. To change the system your senior leadership has to be the strongest advocate. They can't be dragged along." Unless that happened, TQM in the field— "the smart things that we've done in the naval depots—will die away in time."

He could count on Secretary Garrett's support. To be sure, the secretary himself was running into resistance. He had people tell him, " 'This is a dumb idea—I've heard all this before.' " But he was the boss and, if nothing else, military people followed orders. "They don't say, 'I won't do it.' "

But the greatest asset the Navy had might be something else again. The operative word in TQM was "quality." People who entered the military believed in America. "In the final analysis," Garrett said, "I think the motivation is pride."

II. A CASE IN CHERRY POINT

On January 24, 1990, Colonel Jerald B. Gartman got a call from someone in the office of Under Secretary of Defense John Betti in Washington, who needed some numbers for a presentation Betti was to give on Total Quality Management. Could Gartman tell him how much productivity had improved at the naval aviation depot down there in Cherry Point, North Carolina?

Gartman and the TQM force at Cherry Point didn't like to keep track of those kinds of numbers. How much have you saved? Talk about cost savings, and the bean cutters would cut your budget. How many teams do you have? The number of teams meant nothing; it was a measure not of results but activity. Talk about results and you were back to money again.

Still, this was the brass calling. Gartman reached for the plaque on his office wall, dated January 9, 1989, that announced Cherry Point had won a "productivity excellence award" from the Department of Defense. He read off a figure: $39.3 million in savings for 1988. That was what Defense said he had saved. It sounded pretty good. "I will give them back the information they gave me," he thought. It was funny how things worked.

Since 1986 Cherry Point had become the star of the Navy's fledgling TQM movement, with a roster of such awards. The files held seventy reports from successful teams. An innovative gain-sharing program was drawing attention. But perhaps the most telling evidence of Cherry Point's accomplishments was the constant stream of visitors who flowed through the base gates to see how quality procedures could be applied in a military setting. Just the day before, the Under Secretary of the Navy, J. Daniel Howard, had come through for a tour. And a few days later, when Defense Secretary Richard Cheney made a long-awaited announcement on the military sites the department wanted to close, Cherry Point was spared.

There was nothing that preordained Cherry Point for such a role. The TQM overhaul took place in a setting that offered both advantages and disadvantages; often one characteristic could cut both ways. That TQM had taken hold and flourished reflected Gartman's tenacity and the utilitarian model developed by the Navy Personnel Research and Development Center. If it happened there, it could happen elsewhere. That was why everyone was so interested.

The naval aviation depot occupied a corner of the Marine Corps Air Station at Cherry Point, on an inlet not far from the scenic Cape Lookout National Seashore. In 1943, the forerunner of the aviation depot was built for maintenance of World War II combat aircraft. In 1967, it was detached from the airstation and placed under Navy control, though it remained under Marine management. Fewer than 100 employees, however, were Marines. The rest were civilians, who belonged to civil service. With a $100-million payroll and 3,200-employee work force, the depot was one of eastern North Carolina's largest industries and its pay scale made it one of the most desirable.

Into this rural coastal area regularly arrived some of the Navy's most sophisticated aircraft for maintenance and repair. The depot had contracts to work on the F–4 Phantom, a jet fighter/reconnaissance aircraft, and the C–130 Hercules cargo plane, the workhorse of Vietnam. The depot was also a repair site for the medium transport H–46 Sea Knight helicopter, the A–4 Skyhawk jet, the OV–10 twin-turboprop multipurpose Bronco and the AV–8 Harrier, the Marines' vertical takeoff and landing tactical jet fighter.

The 130 or so aircraft repaired each year constituted about a third of the workload. In addition, a power plant division overhauled close to 500 engines a year; while other departments repaired worn and broken aircraft engine blades and vanes, and components such as valves, gauges and pressurization units. Some of the depot's work took place in the field, where teams made emergency repairs, performed modifications and offered training and other services. Altogether the depot did nearly $250 million in business a year. Its "customers" were the Navy, some Army, Air Force and Coast Guard units, as well as the National Science Foundation.

The Cherry Point work force had just two major divisions in addition to males and females—black and white. In that respect, it was unlike North Island, for example, which also had large numbers of Asians and Latinos from different countries. Outsiders often remarked that the homogeneity and stability of the work force—the annual turnover was just 3 percent and the average supervisor had been there twenty years—was an advantage when it came to pulling together, particularly in the increasingly competitive climate. Cherry Point not only bid for work against other depots, but against private contractors as well.

While it was true, conceded TQM coordinator Jack Adams, that people's similar family backgrounds as "farmers, fishermen and retired Marines" provided an element of cohesion, the ingrown eastern North Carolina culture, in his view, was a limitation in one regard. Adams maintained that Cherry Point employees found it difficult to "separate personal and professional issues." If, for example, one person criticized another for something that happened during the course of work, it was interpreted as an insult. "You insulted my family tradition because I didn't give you the right part." And suddenly people weren't speaking to each other. Often the family tradition was well represented at the plant. Adams's father and father-in-law had worked there and now his brother, ex-wife, brother-in-law and a lot of "unclose" relatives were members of the work force.

Workers at the plant not only belonged to civil service, they were represented by seven unions. To be sure, the unions were deprived of their ultimate weapon—a work stoppage—by virtue of the military link, but they could still make things difficult by filing grievance after grievance. Thanks to dual representation, it was next to impossible to fire anyone, and should an attempt be made to do so, the depot paid the legal costs of the appeal procedure provided by the civil service system.

Cherry Point was also one of the smaller depots, and every time the Navy brass talked in the past about closing one down, which they did from time to time in the 1970s, Cherry Point surfaced as a candidate. Unlike the other five depots, Cherry Point was not close to a deepwater port that could accommodate aircraft carriers, normally an advantage because it reduced overland transport costs. Crash-damaged aircraft or others needing work could simply be lowered over the side of the carrier docked at the depot.

Cherry Point therefore had sought with some success, as Admiral John Kirkpatrick put it, "to make ourselves so good, they can't close us." As early as 1980, Cherry Point began to ease away from its practice of massive final inspections, in which the people from quality assurance would swarm over the completed plane with checklists, to an artisan's certification program that made sure people doing each job were certified with the proper training. That sounded simple, but the depot had thousands of tasks to keep track of.

Whether due to fear of closure, the Marine's vaunted fighting spirit, these early quality efforts or some combination of all three, Cherry Point was the acknowledged leader among the depots, capturing a productivity award for three years running. But in a paradoxical way that dampened enthusiasm for TQM. People didn't see why they had to change.

Gartman returned in 1986 to the post where he had been production officer four years earlier, fresh from an all-Navy Deming seminar down in Jacksonville, Florida. At that time, the North Island aviation depot had already stepped out smartly with TQM. Norfolk was starting to move. And Cherry Point had some exposure.

Gartman soon discovered that much of what he had accomplished from 1980 to 1982, or thought he had accomplished back then, seemed to have disappeared. He knew now that Deming would deplore his style as "management by numbers." It was characterized by verbal floggings of supervisors and workers alike to work harder, faster, better. And he had thought it was effective—until he came back. "All that yelling and screaming as a production officer—talk about driving out fear, I spent my two years here driving *in* fear—all those gains we made when I quit yelling and screaming were gone."

Like so many managers hearing Dr. Deming for the first time,

Gartman was most troubled by Deming's insistence that management was responsible for 85 percent of the defects that took place in the system. People work in the system, Deming said. The manager's job is to work on the system. By the time Gartman finished the seminar, the message had sunk in: People truly try to do their best within the system. The real problem is the system.

Gartman's return coincided not only with Kirkpatrick's push for TQM, but also with the pressure for greater productivity in a newly competitive climate. Thanks to the Coopers & Lybrand report, he was aware that the biggest threat was "the view that was held by bosses that we were not competitive, we were not productive." He viewed his first task as "damage control"—to convince Washington that the picture was not true. The only way he knew to do that was to start turning out quality work for the customers.

"If you looked at quality as conformance to specifications, we were doing a very good job. If you looked at quality in meeting our customers' expectations, we had a ways to go. A lot of that was communications problems. We weren't talking to our customers."

First the people at Cherry Point had to figure out who their customers were. "We run the gamut. Our customers start in Washington with the people who go through the budgeting process, with the people who allocate funds. . . . Our customers are also the people who use our products. And in between those two groups of people, there are people at Air LANT/Air PAC (for "Atlantic" and "Pacific"), who are the intermediaries, who actually dispense funds to the people who own the airplanes that we're going to work on."

Gartman sent small groups out to sit down with each. "We went out, we talked to all of them, we got their view of us. . . . We set about rewriting specs to suit customers. . . . We made internal decisions that even though we're not getting paid to do this work, is it an advantage to do this work?"

A decision to paint the cockpit of the C–130s during an overhaul reflected the new way of thinking. Normally that was not part of the job. But it would improve the appearance of the aircraft immeasurably.

"We go through there and we do a tremendous amount of work," Gartman said. "Ninety percent of that, the customer cannot see. You get in an airliner, you can't see inside the wing. . . . The same thing is true when a customer gets his airplane from us. He can't see most of the work that we've done. It's repairing damage that's done internally. But he can see the cockpit. And when he gets in there, what he was seeing was a cockpit that looked just like it looked when he brought it in here. If it was dirty when he brought it in, it was apt to be dirty when it went out. If it needed painting when it came in, it probably needed painting when it came out. That was what we considered squadron-level work. They could do it themselves if they wanted it done.

"So we took a look at that and we said, 'How much would it cost us to rehab that cockpit while it was here?' And we determined that it was a relatively small cost, but it's a cost nonetheless. So should we do it or shouldn't we do it?' What we found is something Deming talks about—pride of workmanship. Our workers wanted to see a nice cockpit in there just as badly as the customer wanted to see a nice cockpit."

The clincher was, he said, "We found out that measuring all the work, measuring the man-hours, measuring the material cost, you probably can't find in the data that we spent a penny more turning out a nice cockpit than one that just met the spec."

Throughout the plant, hourly time standards were removed from the cards that accompanied each work order. Although they were intended to be a planning aid, said Gartman, "We were using standards to say, 'Gee whiz, what's wrong with you? Why aren't you meeting the standard?' Just like Deming said, when we took the standards off the card, we found that standards had been a cap." Afterward, people were as apt to work faster as slower.

The depot had long had a business plan with five-year objectives, drafted by its central planning group. "It was put on the shelf and never paid much attention," Gartman said. Under Admiral Kirkpatrick, the depots began to do corporate and individual plans, with a long-term five-year strategy, shorter-term two- to three-year goals and a set of objectives of a year or less. "It's now a living document. We track it monthly," Gartman said.

In introducing TQM, Gartman followed the model developed by NPRDC and pioneered at North Island. He formed an executive steering group of his civilian department heads and the top military people, which then proceeded to establish some general priorities for action while studying Deming's method and assessing themselves on the Fourteen Points. The blend of military and civilian outlooks worked well, Gartman said. "The military is more used to rapid change. They tend to grab on more rapidly. The civilians are a long-term stabilizing influence."

Gartman at first thought he could get by with a part-time coordinator. Instead he found his appointee, Jack Adams, needed the help of two other assistants, Fred Davenport Jr., to work with a growing flock of facilitators, and Bill Sadler, to work with process control, plus a statistician, Sandra White.

An infrastructure of quality management boards (QMBs) was established, and the boards were trained in how to select processes for improvement and assign process action teams (PATs). Only boards could charter PAT teams. After completing their analysis and making recommendations, said Adams, the PAT team's job was finished. "That team goes away. . . . Some of them work a day or two, some of them work months."

The first PATs were assigned to processes that the executive steering group thought not only needed improvement but would yield big paybacks and build credibility for TQM. They solicited suggestions from the floor and selected the first 20 from more than 100.

The TQM office decided early on that the teams would not be composed of volunteers. Just as Gartman had chosen Adams to be coordinator, the QMBs would select team leaders, then team members. The object was eventually to enroll everyone at Cherry Point on a team. "We don't want 200 stars who are good on PAT teams and that's all they do," Adams explained. "We want 3,000 people who have been on PAT teams."

A facilitator was assigned to sit down with the chairman of the team before the first meeting. Together they would draft a plan. This accomplished several things. Explained Adams's assistant, Fred Davenport, "That calms the chairman down. It keeps the QMB from just throwing resources at a problem. And when experts come in, they know what to do."

Cherry Point had previously had some exposure to quality methods, chiefly some training in problem-solving and a network of quality circles. As elsewhere, the circles "were a miserable failure," said Adams, mincing no words, "because there was no structure of management support for them. These people sat around and did their thing, and they came up with recommendations. Everybody said 'Great job,' and nobody ever implemented the first recommendation."

Perhaps that explained some of the cynicism when Deming's

Fourteen Points were printed on three-by-five laminated cards and distributed to the work force. "Our people are not stupid. The average educational level is thirteen years. They read those fourteen principles and said 'What are you going to do about this? What are you going to do about that?' " Management wasn't ready with all the answers. That gave the critics an opening. "Handing it out was a mistake," Adams concluded.

There were other mistakes. Cherry Point, like so many other facilities, plunged headlong into training workers in the seven graphic tools of statistical quality or process control, including control charts. Afterward, a handful of overzealous facilitators headed out to the floor to promote the new techniques. "Pick something that's an output and we'll try to control it," they said in so many words. In no time at all, recalled Adams, "It was working good in eight of ten areas. We were getting good paybacks. The shops were up and running, so we pulled the facilitators out. Almost immediately, things stopped in seven out of ten. The shops didn't own it. It was somebody else's SPC. Those areas where it took hold, the shops pushed the facilitator aside and said, 'It's our SPC. Lesson learned? You don't do it for me.' "

Sometimes the workers on day crew blamed the night crew for taking down the charts. One worker confessed to Adams that it was his supervisor who had pulled them down. Adams knew then that "the managers didn't understand." When the charts revealed high defect levels, they thought they would be blamed. "Therefore they were threatened by it. The greatest impediment was mistrust and fear in the work force. Workers don't trust managers. Managers don't trust workers. Managers don't trust other managers."

The TQM staff realized that statistical training had to start at the top and be moved down a level at a time, so supervisors would understand its uses. Otherwise, Adams said, "you just frustrate the workers trying to apply it because the boss won't let them." There was no need to promote control charts at the outset. Explained Adams, "We've probably found that our greatest payback is through process flowcharting, pareto analysis, and cause-and-effect analysis. We're applying run-charting and control charting where it works. . . . Just simply doing a flow chart does wonders for you, getting people to really analyze a process." NPRDC did the initial training. Eventually the TQM office took it over.

Over the next three years, the work force was trained on a just-in-time or as-needed basis as set forth in the depot's business plan. The basic course for everyone was thirty hours in structured problem solving and basic graphic methods. Facilitators got forty hours of instruction, plus another eight hours in group dynamics. For new employees there was a forty-five-minute TQM awareness session.

With 3,000 employees, the training took time. In early 1990, the basic three-day course in graphic tools was still being taught to people on the line. And it was expensive. Materials and salaries for trainers was the least of it. Every hour an employee spent in training was a lost man-hour on the job. As such, it cost the plant $20 an hour in salary, plus overhead and lost production. "We hire them to turn wrenches, and if they're not turning wrenches, the perception is we lose money," Adams observed. By 1990, some 80,000 man-hours had been consumed in that fashion. The reaction in Washington was predictable. As much as the bosses there wanted greater productivity, they still viewed training as a frill, and looked askance at the figures.

Gartman ignored them as best he could. Subsequent results would justify his course. The depot had been programmed to lose money in those years under Washington's convoluted budget system, which set depot prices so that they would match what the customers had available to pay. If the customers—the various fleets and squadrons—had not been sufficiently funded by Congress, the depot rates were set arbitrarily low. The difference between those rates and the true costs was the "loss" and it was later made up from a pool called the Naval Industrial Fund. Instead of programmed losses, however, the depot was showing substantial gains, thanks to the way teams were churning out savings.

Among the successful changes prompted by TQM:

—Floorboard components were being primed to comply with the manufacturers' drawings. An engineering investigation revealed it wasn't necessary. The labor savings were $9.23 per unit.

—A "Goldplate" fuel control component ("Goldplate" referred to work done on presidential or other preeminent aircraft, for which top security was required) was being locked before lunch and again at night in a cabinet inside what was called the "Clean Room." Each time this was done, the parts had to be dismantled and inventoried. Merely locking the Clean Room at those times would satisfy security requirements, avoiding labor costs of $88.60 per unit.

—A five-hour abrasive blast process was substituted for a two-stage treatment to remove a coating from turbine blades that required several steps and twenty-four hours, for a savings of $336 each time.

—Damage to Teflon rings on self-locking nuts were rendering a third of them useless. SPC identified the source as the cleaning solution. A manual cleaning process was substituted and the reject rate dropped to zero, for a savings of $20,000.

—One team working on corrosion problems with the H–46 found that among the causes were poor lighting, failure to follow instructions and the use of improper tools. The lights were cleaned, the right tools were made available and instructions were issued. Corrosion was eliminated. "Tangible savings cannot be documented but intangible savings involving increased customer satisfaction are immense," said the summary report.

The results began to add up. Projected revenues in 1988 were $9.4 million. They came in at $12.7 million. In 1989, a loss of $7.6 million was projected; instead there was a $21.5 million profit. The controller's office looked at the savings, looked at the training costs and wondered how Gartman could do both. Recounted Gartman, "They said 'Where'd you get the money?' I said 'I don't know.' I know where it came from. I budgeted it right up front. I said 'I may lose more than they ever anticipated, but I think training will pay.' We think it pays about $14 to $1. . . . So you show me the cost of the training. . . . Training is very, very expensive and ignorance costs more than you can imagine."

On coming to Cherry Point, Gartman had been intrigued with the idea of gainsharing as a way to motivate people. Supporters believed that gainsharing not only encouraged people to be more productive, it created peer pressure for everybody to work harder. Title Five of the U.S. Code gave the government permission to do gainsharing. A Department of Defense regulation limited the employees' share to 50 percent of the productivity improvements.

In December of 1986, Gartman set up a gainsharing committee to study various schemes. Neither he nor the committee, which included two union representatives, wanted to link financial rewards with individual performance ratings. The committee made several basic decisions: that the payouts would come from profits, based on productivity improvements; that everyone would receive the same amount; that people with high absenteeism would be excluded; and that it would be based on three variables—labor, productivity and direct and indirect material savings. Twenty-five dollars would be the smallest payout (amounts less than that would be credited to the next period); if the depot failed to meet its deadlines and quality indexes, there would be no payment.

The first payout was $265, made in March 1988.

At the end of eighteen months, Bill Sadler from the TQM office, who was also cochairman of the gainsharing committee, was undecided about its value. It seemed to him that people needed more education on gainsharing. "Otherwise, after a year to a year and a half, people start to expect it. Then they start losing sight of what generated the payments." His experience was consistent with a study of bonuses by Joyce Nilsson Orsini, an associate professor of management at Fordham University, who outlined four phases of what she called the thank-you bonus: "1. 'Hey, isn't this great!' 2. 'It's about time they did something for us.' 3. 'I wonder if this means they're going to expect more from us.' 4. 'I wonder what we'll get next year.' "

In interviews, fourteen of twenty-seven CEOs whose companies practiced gainsharing noted some negatives but believed the net effect was positive; nine said they'd wished they'd never started it. The remaining four were ambivalent.

But the feeling at Cherry Point, based on an employee survey, was that gainsharing had in fact increased employee understanding of the depot's objectives and how quality improved productivity and reduced costs.

Inevitably, however, there were managers who couldn't or didn't go along with TQM. "I had one division director here I'd known forever," Gartman said. "A top performer. He'd always done very, very well. When we went into this he came in and said 'Hey, boss. You leave me alone and I'll continue to produce for you, but I don't buy into this stuff, and I'm not going to do it.' And we chatted about that for quite some time over a period of about a month. And finally he came in and said 'Dammit, do you want me to turn out engines or do you want me to play these games?' I said 'Both. At the very minimum as a division director, you're going to get involved and try this thing.' He couldn't do that, so he retired. Great. Best for both of us. We're still friends.

"I've got a branch head, he will tell you that he is for TQM, he loves it, he believes it, he does it. And all the feedback I get is . . . he hasn't seen the light yet. I keep working on it and working on it and working on it. And you say 'How is it a person can mouth the words, so you know they've heard them, and if they can mouth them, they should be able to intellectualize them—Hey, this'll work!—and then walk right back and beat the hell out of your people for doing what they're trying to get done?' Those things frustrate me. I would like to have instant pudding." "Instant pudding" was a Deming label for the desire for immediate results.

The hardest thing for him personally, Gartman said, was "the slow pace of change. It makes so much sense, and it's the right thing to do."

Adams, too, was frustrated by some managers, particularly the way they handled teams. Often, they would assign teams to issues they should handle. Or they would tell a team to implement its own recommendations. It was hard to reverse that. "We put out command policy on it. We did training on it. It's still happening."

Despite a sometimes unsteady course, TQM steamed ahead. Said Adams, "If you wait until everything's ready, you never get started. Sometimes you have to jump in, so we jumped in. . . . We kind of pulled rabbits out of a hat. If we didn't like the color of the rabbit, we stuffed it back in and pulled out another."

The colonel's unswerving commitment to TQM, and the knowledge that he was behind them, gave confidence to the teams. Ben Lopedote, a facilitator to a team hammering out a new process on bearings, said some middle-level managers might say " 'We won't go for that.' That's not their place to say they won't go for it. That's upper-level management. If the colonel says 'It'll get done,' it'll get done."

That was one thing about the Marine Corps: Its officers might not appear to be exemplars of "participative management" as the term was generally used, but leaders stood by their troops.

"If you look at what we define as leadership in the Marine Corps," explained Gartman, "there's a couple of things. We keep our troops informed, okay? And we stay very close to our troops. We get a lot of feedback, so in doing our normal leadership as we progress up through the ranks, we are really very, very participative. We're always interacting, and we use their ideas."

As an illustration, he offered the basic problem posed to officers in training: " 'Okay, lieutenant. You've got a sergeant, two PFCs, a flagpole, a piece of rope and a pulley. The colonel has said he wants the flagpole erected in two hours. What do you do?'

"You have some guys who say 'I put the block and tackle here and I hook the rope to it . . .' But the answer is, you turn to the sergeant and you say, 'Sergeant, put up the flagpole.' They decide the process. You're responsible for getting it done. That's the way we train in leadership.

"The other side of that is that we demand immediate and precise compliance when that's required. We don't say 'There's an enemy up on top of the hill. Let's take a vote and see if we want to go up the hill.' You say 'Follow me. We're going to take the hill.' So when it's required, we are absolutely nonparticipative, but we have established our ability to lead. The reason very few Marine lieutenants ever get shot in the back by their own troops is because they have established over a period of time, as have the sergeants and corporals, and all the leaders in the Marine Corps, the trust and the ability to communicate with the people they work with so that everyone knows that when the time comes, the lieutenant isn't going to get down in the hole and say 'Okay, you guys, go up the hill.' He's going to say 'Come on, let's go.' And they're going to go."

Before TQM, said Ray Harper, chairman of a team in the blade/vane repair shop, "We never got anything back. It was always 'Okay. You have a problem? Okay. I'll take care of it.' Lot of times you kept the same problem, or if the problem went away, you never got anything back. With total quality management and collecting data, we're getting feedback. That makes a lot of difference."

By 1990, there were eighty facilitators, forty QMBs and forty or more teams at any given time. In addition there were Process Improvement Teams, organized in work areas.

When he arrived, Gartman had thought they could have TQM in place by the time his tour was up, in four years. Instead, he extended a fifth year, and the job was nowhere near done. "Four years later I can tell you in twenty years we may be where I think I would have liked to have been now. . . . As Deming says, there is no instant pudding." He hastened to add, however, "That doesn't mean it doesn't pay as you go." Gone were the days not so long ago, Gartman said, when an H–46 helicopter would reach the end of the line, quality assurance would inspect it, the workers would fix the defects or "discrepancies," as they were called, and then when Gartman, a pilot, would check it before flying, "I'd pick up eight, nine, ten things on a preflight. Then when I flew it I'd pick up another one or two things. We'd get all those fixed and we'd sell it to our customer. And on the average our customer would come back with anywhere from two to six things on the airplane that he didn't like."

Now that Cherry Point had shifted from inspection to process improvement, "It moves off the end of the line and goes right into flight. It is very, very, very rare that I ever find anything on preflight. I go up and fly it—I average about 1.4 things in flight . . . that I don't like. And these are generally things that could not have been discovered in the rework process. They can only be discovered in flight . . ." Things that "people didn't like" were called "discrepancies." Cherry Point counted only those that were covered by their contract.

In all, by 1990, their aircraft averaged just one discrepancy for every two planes. In 1989, 70 percent went out with no discrepancies. And one customer accounted for 25 percent of those that existed, owing to what Gartman delicately labeled a "communications problem."

Gartman was the first to admit that because the depots were funded by their customers, they functioned much like any other heavy industrial plant, which gave them "some latitude that the poor guy out there on a budget—you know, money from Congress—doesn't have."

But even with this flexibility, the depots were prevented by law from carrying out certain reforms. In the matter of the government's five-tier performance appraisal system, for example, Gartman said he agreed with Deming that "it's one of the most damaging things we do. Everybody thinks they're doing great, so the guy you call in and say 'You're doing great—he knew that, that doesn't help any. And the guy that's not doing quite as well, you call him in and say 'You're not doing quite as well'—well, he thought he was doing great, too, so he tries to mold himself after the guy that got the better performance appraisal and that's probably not within his realm, so you just got more variability."

And as much as he would have liked to trim the number of suppliers to those with superior quality, Gartman said, "The federal government's determined that we will have competition to the maximum extent possible, so we're not able to cleanly go to fewer suppliers." In government contracts, where several bidders met specifications, the contractor had to choose the one with the lowest price.

"Now, how does that affect my quality? A little. I don't lay awake nights worrying about it. We have enough things that are within our control to keep us busy the rest of our lives, fixing those things that we management have screwed up over time."

III. QUALITY STORIES

The Bearing Team: Roll Out the Barrel

Forget the simple ball bearings in roller skates that could take all kinds of abuse and still keep the skater upright. The bearings used at Cherry Point were delicate, finally machined parts that came in many sizes and varieties, weighing from a few ounces up to 15 pounds, with price tags ranging from $1 to $6,000. Whether used and in need of reconditioning or new and being prepared for first-time use, they required extensive cleaning and packing, at an average cost of $140 per bearing. This was why procedures called for scrapping the used bearings that cost $50 or less. It was simply cheaper to use new ones. If, however, as was frequently the case, replacements weren't available for these cheaper bearings, the shop would have to recondition the old ones.

Everybody knew there were two major problems with bearings, whatever the kind and price: They were not always available when needed and new ones were being installed without the proper preparation. The manufacturers packed them in preservatives that had to be blown out and replaced with a specified lubricant. Neglecting to do so could lead to vibration and premature failure.

One team had already looked at the problem, but its recommendations had not made much of an impression. With hindsight, it was clear the team had not done a good job of collecting data, making it vulnerable to criticism. The Quality Management Board in the blade/vane branch set up a new team, with Darleen Roberts from the bearing shop as chairman.

Bearings were distributed either directly by the bearing shops or by "stores"—storage areas manned by production control supervisors, who had the authority to order more bearings. Indeed, one problem was that too many people could order bearings, even a production worker who knew how to place a computer order. In addition, there was a "free store" where frequently used bearings were available to anyone who walked in, no questions asked. "If somebody messes one up, they don't have to go anywhere except to free issue and get another one," said Roberts. She often saw damage caused by mechanics who didn't use the proper tool to remove bearings, popping them off with a screwdriver or tapping them off with a mallet.

After drawing a flow chart, the team could clearly see that too many people had access to ordering bearings. In addition to mapping out the paper trail, the team toured some of the areas where bearings were used. They discovered that mechanics often knew little about the exacting procedures in the bearing shop and would make their own judgments about quality, discarding those bearings they didn't like and using new ones.

Some older mechanics believed they knew when a used bearing could be recycled without reconditioning. Said Roberts, "We had a few mechanics that absolutely refused to send it to the bearing shop because they could 'feel' it on their finger and 'knew' it was good." They could pack it with grease and pop it back in the equipment, saving time.

Said Ann Beck, one of two team members from production control, "This has been done for years and years and years, and it's real hard to break down. The shops have been cleaning and packing their own, right or wrong." At one time, that might not have been so bad. But times had changed. Equipment was much more sophisticated and finely tuned, not to mention expensive.

On its tour, the team found a 55-gallon barrel full of discarded bearings. Said Roberts, "The scary part of it was, if they got in a bind, they might go dig those bearings out of that barrel." With the best of intentions, workers hoarded bearings to make sure they had them when they needed them. One helpful supervisor found $27,000 worth squirreled away in his shop. The team's facilitator, Ben Lopedote, wasn't surprised. "I worked fifteen years on the line out here. When we started running short of fasteners, we found out some guy had two lockers full—almost $10,000 worth of fasteners. And we never would have found that out until he happened to open it up one day and somebody caught a glimpse of them, stacked, two lockers full."

Roberts outlined the worst-case scenario. "If somewhere along the way, these people are heisting bearings out of the stores that are not showing against what they need for procurement, you may have used a thousand bearings and the people that are ordering them say 'Gee, you know, they haven't used any of these bearings' . . . and they don't let another contract and all of a sudden you're *out.* And it's two years before you can get a new one, so therefore you're scrounging in every barrel you can find to reprocess them—at three times the cost. Or you find somebody out in town who knows your dilemma and sells them back to the government at six times the cost . . . and then you pay three times the cost to process them because it's salvage."

Team member Eddie Daniels from operations analysis looked at the costs of processing used bearings under $50, as opposed to buying them new. In the amounts used at Cherry Point, the ratio was two-to-one, and the dollar difference over two years was more than $1 million. That was how much the depot would needlessly spend to recondition bearings if replacements were not available.

The team proposed recommendations that would channel all bearings through the bearing shop and into a bearing pool under its chief of production control. Only a limited few who would have what amounted to a secret computer password could order bearings. The proposed routing would eliminate five steps, reducing turnaround time. Most of the major savings could not be measured in advance, such as a reduction in turnaround time, unnecessary processing and component failure.

AV–8B Repair Team: Joining Forces

The AV–8B Harrier, the Marines' vertical takeoff and landing aircraft, was the first to be so extensively composed of carbon epoxy materials rather than aluminum. The composite material made the plane lighter, stronger and corrosion-proof. There was one significant drawback, however. The all-in-one molded construction was difficult to repair. As more AV–8Bs took to the air, and some inevitably fell down, this became an increasing problem. The plane was manufactured by McDonnell Douglas Corporation—"MacAir"— but that company wasn't in the business of making spare parts for the Harrier. Thus parts were difficult to acquire. Moreover, they were extremely expensive. The cost of a wing or a forward fusillage approached $200,000. On a crash-damaged aircraft, Cherry Point, which had recently gotten the repair contract for the AV–8B, might need to replace only the wingtips. But because the wing was a single, fused unit, it would have to buy the whole span.

The waste bothered everybody. "It cost $180,000 for that one piece and we end up sawing 18 inches off," said Douglas Walling, the lead engineer for composite structures on the AV–8B.

The solution wasn't difficult. Indeed, many people had figured out what to do. But doing it was another matter.

MacAir sometimes rejected for quality reasons the very parts that Cherry Point needed. But that didn't mean the entire part was defective. Problems with porosity in a wingspan, for example, generally occurred in the thicker center portion. Instead of cutting up the part and throwing it away, as was the practice, the company could ship it to Cherry Point, which could cut off the wingtip and splice it to an injured aircraft, provided proper precautions were taken to identify and not use the defective portion.

Efforts to work out an arrangement had failed in the past, resulting in a lot of frustration. "Nobody could sit down and make a decision so it was decided a PAT team was needed," explained another engineer, James Fuss. MacAir agreed. It was Cherry Point's first joint team with an outside contractor.

Relations with MacAir were historically good. This time there was more than goodwill involved. MacAir was pioneering its own version of total quality. The top people there thought it would be educational to work with employees from Cherry Point, and things went well from the start. In just five months, Cherry Point had worked out a flow chart of its proposed procedure for handling, inspecting and storing the parts to ensure no defective portions were used. There would have to be a data base to ensure the parts and the paperwork matched. The depot, of course, would pay shipping costs, but no other expenses would be involved. The process took longer to arrange at MacDonnell Douglas, because the revised procedures would have to apply to all aircraft, which meant that many people were involved with the decisions. And anything that was done had to pass muster with the lawyers. Given the company's positive attitude, however, the Cherry Point team felt confident they would be getting the parts they needed.

Said Fuss, "It was the upper echelon that really pushed this from the very beginning, and that was why we had no problem sitting on the committee. Everybody was very helpful and there were no conflicts, and we think the word came down from the top that this was going to work."

The A–4 Slat Team: Flying High

"The A–3 will pitch up, severely and uncontrollably, if the outboard wing slats do not extend normally as the aircraft is slowed, as in the landing approach," stated the technical article on the A–3 Skywarrior. "The smooth functioning of the wing slats is, consequently, a matter of prime importance to maintenance personnel."

Aerospace engineer John Tyner had saved the article. It described the very problem that Cherry Point was having with a different aircraft, the A–4, for which it had recently won the repair contract. Until something was done about it, the planes could not be delivered to customers.

The slat was the curved forward part of the wing that slipped forward as the plane changed its angle of attack—the angle the wing formed with the direction in which the plane was traveling—in order to slow down and land. The slats on the A–4 were giving Cherry Point a headache. The biggest problem was that they failed to slide forward together, doing so at different times on each wing, sometimes causing the pilot to lose control of the aircraft. In extreme cases, the plane crashed.

The people at Cherry Point consulted those who had rigged slats at Pensacola. The Floridians talked about "getting the right feel" or finding someone with a "magic touch." In their absence, the first A–4 out of Cherry Point required twenty-two test flights before the slats worked properly. And even then, no one knew why they worked.

So many variables were being changed at once that it was difficult to pin down cause-and-effect. At that point a PAT team enlisted two people from the production line, Archie Salters and Allen Anderson, to begin collecting measurement data during test flights. One of the measurements was the distance between the trailing edge of the slat and the upper surface of the wing. Data from flight tests revealed that the lower the slat, the sooner it would come out. With that information and more, it was possible to predict performance based on certain adjustments.

There were also problems with the way reworked slats attached to the wing. The fixture points didn't line up, apparently because of errors in the blueprints. Cherry Point couldn't consult with the manufacturer, MacDonnell Douglas, because the planes were no longer being built. Happily, someone who knew the team was working on the problem alerted them to an original Douglas A–4 slat out in a field that the air base down the road used as a graveyard for old parts. The team retrieved the slat, cleaned it up and tried it out on a plane. It fit perfectly. They were able to rewrite the technical data to correspond to the Douglas slat. They also decided to build prototype slats, with a view to eventually going into production rather than depending on another depot to make them.

CHAPTER SIX

Bridgestone (USA) Incorporated

The truth? You want to hear Americans do it better than anybody else.

They're kicking our butts. And that ain't luck. That's the truth. There's your truth. Sure, the great old American do-or-die spirit. Yeah, it's alive, but they got it.

—HUNT STEPHENSON
Gung Ho

I love Bridgestone. I love my job. I love the people I work with. I love bragging about it.

—LOUIS AMIRAULT
Section Manager

I. HOMEGROWN *KAIZEN*

In 1981, the Firestone Tire and Rubber Company hung a FOR SALE sign on its radial truck tire plant in LaVergne, Tennessee, a rural community 15 miles southeast of Nashville. When a year passed with no deal, the company laid off two-thirds of the work force. The plant began to close down two weeks of every month.

Drawn by the right-to-work climate in the Sunbelt, Firestone had built the plant in 1972 to make both bias and the increasingly popular radial truck tires. But things went wrong from the outset. Demand was less than anticipated, thanks in part to the energy crisis that had created a cost-conscious driving public. Next to gas prices, tires were the highest expense for truckers and they kept very close tabs on how well they wore. By retreading and switching them from the cab to less critical positions on the trailer, they could prolong their use. Unlike other brands, which were good for three or four retreads, Firestone's tires held up for only a couple. And there were quality problems. In 1980, the LaVergne plant could sell only half the tires it was able to produce.

Meanwhile, a corporate command based in distant Akron, Ohio, seemed unable to cope with these issues, nor with others involving the work force. The United Rubber Workers made inroads, and there were two bitter strikes in the late 1970s, one to win union recognition and another to secure a contract.

So a decade later, Firestone announced that if it could not sell the LaVergne plant, it would close it. But who would want to buy a factory beset by labor strife and plagued with quality problems?

Guess.

Japan's Bridgestone Corporation manufactured not only truck and car tires, but also marine hose, tennis rackets, balls and shoes, golf clubs and bicycles. Tires, however, accounted for 70 percent of its revenues. Bridgestone was Japan's largest tiremaker, with twelve plants in that country and others in Thailand, Taiwan, Indonesia and Australia. It ranked third in worldwide production, after Goodyear and Michelin. But if the company were to grow, it needed to produce and sell in the United States, both to the replacement market and to vehicle manufacturers, including the new crop of Japanese-owned auto plants.

The state of Tennessee was openly wooing Japanese companies. Nissan was coming in with a huge auto plant just five miles down the interstate in Smyrna. Komatsu, the world's second largest tractor company, had located in Chattanooga for many of the same reasons Bridgestone was considering LaVergne. There was Sharp in Memphis, and Toshiba in the tiny town of Lebanon.

Although it had ample reason for buying the LaVergne plant, and had entered negotiations with Firestone in 1981, Bridgestone—the "stone" in each of their names was mere coincidence—made the deal contingent on a contract with the union, URW Local 1055.

In the 1986 film *Gung Ho,* the entire town of Hadleyville, Pennsylvania, turned out to welcome the Japanese purchasers of the defunct auto plant that had been the town's major employer. As the new Japanese owners descended from the plane, they were met with a marching band, balloons, a cheering crowd and a red carpet. (The startled Japanese removed their shoes and stepped forward gingerly.) The work force, under the stewardship of foreman Hunt Stephenson, played by Michael Keaton, pledged to work harder than hard.

No such welcome greeted the delegation from Bridgestone that came to LaVergne in the summer of 1982. Indeed, the union leadership seemed to view the negotiations as an opportunity to win concessions, not make them. Both sides dug in their heels. Then, in a moment of ill-advised bravado, the president of the local, Tommy Powell, told the Japanese in so many words that they could just go back to Japan.

Dan Bailey, then local vice president, described what happened next: "The union guys got up and left. The next day Tommy tried to call (the Japanese) and found out they had checked out."

The Japanese had gone home.

Bailey was appalled. It was one thing for union members to say no to the Japanese. But in this case their leaders had acted without telling them. Peoples' jobs were at stake. "When I knew they went back across the water, I thought, 'We have screwed up big time here.' "

The union officers were summoned to Akron to meet with Firestone and officers of the International Rubber Workers Union. In 1980, Firestone had shut down seven of it seventeen plants, and it was clear the company planned to go ahead with this closure as well. In short, the union had no leverage. The Local 1055 executive board decided to swallow its pride and invite Bridgestone back to the table. This time both sides made commitments. Bridgestone pledged to recall laid-off workers. The union eased work rules and promised to lobby for ratification. The $52 million sale went through in January 1983.

What happened in the next four years was documented by Vanderbilt University professor Thomas A. Mahoney in a case study entitled "From American to Japanese Management: The Conversion of a Tire Plant." An excerpt follows.

"Operating results during the period 1983–1987 demonstrated a 200% increase in the output of the plant, relative productivity level of 172.4% in 1986 compared to 144.6% for the industry (base = 1980), reductions of various measures of product errors and scrap of 60% since 1983, and achievement of a 2.2 incidence rate for injuries relative to 14.0 for the industry. These results were accomplished with the same basic work force, many on layoff in 1983, and under representation by Local 1055 of the United Rubber Workers."

Mahoney listed the changes that produced the results, which ranged from modification of machinery to worker involvement to a conscious effort to increase informal communications and to downplay differences in status between workers and management.

After Bridgestone took over, workers who had lived in fear of losing their jobs were suddenly drawn into a giant renewal effort. In the Firestone days, Bailey said, "They didn't want you to bring your brain here, and that's not the case now."

Said mold shop employee Larry Coleman, "It's a company that's got more ideas. They want to help you, and you want to help them."

Firestone had lost the hearts and minds of its workers. Bridgestone won them back.

It wasn't that Firestone had ignored product quality. Far from it. The company had eighteen "roving inspectors" whose job was to do nothing but check for quality. "The main thing we did," said Barry Hill, who was hired in 1972 as a statistical quality control supervisor, "was collect the data to get a pulse of the quality level in the plant— report information, deal with discrepancies, try to make sure components in noncompliance would not be used in production." The inspectors accumulated sheafs of data on various dimensions of the components: length, depth, width, bias angle. They checked machines for pressures and settings. And they went over the finished product. Nevertheless, Hill said, "there was insufficient activity on how to prevent noncomformance. . . ."

After the inspectors had collected the requisite data, they would give a supervisor the results and expect him to "take care of it." Often the supervisor didn't know any more than anyone else what to do about it. Workers regarded the inspectors as company cops. " 'Hey, here's someone to check on us, tell us what we're doing wrong, but not give us any help.' "

Concluded Hill, "We felt some responsibility to try to control quality, but it was very difficult. It has to be built into the product and the only people who can do that is production. This was the system at the time. It was the Firestone system."

Part of the problem, said Bob Clark, who was quality assurance manager at the time, was that Firestone was caught unprepared by the shift from bias tires to radial tires. "Bias tires are very forgiving. You can pretty much throw them together. Radial tires are very unforgiving." Firestone, he said, didn't realize how different they were. "They jumped in very quickly and maybe misunderstood the product."

"Maybe" was being kind. In 1978, Firestone had agreed under pressure to recall some ten million "Firestone 500" steel-belted radials for passenger cars—the biggest recall in history. By that time, the National Highway Traffic Safety Administration had received complaints that at least forty-one deaths and seventy injuries were related to Firestone radial tire failures. The company tried to blame consumers for underinflating the tires. But federal investigators found internal documents dating from 1972 that had alerted management to the tires' tendency to come apart. Even as technicians frantically tried to find a solution, eventually concluding that moisture buildup caused the steel belts to separate from the tread, the sales force continued to push the tires. It was a dark chapter in Firestone history.

Although the LaVergne plant made only truck tires, the "500" episode had given all Firestone products a bad reputation. In addition, Clark said, "after the oil crisis, it got very competitive. Customers could pick and choose on quality and pricing and various other things." With its force of roving inspectors and statisticians "who tried to take all that mountain of data and make something out of it," plus a bank of eight new $250,000 X-ray machines, Firestone's quality assurance "was a 'Catch–22.' We were constantly testing to confirm or recheck production that was first considered to be abnormal. You only have so much capacity, and you're tying it up to retest abnormal lots; that takes away from your production testing, so you're maybe missing something."

Meanwhile, he said, "authority and responsibility for quality really was centered in Akron in the corporate structure. If I had a tire fail, I'd check a second one; if it failed, we would hold up the lot. Decisions made to release it came from Akron."

Dan Bailey remembers that in the late 1970s quality problems routinely surfaced in the final inspection area where he worked. "We'd been telling them about it for years after the '500' fiasco. But it didn't get the same publicity. Then a bunch of truck companies started sending back tires and dropping accounts. You had workers saying 'We told you so,' and they (Firestone) blamed the workers."

Employees told Vanderbilt's Mahoney that unfinished or defective tires were sometimes taken to the warehouse to be counted as output and then transferred back for completion, or even shipped to customers. If they were returned for rework, the same tire could be counted again as output. The emphasis was on production—getting the numbers out.

Into this sea of difficulties waded the new Japanese owners. Bridgestone had already established a reputation for quality in the United States, where it had had a California-based sales operation since 1967. The Bridgestone motto was "Serving society with products of superior quality" and it did more than pay lip service to that credo. The company had won the Deming Prize in 1968, and its quality department was called the "Deming Plan Promotion Department." Twice each year, the company invited winning quality circles from each of its plants around the world to two intense days of presentations. In 1987, LaVergne hosted the first such presentation in the United States.

Encountering shaky oil supplies and a drop in sales in the early 1980s, the company decided to rededicate itself to quality with a new round of training and internal audits. By then, the quality movement in Japan was called "Total Quality Control" to distinguish it from the narrow application of statistical quality control or the promotion of quality circles. Kaoru Ishikawa, Japan's foremost quality theoretician, called TQC "a thought revolution in management" distinguished by such features as "management by facts" and "respect for humanity."

"Set your eyes on long-term profits and put quality first," he admonished.

Given how seriously the new owners took quality, many expected them to clean house in LaVergne. Instead, the company dispatched some thirty "advisers," who were assigned to shadow the American managers. These would be its shock troops in the battle for quality. Young for the most part, they had grown up in Japan's quality-minded industrial system. As one American manager put it, "They had TQC running in their veins." The proof was that no matter to how many advisers a question was put, they all gave the same answer.

Prior to the sale, the Americans had supplied a tremendous amount of information that the Japanese had digested and incorporated into a plan for the future, displayed in the form of a flow chart with time periods and targets. "January 10th was the sale," Bob Clark said. "January 11th, my guy showed up and said this is what we're going to do for the next three or four years." Clark could see that the role of quality assurance would shift from inspection to training and education. "Our job changed from inspectors fighting product problems to promoters, educators, leaders. I was surprised at the detail. I was supportive almost in total."

He had one major reservation. "I thought perhaps it was too aggressive. They did not totally understand the American mind. It's easy to say you're going to train people on the floor in how to check their quality and turn it over to them. I knew there would be resistance. But it was great to have a plan and great to have something to start with."

"Quite frankly, it was a little scary," said Barry Hill. "You mean, all these people are responsible? Nobody's going to be out there double-checking to make sure they know what they're doing?"

The Japanese advisers were themselves role models for the new way of managing. Plant veterans expected them to march in and begin issuing orders. Instead, said Louis Amirault, who began with Firestone in 1981 as a supervisor and rose rapidly to a managerial position, "they advised us, directed us, talked about how to motivate the work force into a new way of thinking. They'd push. They'd make you think. . . . They'd give you a bunch of scenarios—'Have you thought about this?'—they wouldn't tell you what to do.

"We had such a narrow vision. They'd encourage us to be radical in our thinking." At the same time, they were relentless. "They'd keep prodding and prodding." Firestone, in contrast, tended to drop things if the work force opposed them. "They'd let it go. They didn't want to confront it."

The men and women who worked in the plant were trained in the basics of charting and teamwork. In the peak years 1984 to 1986, Bridgestone devoted some 50,000 man-hours to training. Prospective employees each took twenty hours of unpaid training as part of their evaluation process.

The company also devoted considerable resources to upgrading machinery. With a training budget partially subsidized by $300,000 from the state of Tennessee, Bridgestone took a number of people, including the top officers of the local union, to see their plants in Japan. Dan Bailey could scarcely believe the difference. Bridgestone had told the people in LaVergne that they were in the dark ages, and now he could see why. Americans may have been bigger and stronger than the Japanese but that didn't stop them from getting bad backs and shoulder separations from handling 125-pound truck tires. They had been stacking tires six high, for example. The Japanese had machines that did the job. In one case, a tabletop controlled by a foot pedal would tip 45 degrees so a tire could be rolled onto it. Back in Tennessee, Americans were hoisting tires onto tables. The Japanese also moved quickly, but without wasted motion.

Bailey was impressed by the charts he saw everywhere. And something else: Here and there were fish ponds filled with recycled water from the plant. It was the company's way of testing the purity of its water. If the carp survived, the water was good.

Tokyo was "so clean" and people could leave bikes and motorcycles unlocked. The whole society worked together. Bailey explained to one Japanese why things like that could happen there and not in the States. "All you have is Japanese. We got everybody." Although he had started but never finished college, he would later reflect he had gotten "more out of this whole experience than I could have gotten with a master's degree."

The public tended to think that tires were produced by taking a lump of black rubber and stuffing it into a hot mold, kind of like a waffle iron. In fact, the creation of a tire was a complex process, beginning in "the Banbury," a six-story mixer in which raw rubber, carbon black, sulfur and other chemical agents were mixed together. The finished tire consisted of a tread, a belt, the carcass or main body and the bead, each with its own production line.

The one-man machine on which some sixteen components eventually came together was called a tire assembly machine. Before the Japanese bought the LaVergne plant, they bought a single machine, took it to Japan and modified it. After the sale the machine came back to LaVergne as a model for the others. By the end of five years, production on each tire machine had risen from twenty to forty tires a shift. While some of the changes were major, many were as small as repositioning a button or a pallet of components for easy access.

The Japanese were very big on "visible standards"—things that made it physically difficult to make mistakes. For example, components arrived at the tire machine accompanied by tags punched with holes in a pattern that matched pre-set pegs on a board. The pegs were positioned for each component, per order. If the tags didn't match the pegs, it meant that the wrong component had been delivered.

The Japanese told the Americans that if they concentrated on quality, productivity would take care of itself. In small and not so small ways they let it be known they were serious. Not until March of 1984, more than a year after the sale, did a tire leave LaVergne bearing the Bridgestone label. It was that long before the tires met Bridgestone standards. Gone were Firestone's three tire grades. Now there were only two, Grade A and scrap. Bridgestone wanted to be known as a company that made only first-class tires.

In the first four years of operating the truck tire plant, Bridgestone spent $68 million on training and upgrading. In 1985, it hired its first new American executive as director of human resources. Sam Torrence had worked for an earthmoving equipment company called Terex. "The first month I was here was the first time since 1983 that Bridgestone made money," he said. "No one seemed disturbed. It was the long-term approach."

Bridgestone emphasized that everyone was part of a team. Executives who once had reserved parking spots now took their chances with everyone else. The only people who wore ties anymore were the computer consultants and purchasing agents. Engineers' offices were moved to the factory floor. And in the offices of the support staff, the walls came tumbling down. Meeting areas were located throughout, and at any given time a visitor would see animated groups of people clustered around tables, going over charts or drawings. When in 1988 Bridgestone (USA) moved into corporate offices in a handsome, flower-bordered pink granite building on the outskirts of Nashville, the same thing happened. Walls were ripped down and replaced with partitions.

"Really, those walls became barriers," said Torrence, who did have his own office, albeit one with glass walls that maintained the open atmosphere. But not everyone was happy about these physical changes. Supervisors complained that it was difficult to talk to employees about confidential matters. Management pointed out that conference rooms could be used for those discussions.

Back at the plant, Barry Hill was among those who missed his office. But he had to confess that one reason was that offices "gave you an air of superiority over the people you work with. Once you got used to it you learned to cope. . . ." While there were more interruptions working in an open space with other people, "It brings us closer together so we can have mutual respect for each other. I'm not the boss in the office." He noticed when he visited Bridgestone's Yokohama plant, only the plant manager had a private office.

The Japanese thought it was important that employees get together outside of work. Money was budgeted for employee activities. There were also funds for token awards such as caps, sport shirts and jackets. And they promoted sports.

Bridgestone overhauled more than just the machinery. Management was thinned from eight to five levels. And the Japanese also introduced a form of policy deployment they called "management by objective." Americans, of course, had MBOs—a performance rating system for managers in which a person set goals in consultation with the manager above and was rewarded with a bonus to the extent that those goals were fulfilled. This lead to various forms of "gaming"— goals worded with deliberate vagueness, or, even better, ones proposed that had already been met without the knowledge of the person above.

Bridgestone's MBO was a system of goalsetting not linked to pay. It began with the president's annual message, announcing a set of targets. Those were assigned to managers in the form of "implementation plans" and to the manager's troops as "itemized implementation plans."

Dr. Deming admonished against goals without methods to reach them. "There are no objectives without a plan," Barry Hill explained. Moreover, "If you follow a plan and don't achieve the results, you're still looked upon favorably, if it was a good plan." The shortfalls were a signal for analysis and countermeasures.

In time, Japanese words, or their translations, began to creep into the language at LaVergne, reflecting the new way of thinking. There was "rootbinding," for example. As Sam Torrence came to understand it, it meant that "the little invisible, overlapping roots of a tree underground are what anchor it. It's important they work together." Applied to people and their activities, it meant that "when my office has ideas, we have to be sure that solving a minor problem for us doesn't create a major problem for someone else."

In the case of implementation plans, for example, Barry Hill explained, "All that has to be rootbound with other people. It does me no good to say we're going to have one hundred quality circles if the production department says we can't handle one hundred circles."

Then there was *genbutsu genba*. *Genba* meant "actual place" and *genbutsu* meant "actual product." As used at Bridgestone, it meant acquiring firsthand knowledge of a problem by observing it and gathering data. Managers were always being urged to practice *gen-butsu genba*.

Kaizen was another common word, which referred to the Japanese practice of continuous improvement through small incremental changes, rather than the big leaps forward Americans liked so much. In the early days, as employee teams tackled monumental process improvements, they often got stuck. Both workers and managers had come to recognize the value of *kaizen*. The idea was to break large problems down into small ones. Bridgestone also taught the Americans the "Five Why" approach developed by Toyota. One began with a large problem and asked "why" five times in succession. The result was a number of small problems, more easily addressed by workers.

Bridgestone called this aspect of its improvement process "small zero defects." The LaVergne plant originated a two-page form for simplified problem solving, which it presented in September 1989 at the 94th Deming Plan presentations held in Yokohama. There an employee team called "The Bounty Hunters" gave a presentation on two measures they came up with to reduce the time it took to change tire molds. Since 1986 there had been eighteen such improvements, reducing by 40 percent the mold change time. (See pp. 202–204.)

Not everything went as the Japanese had hoped. The slow pace of quality circle formation, for example, was a major disappointment both to them and to their American converts. As in many other American companies, quality circles had a bad name at LaVergne. Firestone had set them up in the late 1970s, making the common mistake of bypassing the union. As a consequence, the union was hostile to the idea. Even when Bridgestone changed their name to "Employment Involvement Groups" and restructured the steering committee to give the union equal representation, employees were slow to join. The EIGs numbered thirty-three in 1989, with participation by just over 20 percent of the work force.

Bridgestone also generated ill will by doing away with Firestone's lucrative suggestion system, which awarded individual employees 10 percent of the first-year savings from their ideas, if used. That could amount to thousands of dollars. Instead, the Bridgestone suggestion system gave recognition awards of a few hundred dollars, causing a drop in suggestions and perhaps some resistance to other forms of employee involvement.

As much as the American workers preferred the new quality-minded environment, old feelings died hard. Witness the matter of the flags.

Bridgestone flew three flags at the plant entrance: the Stars and Stripes, the Tennessee flag and the company flag. Why not a union flag as well, the United Rubber Workers wanted to know? As Sam Torrence would later tell this part of the story, Bridgestone was willing to compromise by flying the URW banner not at the entrance, but among a new row of flags from countries where the corporation had plants, which would represent the "friends of Bridgestone." Among them, of course, was Japan.

But the sight of Japan's familiar red sun fluttering in Tennessee breezes offended people in the community. Local president Dan Bailey was offended too. "I felt the same way. My father fought in World War II. After fighting Germans he was sent to Japan." Bailey said he told people that "it was becoming a real issue. No one would listen to me." On the eve of a visit by the Bridgestone chairman and other dignitaries, Bailey found himself outside the plant. "I kept looking at the flags." On impulse, he decided to act. "I just took the flag off the pole.

"That got some attention."

Indeed, it did. The missing Japanese flag triggered a desperate attempt to find another four-by-eight-foot banner suitable for flying before the dignitaries arrived. People thought they were onto something when the state of Tennessee said it had some Japanese flags that size. The four-by-eight part was right. But the measurement was inches, not feet.

It was no secret that Bailey had taken the flag. Several workers told management they had seen him do so. But no one wanted to fire the local president for stealing company property, particularly right then. Intermediaries reasoned with Bailey. The next morning Bailey returned the flag to the top-ranking Japanese at LaVergne, a well-liked executive named Nori Takeuchi, who was president of the tire sales group. "I didn't deface it or anything like that," Bailey said. "I folded it up just like American flags." Takeuchi understood perhaps more than anyone else at that point Bailey's need to save face with a compromise. The Japanese flag would stay, but Bridgestone would fly another American flag with the "friends"—higher than the others. In retrospect, Bailey said years afterward, "it seems kind of funny now, but it was pretty emotional at the time." Takeuchi "looked like he was about to cry, and I was choked up."

In 1986, Bridgestone announced that it planned to expand the LaVergne plant to add passenger tire production. But the company wanted changes in contract work rules, primarily related to mandatory overtime for training, meetings and other activities. If a worker's replacement had not reported when his shift ended, for example, Bridgestone would require that worker to stay a half hour longer. But many Bridgestone employees traveled in car pools. That meant they could miss their ride.

Once again, Local 1055 vetoed the plan. The vote was 170 to 40, with just over a 30 percent turnout of the 600 members. The results took those who had not voted by surprise. So once again, petitioned by the membership, the local reconsidered and approved the arrangements, this time by a vote of 314 to 190. Bridgestone gave the go-ahead. The $77 million plant addition opened in 1988, increasing employment to 1,000. In retrospect, Dan Bailey said, the overtime provisions had not turned out to be a problem.

In May of 1988, Bridgestone bought Firestone Tire & Rubber Company. The purchase was diplomatically termed a "merger," although some noted that Bridgestone's $2.6 billion payment—the largest sale in history at that time of a U.S. firm to a Japanese corporation—scarcely constituted anything but a takeover, albeit a friendly one.

The news was greeted with considerable enthusiasm by most of Firestone's 53,500 employees—exactly half the 107,000 who had worked for the company as recently as 1979, before all but five North American plants were closed. Bridgestone pledged to invest $1.5 billion in those plants and the 1,500 retail stores. The advisers who had been at LaVergne moved on to new assignments.

It wasn't long before Dan Bailey was getting calls from other Firestone locals around the country, wondering what was going to happen. He advised them to be patient. "It's going to take time," he told them. "You're going to see slow steady stuff."

On February 2, 1989, Bridgestone announced plans to build a new facility, a $350-million truck tire plant in Warren County, Tennessee, about 60 miles from LaVergne. With Torrence in charge, the Bridgestone labor management staff had worked hard to build a good relationship with the United Rubber Workers, not just at the local level but with the international leadership as well. It did not plan to jeopardize this relationship now. The company agreed to give the union liberal access to the new employees. If a majority signed cards asking for union recognition, Bridgestone would grant it.

In return, the union agreed that the work force in the Warren plant could be structured quite differently from LaVergne. Warren would join others using self-directed work teams, or "star" teams, a system pioneered by Procter & Gamble. Divided into maintenance and production, members would be cross-trained to do all the jobs on a process. They eventually would take charge of administrative functions such as scheduling and training and be part of the hiring process, thus eliminating the need for a supervisor.

Bob Walsh, who was appointed plant manager, explained that he had pushed for the idea as the logical realization of TQC. Formerly LaVergne's chief chemist, Walsh had switched to production after the Bridgestone sale, recognizing that "in the Bridgestone philosophy, the center of the universe was production." Until he became a production manager, and went from dealing with things to dealing with people, he said, he didn't fully understand TQC.

In his view, TQC at LaVergne had hit a plateau after the gains of the initial four years. He could see that what was needed was total dedication to *kaizen*—he even bought author Masaaki Imai's text on the subject—and he could also see how difficult that was going to be. "For it to work, everybody has to be involved. Now we're getting to the hard part: how to get the same level of involvement in the new plant as they have in Japan?"

He asked himself "What is it that's different in Japan than in America?" He went through a half dozen of Bridgestone's Japanese plants for the second and third time with that question in mind. Many people thought it was the culture. But he concluded that was only partly the reason. More significant was that "the average ability of the staff is much higher—the way they do their job. They're good, they know what they're doing."

Why? "The way they do their selection process, and ten times more training."

The difference in the two work forces was illustrated by how supervisors were selected. "Here, when we want to promote supervisors, first we do an interview. Then we pick a guy, put them in training for a month and they take over.

"In Japan, they decide how many supervisors they will need.

Candidates sign up, get interviewed and then they're tested rigorously. They're pared down, then sent to Tokyo to train. . . . They're trained in business, safety, engineering. In my opinion they get a hundred times more preparation. Our guy will spend the first five years getting the training they have on day one. At the end of five years they might be equal."

It seemed to him that self-directed work teams offered "an environment in which continuous improvement is a way of life and working in teams is natural. You won't need quality circles because everybody in that plant is on a team. . . . Not 20 percent but 100 percent of your people involved in team activities."

The other part of the equation was the hiring procedure. At La-Vergne, applicants were drawn from a pool of people recommended by the current work force. That had some disadvantages, not the least of which was the large number of relatives employed as a consequence. If someone was turned down, too, it created hard feelings.

For the new plant, Bridgestone wanted people who not only had sufficient education but also had demonstrated an ability to work in teams. The company established an assessment center to process the hundreds of applicants who came to them only after first passing a four-hour general aptitude test administered by the State of Tennessee. Fewer than one in five made it through that test.

Next there was a four-hour panel interview with three team leaders and a technical test, which weeded out another 50 percent. Candidates who cleared those hurdles reported to the assessment center for seven and a half hours of simulated group–problem solving, in which trained assessors judged them on participation, leadership abilities and mediation skills. In the end just three of one hundred initial applicants were hired.

Researching the star-team concept and setting up the assessment center, as well as making a $100,000 video to be shown at job fairs and other forums, occupied human resources manager Mark McLaughlin for more than a year before the first tire was built. As far as he knew, Bridgestone's Japanese plants had not ventured into this realm. For once the Americans were out front. That do-or-die spirit evident in the movie *Gung Ho* had finally kicked in.

Said McLaughlin, speaking for himself and others, "Our ambition is to have the Japanese over here in five years, so they can learn from what we're doing."

II. QUALITY STORIES

Kokai Watch

One morning in late 1989 a group of people gathered around a loud, towering machine called a quad cold tuber, which made the tread component of passenger tires. A compound was fed through one end and forced over a die; it emerged from the other end in a narrow strip that was color-coded by four canisters of paint as it moved along on a conveyor belt. The one machine ran up to twenty different treads. In what was known at LaVergne as a *"kokai* watch," the group would observe two workers change the incoming material and the die to produce a different tread.

The *kokai* watch was yet another import from Japan. The idea was that people could observe a process, even those who were strangers to it, with fresh eyes, seeing things that closely involved workers might not. Their suggestions could thus be helpful. Mark Fox, a foreman in the passenger tire department, credited the *kokai* watch with many of the improvements that had reduced the changeover time in treads on the quad cold tuber by 80 percent.

As it happened, the *kokai* watch was not a technique that the Americans had learned from their Bridgestone advisers. Instead, when he was dispatched to Japan to study productivity improvements, Fox saw one take place at a Bridgestone plant there. Back at LaVergne, he targeted the quad tuber as a maiden site. But soon, people found other applications. When a worker suffered a partial loss of two fingers using a piece of new machinery that was supposed to be safe, for example, Louis Amirault, passenger tire section manager, suggested a *kokai* watch. Because the machine, a body ply cutter, was new, he recalled, "People said, 'My God. It's brand new, not a thing wrong with it.' " And, as it happened, the injured worker had not been following the proper procedures. The old way of thinking was to say the accident was his own fault. Instead, Amirault wondered in what other ways the cutter might present a hazard.

About a dozen people gathered on the midnight shift, divided the machine into four sectors and proceeded to conduct a four-hour "SST *kokai*"—for "safety sensitivity training." They found no less than 63 potential dangers, including 6 places, Amirault said, "without machine guards where a guy could get caught bad by it."

The watchers gathered afterward to list their observations and assign priorities and countermeasures. Since then, there had been many *kokai* watches, including follow-ups to earlier ones. Usually, top managers were invited as well, to familiarize them with activities in the plant.

Amirault was a big fan. "You cannot believe what we generate in a *kokai* watch." In addition, he said, "You do not know what a morale booster for a guy on the midnight to 8 A.M. shift to have the vice president for production there."

The *kokai* watch on the quad cold tuber was organized by Mark Fox, who had become something of an authority on how they worked. He cautioned that it was inadvisable to involve more than a half dozen people. The first *kokais* at LaVergne had drawn as many as twenty. Not used to such attention, nervous workers made mistakes. By the same token, a *kokai* watch would not be successful when employees did not trust the bosses, because they would suspect that the watches were merely a device to find fault with them.

Today there were five "watchers." In addition to Fox, there was a plant visitor, a member of the human resources staff, a chemist and a project manager.

"Write down anything," Fox said over the roar of machinery. "Just watch with an open mind and jot it down. 'Hey, looks like this guy is walking too much,' or 'Looks like he's not handling the knife right.' That's what you're going to do."

The watchers were not to ask questions of the two men on the machine. "You want to see what happens. Let them do their job. We're trying to see the real world, not something manufactured just for us."

For eighteen minutes the little group watched and took notes, focusing principally on a worker who scurried about changing computerized machine settings for the new lot, slicing off the old stock with a knife and prying its remains from the tuber with a crowbar. Then they reassembled in a conference room above the factory floor, where Fox quickly scrawled three headings across a broad sheet of paper: "Problem/Countermeasure/Who."

He went around the watchers one by one, asking for their observations. Someone said that worker seemed to spend a lot of time flipping through a book of computer codes looking for the correct one. Perhaps they could be flagged. And because of the manual labor involved with the die change, he was wearing gloves, which made the job more difficult. Fox assigned a countermeasure: "Do as much paperwork before change as possible."

The worker had a hard time pulling out the stock. "Use head lube each time—check effectiveness," Fox wrote under countermeasures. The crowbar he used to pry loose the old stock hung a few feet away over a rail and looked dangerous. "Prepare holder," he wrote. Perhaps the holder could be welded to the machine near the die itself. The worker had also forgotten to prepare certain die numbers in advance. "Review method," Fox wrote.

Each countermeasure was assigned to a person in the "who" list. Explained Fox, "I'll send out a copy to everyone involved and ask for dates when they can get it done. In a week, I'll call back to check. And probably in a couple weeks we'll do another *kokai* watch."

He continued, "I would strongly suggest that any company should have a *kokai* watch. The main thing is that you want to get your boss involved. Instead of saying 'Why's everything so screwed up?' he'll say 'I know why Mark's having that problem. I saw it myself, and I've got to get him some resources to help.' "

When the watches began, Fox said, the countermeasures considered worthwhile were those that saved ten minutes. "Now we're looking at things that took two minutes." In Japan, however, they would say "Man, that took six seconds."

Small Zero Defects

In a tire plant, the unit that cleans and changes the two-ton iron molds that fit into presses and give the tire its distinctive tread is the "mold shop." The "Bounty Hunters" team from Bridgestone's passenger tire mold shop had become adept at the plant's simplified problem-solving format. To illustrate the format, the team presented two improvement projects at Bridgestone's ninety-fourth Deming Plan presentation in Yokohama in September of 1989. They were the two most recent improvements on a list of eighteen that had reduced mold change time by 40 percent.

Project I

(1) Theme: The team chose to "improve in/down loader adjustment." (This was the means by which the mold was loaded and lowered into the press.)

(2) Reason for theme's selection: to reduce cost and improve morale and productivity.

(3) Date started: February 1989.

(4) Current state: It required too much time to load each of the thirty-nine presses. The process involved using a large wrench to turn a threaded bolt to the proper setting, located by trial-and-error.

(5) Frequency: The shop averaged four loader adjustments per day.

(6) Objective: The team hoped to reduce the adjustment time by 75 percent.

(7) Target date: May 31, 1989.

(8) Cause analysis: Often bolts became worn and rusty and therefore hard to adjust. Sometimes the person changing the mold had difficulty finding the wrench. "The method had been used for seventeen years, but the group felt not anymore!" the team declared. "There has to be a better way."

(9) Countermeasure: The threaded shaft was replaced with a bar with set holes and a pin. The person changing the mold could move the bar up and down to the proper position and lock it in place with a pin. Gone was the wrench. The team went through the Plan-Do-Check-Act Cycle again and decided to attach a limit switch to the loader, which further reduced the time.

(10) Results: The adjustment now showed a 95-percent improvement.

(11) Date of completion: The team met its May 1989 target date, working four months.

Project II

(1) Theme: "Improve cake pan change time."

(2) Reason for theme's selection: To reduce cost and improve morale and productivity.

(3) Date started: February 1989.

(4) Current state: The "cake pan" was a rounded mold insert that held a "green" or uncured tire in the proper position so it could be picked up by the loader. There were two sizes that were switched depending on the size of the tire being run. To change the pans, eight bolts had to be removed, then reinserted—a step that took twenty-five minutes.

(5) Frequency: Cake pans were changed approximately twice a week.

(6) Objective: To reduce the change time by 80 percent, to two minutes.

(7) Target date: June 1989.

(8) Cause analysis: The team used the "Five Why" method to zero in on a cause. It needed to ask "why" just three times:

> FIRST WHY—"Does changing the larger cake pan to the smaller take so long?"
> ANSWER—Must remove bolts and move large cake pan, then install small cake pan.
> SECOND WHY—Does large cake pan have to be removed?
> ANSWER—Can't put small cake pan on top of large cake pan.
> THIRD WHY—Can't put small cake pan on top of the large cake pan?
> ANSWER—Maybe we can put small cake pan on a large cake pan.

The group decided to try it.

(9) Countermeasure: The team devised a way to attach a plate and a nut to each large pan to anchor and center a smaller one. The small pans were modified to sit properly, once bolted in place. No longer would one have to be removed and replaced with another.

(10) Results: The team met its 80 percent objective. The new setup took just five minutes.

(11) Date of completion: June 1989.

CHAPTER SEVEN

Globe Metallurgical Incorporated

American business and industry are beginning to understand that poor quality costs companies as much as 20 percent of sales revenues nationally, and that improved quality of goods and services goes hand in hand with improved productivity, lower costs and increased profitability.

—THE MALCOLM BALDRIGE NATIONAL QUALITY IMPROVEMENT ACT OF 1987

Up a winding dead-end road just north of the ramshackle little river town of Beverly in southeastern Ohio stood the twin sheds of Globe Metallurgical Incorporated. They looked like oversized red barns bristling with ducts, hoppers and chimneys. Piles of wood chips, gravel and coal, the raw ingredients for ferrosilicon and silicon metal, were heaped in the yard.

Next door were the two high stacks of a power plant belonging to the American Electric Power Company. Steam billowed from its concrete cooling tower. A web of transmission lines spread from the plant. Nothing about the site would prompt a driver to stop and remark "My God, I bet that place just won the National Quality Award."

After Globe did, in fact, win the Malcolm Baldrige National Quality Award in 1988, named for a U.S. Secretary of Commerce who died in a rodeo accident, vice president Kenneth E. Leach was in demand to explain how it had happened. At presentations he would flash a slide of the plant and deliver that line. It always got a laugh because it was so true.

On days visitors were expected, the blue banner with the silver Baldrige logo flew with the American flag and two others, from Ford and General Motors, bearing quality insignia. Otherwise Globe raised only the Stars and Stripes because the flags got dirty so fast and the company didn't want to keep asking the Ford and GM and Baldrige people for replacements. Besides, the only ones who saw them were employees, and they knew they had won.

Of late, however, the flags were almost always up, because there were so many visitors.

The Globe quality story appealed to people because it suggested that even a small company could, with sufficient effort, succeed in the most adverse circumstances, just like the big guys. The other 1988 Baldrige winners were high-techers Motorola Incorporated and the commercial nuclear fuel division of Westinghouse Electric Corporation. In contrast to these industrial giants, with million-dollar budgets, large human resources departments and armies of technicians, little Globe undertook its quality improvements in isolation, with a skeleton staff and an equally lean budget, amid a bitter strike and a leveraged buyout.

Globe's achievements not only demonstrated that quality systems were within reach of everyone, but also that they could be applied in an environment that couldn't get much more low-tech. Leach, whose deadpan delivery invited comparisons to Tom Bodett and Garrison Keillor, would get another laugh when he told audiences "You won't catch our employees wearing a surgical mask to keep from sneezing on the product. They wear respirators to keep from breathing the product in." That also was true.

And although the Baldrige Prize had its critics—among them Dr. Deming, who worried that it was too results-oriented, fostering a short-term attitude—it did focus national attention on quality at a time when the nation desperately needed a dose of it. As the 1990s dawned, Baldrige criteria were being used as guidelines for improvement by many companies who might otherwise begin the quality expedition in the dark.

Although small, Globe had been around since its founding in 1873 as the Globe Iron Company in Jackson, Ohio. During the Civil War, its founder had owned a single furnace, which made the iron used by Confederate forces to sheath the *Merrimack*. The battle between the *Merrimack* and the Union's *Monitor* was the first between iron-clad ships, a milestone in naval history.

In modern history, Globe was owned for nearly three decades by Interlake Company. In 1984, that company sold it to Moore McCormack Resources. By then the Globe had two plants—the one in Beverly, equipped with five electric furnaces that could produce both silicon metal and a full range of ferrosilicon products; and a smaller one in Selma, with two furnaces specializing in high-grade silicon metal. Globe's silicon metal was used by the aluminum industry as an additive and by the chemical industry for a wide variety of bases, from food to cosmetics to caulking compounds. Its principal outlet for ferrosilicon was steel mills, which used it for oxidation in the steelmaking process.

The company had a good reputation for quality. Its laboratory in Beverly was equipped with sophisticated X-ray and atomic absorption equipment that was used by the U.S. Bureau of Standards to develop standards for ferrosilicon and ferrochromium. Globe sampled everything that went out the door. The 100-percent inspection was costly but effective.

Globe's comfortable market niche began to shrink in the early 1980s, however, as the domestic auto industry shriveled, taking the steel industry down with it. Even more damaging was a tide of low-priced imported material from Brazil, Argentina and Canada. Suddenly there was a glut on the market. Globe's annual losses were in the millions of dollars. At Beverly, only two of the five furnaces were operating and more than a third of the work force was laid off.

As a way out, the company could expand its silicon metal sales to the chemical industry and sell ferrosilicon to auto industry foundries, both of which required higher quality, well-controlled alloys than those from abroad—if Globe, in turn, could raise quality levels.

Spurred by Japanese competition, Ford had taken the lead in pressing its suppliers for better products. In 1979 it issued a document called Q-101, a manual of quality specifications widely regarded by suppliers as an instrument of torture because they had no idea how to meet them. To help, Ford had established a training institution called the American Supplier Institute. Then, in 1985, Ford approached its suppliers with a quality certification called Q-1. The first step to certification was to pass a Q-101 audit, with a score of 140 or better out of 200.

Globe decided to go for it.

Leach, a West Virginia University graduate with a background in human resources, came to Globe from a competitor in 1985 as director of corporate services. He was handed the quality mission by CEO Arden Sims, who had joined the company the year before. It was clear to Leach that Globe was deficient in major areas delineated by Ford Q-101 criteria. Ford wanted evidence of quality through a defect-prevention system, not a defect-detection system; it also wanted statistical process control, a quality plan and employee participation.

Globe had none of those.

Globe took a further cue from Ford, whose leadership was committed to the principles of W. Edwards Deming. The corporation not only sent people to his seminars, but frequently brought in Dr. Deming himself to do private sessions for its people.

Globe rented the videotapes.

Produced by the MIT Center for Advanced Engineering study, the tapes were a synopsis of a Deming four-day seminar. But there was a big difference. With a live audience, Leach would later note, Deming "liked to snap at people and jump all over them, and it kind of keeps you on the edge of your seat." Produced in a studio, the videotapes were a tad on the dry side. "If you have trouble sleeping at night," Leach quipped, "you can take these things home and slip them in the old VCR." As a general rule, it made symbolic sense for the CEO to sit through the same training as employees. That both management and supervisors watched the Deming tapes was particularly meaningful, Leach said, "because we subjected ourselves to the same torture we were subjecting them to."

No sooner had Globe shown the Deming tapes and launched an SPC training program for supervisors, however, than one of their customers criticized them for excluding hourly workers. Lynchburg Foundry had already won the Q-1 award that Globe was seeking. "There's no way you're going to get it," a representative told Leach during a visit to Globe. When their plane left for Lynchburg the next day, Leach was on board with the foundry people to see what they were talking about. "A lot of what we do is based on what they did," he said much later. "They gave us a lot of good ideas on how to start." Without understanding all that he saw, it was clear that a big difference was the level of employee involvement. The hourly workers had to be drawn into the quality process.

That was not as easy as it sounded. Hourly people often responded negatively to classroom instruction in charting. Globe did have one persuasive argument. Said former chief chemist Jim Cline, who had been appointed SPC trainer, "We were able to tell our people it's a matter of survival."

Globe enlisted the services of an instructor from the American Supplier Institute and asked that the training be tailored to plant processes. Explained Leach, "Rather than talking about the generic—if you average the height of all the guys in the army, you get a normal distribution and a histogram and all that—we were afraid that might not carry out to the pouring temperature of 50-percent ferrosilicon prior to making a magnesium ladle addition, so we trained them on that pouring temperature."

The trainer arrived a day in advance to familiarize himself with data collected in the normal course of events so that he could build the training around it. "As we started to construct charts from that historical data, right before their eyes," Leach explained, "they realized that 'Gee, we're out of control here. We're not as good as we thought we were.' I think that was meaningful for them."

Globe bought every worker a calculator. One guy complained after the training that his calculator didn't work. The trainer discovered he didn't know how to turn it on. He was not the only person who had never used one before.

When it came to empowering the workers with statistical tools, however, the biggest stumbling block was the supervisors. Said Leach, "These were the middle management that Dr. Deming would call 85 percent of the problem. They already knew how to make silicon metal and they didn't need SPC or Dr. Deming or employee involvement or whatever."

In addition, there was an adversarial relationship between management and labor, represented in Beverly by the United Steelworkers of America. The last thing the supervisors wanted to do "was go out there and empower hourly people to start calling shots on the shop floor based on a control chart, which they really didn't have any confidence in anyway."

Leach, in retrospect, would call the resistance of middle management "the most difficult bridge we had to cross." Overcoming it was critical. "These people can't be out on the shop floor telling hourly people this is all going to blow over, it's the flavor of the month or whatever." When persuasion didn't work, "we went in there and knocked some heads and hammered some people. . . ."

In December of 1985, a Ford representative conducted the Q–101 audit. Globe was one point short of passing, though 139 was still a high score for a first-time review. The auditor returned in January, after Globe had followed some of his suggestions. This time Globe passed, the first ferroalloy producer to be awarded the Q–1.

There was little time to celebrate. In June of 1986, the same month the Q–1 was awarded, Moore McCormack Resources announced the company was for sale. In October the union called a strike.

The labor issues were fundamental ones of job security and pay. As management saw it, there was simply no way the company could be profitable without a drastic reduction in labor costs. There were two ways to achieve that, by thinning the work force or by lowering wages.

Rigid work rules governing twenty job descriptions stood in the way of efficiency. Under the union contract, the supplier down the road couldn't unload a delivery of wood chips directly into the bucket elevator that fed the furnace. Only a union member could do so. That meant Globe needed to have a front-end loader and someone to man it, and someone else to maintain it. The person who operated the front-end loader couldn't drive a fork truck. A foreman couldn't help out a furnace tapper. And so on. As a result, often people sat around with nothing to do. Globe wanted to cut the number of jobs in half. Deeply committed to job security, the union was willing to yield, but not that much. If Globe were to give in and keep the same number of people, however, it wanted to slash the $19.23 wage-and-benefit package by $5.43. That, too, was unacceptable to the union.

Globe remained open during the strike with a salaried work force of sixty-five. After six months the company hired permanent replacements.

It was a bitter strike. "It was like the Civil War," Leach said. "You had a father in the plant and a son on strike. Or a son working and the father out. Or one brother working and one not." Fearful of violence, Leach had a round-the-clock armed guard at his home.

Inside the plant, anxiety levels ran high, not only because of the strike but also over the company's uncertain future. Managers and workers alike worried that no one would buy Globe and the company would fold. "It was in that climate," Leach said, "that we had to keep the focus on quality." Having been certified by Ford, Globe was now seeking a similar endorsement from General Motors, which audited its suppliers on quality, delivery, management, cost and technology—"five targets for excellence."

A General Motors delegation arrived for the audit. Recalled Leach: "We had to get them across the picket line, get them into the plant. We had a whole new work force that wasn't there when Ford was there. And we had to go through the targets, which is not a great day at the beach in itself. . . . You can't really use 'We have a bad union situation' as an excuse to just not do some of the things that needed to be done." Globe received the highest point score given to date by the GM central foundry division.

In October of 1988, the union called off the strike. Eventually forty-three union workers came back. A petition for decertification was unchallenged. For all the ill effects, Globe now had license to restructure its work force dramatically. Moreover, the four top managers, including Leach, had put together a leveraged buy-out, and the future suddenly looked promising.

Front-line supervisors were absorbed into the work force and paid an hourly wage. Where once a furnace might have had eight operators and two supervisors to cover three daily shifts for a week, there were now just eight operators who were responsible for scheduling the work, carrying it out and making adjustments if something went wrong. Workers could help out in other jobs as needed.

Whereas the Beverly plant once had 262 hourly workers and 65 salaried workers, three years after the strike there were 104 hourly workers and 28 salaried employees. In Selma, hourly workers were represented by a different union, one that proved more amenable than the Steelworkers to the changes Globe wanted. There Globe engineered a reduction in the hourly work force from 90 to 57. The company pledged that henceforth no one would be fired if productivity gains eliminated jobs. The company would find something for those people to do. At Selma, for example, Globe replaced security guards from an outside company with its own people.

Leach was often asked whether there was a difference between the two plants, one now union and the other nonunion. If anything, he said, the Selma work force was the more involved of the two.

In addition to training its own people in SPC and employee involvement, Globe also trained its suppliers and set up its own certification system. But how, suppliers wondered, could SPC work in a company such as theirs, engaged in such primitive operations as mining gravel or coal or chopping up wood into chips. "We have the greatest SPC going," a coal supplier told Jim Cline early in the game. "Safety Prevention Concept."

Their attitude was understandable. As Cline summed it up: "The Lord made gravel and put it in the ground. The Lord made coal and put it in the ground, and there's nothing we can do."

But wherever there were variables, there were opportunities for consistency. Coal varied in the amount of fixed carbon, the amount of ash and size distribution. The size of wood chips varied according to the sharpness of the blade and its rpms. Those variables affected Globe's product.

One supplier, for example, frequently shipped the Beverly plant undersized quartzite, which was undesirable for silicon metal production because it burned too quickly. Because the supplier's quartzite was extremely low in impurities, however, Globe continued to buy it, screening out the small pieces upon delivery and using them in ferrosilicon production. Globe not only paid for the screening, but it was using the expensive quartzite in a process where a cheaper, higher-iron product was available.

After Globe trained the supplier's employees in SPC and began to require control charts with the shipments, undersized quartzite disappeared from the lots. It cost Globe $2,500 to dispatch the training team. The savings were $250,000 a year.

Where once Globe had inspected all incoming shipments, now it did so only randomly. Moreover, because the quality of supplies was now such that they could be delivered directly to the furnaces for same-day use, a just-in-time system of delivery evolved among suppliers, yielding more savings.

Globe had come a long way by 1988, when Jim Cline and Ken Leach found themselves at a quality conference in Dallas. It was there that Cline noticed an application for something called the Malcolm Baldrige National Quality Award. "Do you think we ought to try for this?" he asked Leach. There were three categories: manufacturing; service; and small business, defined as having fewer than 500 employees. Two companies could win in each category.

The idea for the prize had originated with a congressional fact-finding expedition to Japan in 1986, led by Representative Don Fuqua, a Florida Democrat. There the delegation met with Kaoru Ishikawa, Japan's foremost quality expert and a counselor with the

Union of Japanese Scientists and Engineers, which had initiated the Deming Prize. Ishikawa encouraged the Americans to come up with a similar award as a way to boost quality. Indeed, in the absence of a domestic award, an American company, Florida Power & Light, already had decided to seek the Deming Prize. Its chairman, John Hudiburg, lobbied vigorously for legislation creating an American counterpart. It passed in 1987, and was named for U.S. Commerce Secretary Malcolm Baldrige, who had died while the legislation was being debated. Private industry contributed $9.9 million to fund the program.

Leach liked the idea of competing for a national prize. Although the awards Globe had won from its customers were widely recognized within the industry, outsiders hadn't heard of them. This was a chance for greater recognition. But there wasn't much time. The pair from Globe had discovered the application on a Thursday; it was due in Washington the following Tuesday. "I've got to go to Montreal tomorrow," Leach told Cline. "What are you doing Saturday morning?"

That weekend, Leach huddled over his Apple computer, filling out the Baldrige application, as Cline supplied documentation. On Monday, they sent it by overnight mail to Washington.

There were seven examination categories: leadership; information and analysis; strategic quality planning; human resource utilization; quality assurance of products and services; quality results; and customer satisfaction. Companies that scored more than 601 of 1,000 points rated a site visit, the second stage of the competition.

Leach laid out the essentials of Globe's quality system, which was called QEC, "Quality-Efficiency-Cost," so-called for the three areas of ongoing improvement. Not only had the entire work force been trained in SPC, along with a number of suppliers, but the company had assembled a quality manual divided into five segments that detailed procedures in both plants; specific instructions for carrying them out; "critical process variables," which were monitored on the shop floor; agreements between Globe and customers on product requirements; and failure mode effects analysis, a numerical system for ranking the potential for failure on various plant operations, which translated into priorities for corrective action. Broken down by departments, the manual was used both for training new employees and as a reference.

As an organization, Globe was guided by a QEC steering committee of top managers who met monthly. Each plant had a QEC committee of department heads, chaired by the plant manager, that met daily. Among its duties was a review of such critical process variables as the molten temperature of the ferrosilicon, which affected how well additives melted and mixed, and the percentage of fines in the coal, which could result in too little carbon and too much slag. In the beginning, when Globe wanted to impress its auto industry customers, it had slapped control charts on hundreds of process variables—far too many to be truly useful. Those had been narrowed down to a more manageable number.

In addition to being organized as work teams, with responsibilities for scheduling and monitoring production, Globe's hourly employees belonged to quality circles both within and between departments, which met periodically to generate ideas for improvement. It was not unusual for a meeting to produce ten suggestions.

Management saw that it needed to act quickly on ideas, most of which were small and inexpensive. Explained Leach, "We find the best way to turn people off is to get back to them three months later on some $20 idea." The ideas were either accepted or rejected by the QEC committee the next day, and the decision posted in the plant immediately. "Quite often," Leach said, "we will implement the entire list within twenty-four hours."

Ideas that were promising but required more work might be assigned to a project team, with members picked by management, who made it a point to include hourly workers. "Historically we would never have included hourly people on project teams," Leach said. "We would have done that with all of our 'smart guys,' all of our engineers and metallurgists. . . . Then when we tried to implement something out on the shop floor that all the smart guys came up with, we found that maybe we weren't so smart . . . that the hourly people would resist some implementation of some things that they just weren't involved in. Nobody asked their opinion, so they weren't going to help. Today we involve them very much, right up front."

One project team worked with researchers from the Batelle Memorial Institute in Columbus, Ohio, on a process for casting metal that saved as much as $1 million a year. Another improvement replaced a sampling process for magnesium that required testing each of fourteen cooling containers. Independent of the product, the sampling process itself produced a lot of variation, which could prompt people to make unnecessary corrections in production. It was also time-consuming for employees in both the plant and the lab. The new method would involve a single sample, reducing labor and ensuring consistency.

In addition, there were several joint teams with rotating membership from Selma and Beverly that exchanged information and technology. The worker involvement had paid off in a big way. Leach credited the teams with a big chunk of the $10 million each year the company was realizing in productivity gains.

When it came to rewards, Globe had decided against giving money for suggestions. Explained Leach, "Invariably we found the employees thought management grossly underestimated the value of their share. So we give somebody a check for $1,000 and they're mad at us because they're expecting $1,500 or $2,000. . . . Also, the people that worked with this employee were mad at him for getting the $1,000, and they were mad at us for giving it to him. Then three or four days later somebody would come in to us and say 'You know, I talked about this to old Bob in the locker room a month or so ago and damned if he didn't turn my idea in.' So what do you do then?"

What Globe did instead was to allow workers to share equally in the increased profits, through quarterly bonuses that averaged $5,000 a year. It passed out jackets, caps, tee shirts with the company logo, honey-baked hams, golf shirts, golf balls. In tandem, the two things seemed to satisfy people. "We haven't had anybody come up to us and say 'Gee, I gave you an idea that saved $100,000 and you give me some lousy $60 ham.' We haven't had that problem because they all are rewarded through the bonus system."

To furnace operator Garry Silvus the bonus represented "a piece of the rock." But he stressed the other rewards of working for a quality-minded company, chief among them a sense of security. Silvus had no sooner started working for the company in 1966 than he was laid off. Even twelve years later, when he had thought he had enough seniority for security, he was still laid off when business took a downturn. Today he said he not only felt more secure, but he was making more money than before the strike, roughly $14 an hour.

Silvus said he welcomed the added responsibility of computers and control charts in a job that no longer required him to punch a time clock. Removing the time clock had an effect he hadn't anticipated. To his surprise, people arrived earlier, if anything, than they had before, just to get a feel for the product being run on their shift that day. Although he had belonged to the union, Silvus conceded that he had thought many of his former coworkers were "deadheads." He was amazed at how they had shaped up in recent years. "Some of the deadheads got back, and they've changed. That's the main thing. They do their job. Everybody does their job. . . . Like a clock—everybody's got to tick or it's not going to work."

Salaried employees also received a bonus, proportional to their pay. Meanwhile, Globe had done away with the performance ratings that previously governed raises. Everybody in the plant, hourly and salaried alike, got the same percentage annual increase.

Globe also took workers by the busload to visit customers, so they could see how their products were being used. Customer satisfaction with Globe was reflected in a decrease of complaints—44 in 1985 (when there was 100 percent inspection) to 3 complaints in 1988. Returned sales tonnage had declined from .02 to .03 percent in the mid–1980s to zero in 1987.

In addition to the strategic business plan that Globe had always written each year, there was now a continuous improvement plan that addressed quality issues. In 1987, it numbered twenty-nine pages with ninety-six objectives. Each objective was broken down into projects, a goal, responsibility and target date. For example:

42.
OBJECTIVE: Develop an ongoing program to certify and further develop and consolidate the supplier base.
PROJECT: a) Develop a certification system for suppliers;
b) Revisit all suppliers in 1988 to work on training and development of their quality programs;
c) Reduce the number of suppliers by 20 percent.
GOAL: Improve the plant operation through the improvement in raw materials received.
RESPONSIBILITY: a) Cline
b) Cline/Leach
c) Leach/Coley
TARGET DATE: a) 12/31/87
b) 06/30/88
c) 08/30/88

The plan was circulated among hourly employees and they were invited to attend planning meetings.

* * *

In 1988, sixty-six companies competed for the Baldrige. Some might criticize the award because it was competitive, creating a class of winners and losers, unlike the Deming in which any number could win. Only two could win the Baldrige in each category. But with just three winners that year, it was clear that many applicants had not attained even minimal standards in the eyes of the examiners.

That only forty entered in 1989 suggested that companies realized how tough those standards were. There were only two winners in the second year of the prize, both in manufacturing: Milliken & Company and Xerox Corporation Business Products and Systems. None of nine applicants won in the service industry, nor did any among eleven small businesses that applied. Ford's North American Automotive Division lost, as did two General Motors divisions, both Globe customers. At the same time, the number of requests for application guidelines soared from 12,000 in 1988 to 65,000 in 1989 to 70,000 in the first three months of 1990, as companies sought to unravel the mysteries of quality.

Winning the Baldrige spurred Globe sales, which increased over the next two years from $80 million to $115 million. And it changed Leach's life. Part of winning the Baldrige was a mandate to share the company's expertise. It seemed as if every public and private quality conference wanted a speaker from Globe, the little company that could.

In 1989, Leach made 120 appearances, beginning in London with International Meehanite, an engineering firm, on January 17, and ending with a tour of Australia's major cities in the second week of December. In between he gave talks at universities, professional societies and organizations as diverse as Procter & Gamble, Stouffer Hotels and Restaurants and the American Society of Interior Designers.

Leach was also in constant demand by both Globe's suppliers and customers. Not only did the company have an enlightening story to tell about its quality journey, but Leach himself was now a senior examiner for the Baldrige. Those who entertained the notion of following in Globe's footsteps hoped he could offer them pointers. Leach's expertise was actually a competitive advantage with customers, something that no other metallurgical company could offer.

And what lay ahead for Globe itself? In 1989 it was the sole winner of the first Shingo Prize for Manufacturing Excellence, presented by Shigeo Shingo himself, a respected productivity expert. Globe was also seeking a new U.S. Senate productivity prize. Each competition offered the opportunity to learn something useful. Leach even thought Globe might go again for the Baldrige in 1993, after waiting the requisite five years for former winners. They were already using the Baldrige guidelines to monitor themselves. After all, quality was continuous improvement, and, he said, "We still have a lot of room to get better."

CHAPTER EIGHT

Doing Without Performance Appraisals

Deadly Disease #3:
Evaluation of performance, merit rating, or annual review. . . .
It nourishes short-term performance, annihilates long-term plan-
ning, builds fear, demolishes teamwork, nourishes rivalry and poli-
tics.
It leaves people bitter, crushed, bruised, battered, desolate, de-
spondent, dejected, feeling inferior, some even depressed, unfit for
work for weeks after receipt of rating, unable to comprehend why
they are inferior. It is unfair, as it ascribes to the people in a group
differences that may be caused totally by the system that they work
in.

—W. EDWARDS DEMING
Out of the Crisis

Using performance appraisal of any kind as a basis for reward
of any kind is a flat-out catastrophic mistake. It is a sure road to
demoralizing your work force. Employees' income becomes depen-
dent on capricious factors well beyond their ability to influence. Just
don't do it. Base your organization's salaries, wages and bonuses on
other things.

—PETER R. SCHOLTES
"An Elaboration on Deming's
Teachings on Performance
Appraisal"

One foggy evening in Portland, Maine, some two years after the S.
D. Warren Company, a large manufacturer of printing and specialty

papers, did away with performance ratings for its 1,500 salaried employees, several managers from the Westbrook mill reminisced over dinner about what it had been like under the old system of "P & Ps" as they were known. Did the letters stand for potential and performance, or performance and potential? Or something else altogether? Performance and promotability? No one could quite remember.

But they would never forget how it worked.

Badly.

There were ten tiers, but only the middle range was ever used. "Anything less than a four, and you'd probably already been fired," said Jim Folsom, manager of organizational effectiveness.

"To get a ten, you had to be God," volunteered Larry Finkelman, one of the mill's four business systems managers.

"To get a nine you had to *know* the Good Lord," Folsom chimed in.

There was, as it happened, a year that Finkelman got a ten. But even that was no cause for celebration. "It was so good I couldn't live up to it."

High ratings, Folsom said, "put you on a pedestal, where you could only fall. You couldn't get an eleven the next year."

There was also a year when the company declared that ratings had been running too high. Everybody had to cut back a point or two. Some people thought that kind of manipulation proved what they had known all along. The ratings were a sham.

With the decision in 1987 to break with its rating system, S. D. Warren joined a handful of employers struggling to do as Dr. Deming prescribed: drastically reform their recognition and compensation systems. Among eight quality-minded firms studied by Navy consultants, it was the only one to abolish ratings completely. Of the others, an AT&T computer technology lab reduced its levels from seven to three, and a General Motors transmission division from five to two. Many of the companies had broadened the appraisals by including the views of peers, customers and suppliers, in addition to the usual contributions from supervisors and employees.

The eight were by no means the only companies to tackle the issue. In Brighton, Michigan, three plants belonging to a General Motors Power Train Division threw out a six-tier rating system that determined raises, promotions and staff reductions, and substituted a process requiring feedback from peers, subordinates and customers.

In Sacramento, an Air Force installation junked its 81-point evaluations along with a rigid bureaucratic organizational chart that had 66 different categories and 15 pay grades. But there were not many others.

Even those companies that in other ways subscribed to Deming principles were wont to improve every process other than how they paid and promoted their employees. "Performance management tends to be the last component addressed in TQM transformation," concluded the Navy consultants. At the same time, it was a "dissatisfier"—"As a result, most organizations change their performance management systems every three to four years."

At stake was no less than what a corporation valued in people—what counted and what didn't. A seemingly insignificant matter, such as whether a skilled worker could earn more than a foreman or whether profit-sharing should be dispersed as an equal payout, equal percentage of pay (5 percent to everyone) or a graduated percentage according to position could prompt something close to class warfare.

No issue was more volatile than pay. And no aspect of W. Edwards Deming's teachings was more controversial than his opposition to performance ratings, one of the "Seven Deadly Diseases" that plagued American management. The belief that by varying compensation a company could reward excellence or stimulate laggards was deeply ingrained in the corporate psyche. And understandably so. The American educational system operated in much the same way, with grades as the measurement. Deming, who taught at New York University's Graduate School of Business Administration, gave only P for pass. "How do I know who will be great?" he often said.

Deming well understood the appeal of ratings when he wrote, "The idea of a merit rating is alluring. . . . The sound of the words captivates the imagination: pay for what you get; get what you pay for; motivate people to do their best, for their own good."

But he insisted that they had precisely the opposite effect from what was intended. As a result, the individual "propels himself forward, or tries to, for his own good, on his own life preserver. The organization is the loser. Merit rating rewards people that do well in the system. It does not reward attempts to improve the system." It discouraged risk-taking and innovation. Employees tended to play it safe.

Followers of Deming elaborated on the devastating effects of performance appraisal systems. One in particular, Peter R. Scholtes, a Madison, Wisconsin, consultant, began to do battle against ratings systems. It was not a role he relished. "I kept waiting for someone else to do it," he said at one point. "I finally saw I was going to have to spend time on the subject, there was such a demand for people to speak to the issue, and I had some opinions about it."

Like Deming, Scholtes argued that performance appraisals did nothing they were supposed to and much they weren't. Among his points:

—Performance evaluations focused on individuals, overlooking their dependence on other people, equipment, supplies and environment—factors, in other words, that were subject to influences beyond their control but that nevertheless affected their performance. By pretending that people operated in a vacuum, performance evaluations actually encouraged "lone rangers," Scholtes said, and were thus "a divisive influence. Having a system where it is individuals who are rewarded or recognized will force workers to choose between the personal reward and recognition or the teamwork."

—No matter how they tried, the people doing the appraisals could never be objective and consistent. Everyone reacted to such characteristics as age, race, sex, sexual preference, religious preference, attractiveness or educational credentials. "These reactions can work to the advantage or disadvantage of the employees evaluated," he said. Moreover, evaluators were influenced by how their subject was perceived by the rest of the organization. And they were also swayed by whether they had to show the evaluation to the person being evaluated. Thus appraisals varied considerably, depending on who was doing them and to whom.

—To the extent that performance appraisals were based on measurable goals, they also tended to be both short-term and short-sighted.

Rather than use performance appraisals, Scholtes suggested that a company could base employees' pay on market rate, seniority and the company's prosperity. He had once had skills and responsibility on the list, but later concluded they figured into the market rate and, besides, could create big measurement problems.

But surely, people always wanted to know, in the interest of fairness there had to be *some* way to reward superachievers or to encourage underachievers. Deming readily admitted there were such people. If performance were viewed as a process and tracked with a control chart, the work of most people would be within the upper and lower limits—within the system. But there could be "outliers" on the high and low side.

Dr. Deming addressed that point, suggesting, "If he is outside the limit of variation of the system on the good side, there is rational basis to predict that he will perform well in the future: he deserves recognition." But it didn't necessarily have to take the form of money.

Someone chronically on the low side had a problem. Perhaps he couldn't learn the job. "The company hired him for this job, hence has a moral obligation to put him in the right job," Deming said. Or to find some other way to make that person productive.

At McClellan Air Force Base in Sacramento, Deming's words hit home with Ardel Nelson, a civilian personnel manager in the Directorate of Distribution, an Air Force supply center for aircraft, missiles and radar, with a $5 billion inventory of some 3,000 replacement and supply parts that rolled over four times a year, with more than 3,000 daily transactions.

As he organized quality circles in the early 1980s among the 2,000 employees, Nelson found that the byzantine bureaucratic structure actually discouraged productivity. A manager's civil service grade, for example, depended directly on the number of people he managed and their rank. The more the people and the higher their rank, the more he earned. If his unit found a way to carry out its responsibilities with fewer bodies, the manager would work himself right into a pay cut. By the same token, "If he could figure out a way to get more people he could get himself a raise," Nelson explained.

The organization had 66 job "series" or categories that were enforced by the personnel office as rigidly as work rules in union contracts. They prevented one skilled worker from doing the job of another, though he or she might know how. Cross-training was out of the question. "You were not allowed to work outside a series," Nelson said. That meant that someone called a "packaging specialist," who determined the best way to ship an item—air, rail, truck, for example—could not reach for the book used to calculate rates. That was the job of a "transportation specialist." There were people who did wood-working, people who did wood-crafting, and people who did carpentry. But they were not the same people.

The 1978 Civil Service Reform Act, however, contained a proviso for demonstration projects related to personnel issues. With that in mind, Nelson began to explore ways to reform his organization, writing for advice to Kaoru Ishikawa, the founder of quality circles in Japan. Ishikawa advised him to contact Dr. Deming. Nelson and other managers, including labor leaders, began attending Deming seminars.

Eventually a plan took shape to restructure the directorate around five processes: material handling, distribution, maintenance, administrative and engineering, with a separate category for managers. The fifteen pay grades in the old job series would be reduced to four ranges. A person progressed through the range according to seniority. No longer would employees be evaluated as before, in nine areas with marks ranging from one to nine—for a potential maximum score of 81 points, which were then translated into the federal government's one-to-five ratings.

When the directorate proposed what became known as "The Pacer Share Demonstration Project," a five-year plan, the directorate encountered substantial opposition from the Office of Personnel Management, the federal agency whose approval was required. OPM was strongly invested in the administration of the current system. Were the Sacramento demonstration project to prove successful in developing a model for other federal agencies, Nelson pointed out, the implications for OPM were enormous. "Up to 75 percent of their mission would disappear." With a boost from California Democrat Representative Vic Fazio and strong support from their union partner, however, the plan was approved and the new system was introduced in 1987. "I don't think anybody would go back to the old way," Nelson said after two years.

Thanks to another provision of the Civil Service Reform Act, productivity savings could be divided between a federal agency and its employees. Through its Total Quality Management (TQM) effort, in 1989 the depot returned $4.1 million in savings to the Air Force and gave each employee a $502 gain share. This naturally helped to build support for the changes.

Employees still needed to know how they were doing, however. In 1990, the directorate had 134 process improvement teams, whose format called for feedback to individuals as assignments were discussed and evaluated. To educate managers on how to guide and encourage employees, as well as on other aspects of the quality movement, Nelson initiated a "TQM Leadership Management Institute" of monthly day-long study sessions for the directorate's 174 managers.

Like Peter Scholtes, Nelson began to write and speak out against performance appraisals to a broader audience. His research led him to the conclusion that "all the appraisal system 'rated' was 'the system,' not the person."

Moreover, he wrote in one paper, "Appraisal is focused on the past. . . . The conception of using the appraisal for positive guidance and direction is somewhat like proposing we drive forward while only looking at the rear-view mirror."

An organization had a responsibility to get a worker the help needed to perform a job. If the worker was unsuited to the job, then he or she required placement in another. If an individual was will-fully not performing a job, Nelson said, then "we are no longer dealing with a 'performance problem'—a person who can't—but a 'discipline problem'—a person who won't." A manager in that case could forget about performance appraisals, and need only "exercise the organization's disciplinary process."

Based on the early results of the Pacer Share project, which in-cluded an 80-percent reduction in personnel department paperwork, Nelson argued for the elimination of the appraisal system throughout government. "It will free all the resources of all the people who make the appraisals, justify the appraisals, log the appraisals, study the appraisals, write up the studies of the appraisals, write regulations on the appraisals system, maintain the regulations on the appraisal system, develop a procedure to appeal the appraisal, appeal the appraisals, adjudicate the appeals of the appraisals, develop new appraisal systems (the life span of most seems to be three to five years, maximum), print the appraisal forms, stock and issue the appraisal forms, review the appraisals, approve the reviewed apprais-als, type the appraisals. . . . It will free up a 'whole heap of folks' who will be available for real work. . . ."

In classes he taught at a nearby community college, Nelson gave his students just two marks, an "A" or an "I" for incomplete. "If they don't understand, I should look to myself," he said.

In 1986, the Power Train Division of General Motors' Buick-Oldsmobile-Cadillac group formed a task force of fifteen supervisors and employees to develop an alternative to the old six-tier appraisal system, one that would be more clearly aligned with the Deming philosophy. The rating was a powerful instrument that determined not only merit raises, but also promotions, transfers and eligibility for staff reductions. "It was really the core for all of the personnel system," observed personnel manager Mary Jenkins, who chaired the task force.

A statistical study of the old system showed that 75 percent of the 1,600 people it covered were in the top two categories. What made that ironic was that the sixth category had been added just three years earlier precisely because a previous five-tier system had grown similarly skewed. The task force concluded that without a forced distribution, ratings systems would always become top-heavy over time. That was due in part to the phenomenon that Peter Scholtes had pointed out: In cases where managers had to share their evaluations with employees, as was the case at GM, they tended to rate higher. "Managers would rather err on the positive side than risk losing a person," observed Mary Jenkins.

The Navy consultants found that supervisors sometimes avoided giving low ratings because they required documentation. Moreover, giving a high rating was one way to promote a poor performer out of their jurisdiction.

Agreeing at the outset that the only justification for performance appraisals was to help people develop, the GM task force came up with a dramatically different variety that both eliminated ratings and divorced compensation from appraisals except for outstanding employees, who numbered just four in 1989.

Under the new system introduced in 1989, at the beginning of the year, the employee and supervisor met and agreed on job responsibilities, priorities, opportunities and training needs. Ten months later at another meeting, it was the employees' turn to tell the supervisor what he or she had accomplished, to suggest what could be helpful for improvement and to recommend specific actions. At that same meeting the supervisor and employee agreed on a list of other employees to be asked for feedback on the employee's performance. Generally the number ranged between three and ten. The supervisor subsequently met with them, then summarized their views in writing. At a third meeting, the supervisor and employee discussed those views, then moved on to writing next year's plan, beginning the cycle again.

Early concern about the feedback mechanism proved unwarranted, Jenkins said. "It's proved to be one of the most popular features." In all, she said, the new method seemed to reinforce teamwork. And because employees were taking more responsibility for developing and carrying out their assignments, she said, the system tended to plug into the division's business plan more tightly than before.

The new approach, of course, required supervisors to be coaches and counselors. They received two days of training on their new role. And other employees were given a half day on how to participate in the feedback sessions. Meanwhile, another task force began work to standardize salaries according to a person's position and longevity in a job category, with rates determined by skills, job complexity and experience. A third task force on promotion sought to define job requirements.

Peter Scholtes sometimes said that it was better to have no performance appraisal system than the kinds most companies had. "Before getting into what to do instead of performance appraisals, consider one overall suggestion: Just stop doing them."

At S. D. Warren, a Scholtes client, that's what happened. Deming's critique had hit home with president Robert McAvoy and others from the paper company, who realized that their "P & P" rating system ran counter to the route the company was taking toward quality.

Headquartered in Boston, Warren owned three mills besides the one in Westbrook that made both coated and uncoated papers for magazine and book publishers, as well as a variety of specialty papers, such as embossed "release" papers that served as a mold for patterned vinyl materials such as those used for shoes and car interiors, and pressure-sensitive adhesive papers, used for peel-off labels.

Although the company had long enjoyed a reputation for quality—bestselling author James Michener specified that his books be printed on Warren paper—cost and innovation were two big issues in the 1980s if the company was to remain competitive.

As the company's executive team hammered out a vision and strategy in 1987, the word "team" kept popping up. "The key concept in implementing our strategy is to fashion an open, creative, team environment in which all people understand our vision, are motivated to contribute to its success and are able to continually improve both business performance and personal growth based on these commonly held principles." One of those principles was "Teamwork is our way of life." Another was "Our people will make the difference."

But the company was saddled with a performance appraisal system that pitted individuals against each other for favorable consideration. It made the wrong person the customer—the boss, not the next person in the process. What else was wrong with it? Just about everything, said Bill Sterritt, vice president for human resources.

For one thing, it had never functioned as designed. Although there were tiers numbered from one to ten, in practice only the middle range was used. For the most part, people ended up being "six's" or "seven's."

"Five was supposed to be average, but if you ever got rated average, you were a problem," Sterritt explained. At the other end, "nine's" and "ten's" were similarly scarce. Thus, Sterritt said, "even though we said we had an evaluation system that rated individual performances and a salary system that reflected individual performances, everybody was pretty much the same." The system made cynics out of people and bred disrespect for the company.

Moreover, it was a fact of life that most people believed they were doing a pretty good job. (At GM, said Mary Jenkins, they called this the "80-30" dilemma, "which is that 80 percent of us think we're in the top 30 percent of contributors.") A high rating might please people, but it would neither surprise nor motivate them, since they already thought they were doing their best. A low rating, on the other hand, caused people to lose confidence in their boss, and perhaps even themselves. There was always the danger, Sterritt said, "that people will believe they're average and start performing that way."

He believed, moreover, as Deming said, that "people in the end were mostly being rated for things not under their control."

The more the executives talked about teamwork, Sterritt said, the more the P & P system "was perceived as a barrier." So it was that later that year, Warren jettisoned the compensation system it had used for some 1,500 salaried employees. The company substituted job rates based on market value, combined with a variable compensation bonus system related to overall business performance.

The company had both exempt and non-exempt salaried employees. The latter occupied the lower-paid job categories, worked regular hours and earned overtime pay. Their salaries were pegged to the prevailing rate of pay for comparable jobs in the community. Salaries for exempt jobs were set using an evaluation system created by Hay Associates, a management organization, which assigned points based on such elements as know-how, problem solving and accountability. Every job carried a salary range. Warren set theirs at the midpoint, and pledged to bring everyone to that point within three years. As it happened, some 70 percent of salaries were below the midpoint, exposing yet another contradiction in the old system.

"Even though we had a system that was recognizing individual performances," Sterritt said, "70 percent were being paid below the prevailing rate."

Based on the improvement in the company's profits, the bonus varied from year to year. The payout rate varied as well, increasing with the level of responsibility. The reason was twofold: Large executive bonuses have long been an American tradition, the theory being that if executives derive a large part of their pay from company performance, they will work harder to improve it. In addition, the bonuses gave Warren the flexibility to remain competitive in the marketplace.

The new system took effect in 1988.

What happened next could charitably be labeled a profound learning experience.

For one thing, people missed their yearly sitdown talk with the supervisor. "Although people didn't feel good about the old system," Sterritt explained, "at least the supervisor sat down once a year and gave them some feedback. At least they knew someone was paying attention to them. . . . People have the strong feeling that in fact they are individuals. Under the old way, they were treated as an individual. Under the new, they're treated as a team."

Some managers continued to talk to their employees on a regular basis. But many didn't know how to do so without brandishing P & P guidelines. "Managers were encouraged to do it," Sterritt said, "but many managers were not good at it, or disliked it. They saw it as an opportunity to stop. One of the mistakes we made was not having the capability in place to provide good coaching, counseling and feedback."

Two other issues surfaced immediately. Non-exempt employees felt they were being paid too little under the new job rates; and foremen sometimes found themselves earning less than the hourly workers they supervised, who were covered by a union contract. In both cases, Warren formed a task force to find solutions. The jobs of non-exempt employees were reevaluated and market surveys on salary levels were updated; in some cases certain skills had been overlooked in the evaluation and salaries were adjusted. In the case of the foremen, the company accepted the task force recommendation to pay them either the job rate or 5 percent more than their highest paid employee, whichever was more.

Another concern was not so easily addressed. "Individual achievers don't get fairly compensated or rewarded," observed Tom Burns, one of the Westbrook plant's quality advisers, who were people trained to assist quality improvement teams. He and some other Westbrook employees gathered one day to discuss the new salary structure. "There's an effort now to take a closer look at succession planning . . . a closer look at performance and how people should be trained for the next job up." At the same time, no one wanted to go back to P & Ps, he said, which were a "total atrocity. There was a lot of bias from manager to manager, mill to mill." Marilyn Walsh, who worked for Jim Folsom as administrator of organizational effectiveness, no doubt spoke for many when she said, "I don't miss them at all. If you hit it off well with your boss you got a great P & P."

"I never liked the damned things," said Woodlands manager Dave Clement, who did not supervise salaried people. "I was always afraid I'd have to fill them out."

There were mixed feelings about the new bonus system, which management hoped would foster team spirit. Clements said he had been motivated as a result "to take a lot harder look at what's going on in the business. I used to feel I didn't affect it that much." But Marilyn Walsh, speaking for non-exempt people, said the graduated payout rates were a "sore spot" because people at the bottom felt they worked just as hard as those at the top.

If nothing else, the difficulties at Warren suggested how sensitive the pay issue was. And while the new system came up short in some ways, employees gave Warren high marks for trying. People did, in fact, believe Warren was seeking improvement. "They want you to get involved and to stretch," said Susan Whitney, a cost analyst who had been with the company for nineteen years.

At the Westbrook mill, where Warren was founded in 1854, there were a dozen part- or full-time quality advisers working with teams. A full-time statistician, Nancy Forrester, who had trained under

Deming, was on board as total quality resource leader. Elsewhere, at other Warren mills, similar quality initiatives were underway. But the abolition of P & Ps more than anything else signaled the desire for change. "It was important to have a symbolic event that said we're not doing business as usual, troops," observed Jim Folsom that night in Portland at dinner. "When you affect their pay, when you suddenly tell them that now their pay is dependent on how the team does, that gets attention."

CHAPTER NINE

Lessons Learned

What should a school of business teach? The answer is, I believe, that a school of business ought to teach profound knowledge. A school of business has the obligation to prepare students for the future, not for the past. As constituted, most schools of business teach students how business is conducted, and how to perpetuate the present system of management—exactly what we don't need. Most of the time that students spend in a school of business today is to learn skills, not knowledge.

—W. EDWARDS DEMING
"Foundation for Management of Quality
in the Western World"
October 1989

It should be evident by now that this book is about change in organizations. It is not theoretical. On a daily basis, the organizations profiled here are struggling with new ways of doing things. Their goals are different, but in many respects the process is the same. And the overarching goal of greater productivity applies not just to money-making enterprises, but to those with other missions as well.

On the one hand, their leaders are changing both management structures and their personal styles of management. And on the other, everyone within the organization is learning to live with change. Continuous improvement is nothing but the development of ever better methods.

This book also documents the successes of teamwork in a country built on individualism, and the elevation of data over beliefs and instinct.

None of this is hard to understand. None of it is easy to do. Change is threatening. There is no right way. There is no learning without mistakes.

Still, the foregoing chapters suggest how it happens. As with life itself, there are stages to the quality transformation. Although an organization may skip over one, inevitably it realizes it must retrace its steps to cover the missing ground.

Stage One: The Decision to Adopt

The CEO accepts the premise that fundamental changes are necessary, then builds a consensus. This seems to be easiest where failure is imminent. The old way of doing business is no longer an alternative. Everyone in the company is aware of the situation; the majority of people are ready to try something—often anything—for survival. Such was clearly the case with Bridgestone's LaVergne plant, the Kingsport Foundry and Globe Metallurgical. All of Japan, of course, was in this situation after World War II.

Sometimes, however, there is no crisis, merely a clouded future. Florida Power & Light could look ahead and see competition from cogeneration, the specter of deregulation and ratepayer rebellion. . . . The future is for a smaller Navy, in which not all installations will survive. Jerald Gartman wanted Cherry Point to be a survivor. . . . Little Cap Snap was on top and Claudia Leonard wanted to stay there in a fiercely competitive environment. . . . Though Hospital Corporation of America was not itself in need of emergency care, troubles in its industry prompted Tom Frist to take action before his company was overtaken. . . .

In opting for a transformation, CEOs seem to respond more to other CEOs who have discovered that quality works for them than to impassioned pleas for change from others in the organization.

Dr. Noriaki Kano, the Japanese quality sage who advised Florida Power & Light, was questioned on this point at the 1989 annual GOAL conference. "How can concerned middle managers help their senior management understand some of this complexity, and get them to take a stronger leadership position?" asked the questioner.

Kano: "In this case is very, very difficult. Successful people do not listen to the voice of middle managers. . . . How do top executives get convinced of TQC? There are very few top executives that get started by the recommendation of the middle manager, but by the recommendation of his friends, top executives of another company. In this case you must patiently wait. . . ."

In other words, if you are a middle manager avid to begin a quality initiative in a company ruled by an executive from the old school, look elsewhere for a job.

For FPL people, the "road to Damascus" was a trip to Japan, said Frank Voehl, a veteran of the early days of the quality movement. "It always worked. Everyone who went over skeptical came back convinced." Voehl went on to QualTec, the corporation's training subsidiary. "Whenever I have skeptical clients, I recommend that they go."

Stage Two: Incubation

The CEO convert takes an active role in quality promotion to overcome a legacy of doubt and hesitation. The job cannot be delegated. Voehl remembered that when FPL chairman Marshall McDonald was touting quality: "Many people were waiting for it to go away. McDonald made it clear that wasn't going to happen."

The executive leadership reconstitutes itself as a quality council with regular meetings. In this stage, managers read books, watch videos, visit quality companies, invite speakers and attend seminars. In large companies, these discussions are often the first time the senior managers have come together on other than a social occasion. Union leaders are included in at least some of these sessions. Usually it is beneficial to hold some meetings at a retreat, away from beepers, telephones and meetings. Secretary of the Navy Lawrence Garrett required attendance. The seats of no-shows were conspicuously empty.

After a certain period of incubation, the leadership often writes a "vision statement" (what we want to be) or a "mission statement" (what we plan to do) or both. Sometimes they formulate a set of values. These address such questions as:
—What is our aim?
—Who are our customers?
—What do we want to become?
—How are we going to get there?
—What are the barriers?
—How will we know we are making progress?
—What are our principal processes?

—Which are most in need of improvement?

—Do our compensation and recognition systems further our objectives?

W. Edwards Deming's Fourteen Points offer a good basis for discussion. Attending a Deming seminar can be mind-altering. Navy Under Secretary J. Daniel Howard talked about "the light bulbs going on." Don Berwick recalled attending a Deming seminar when he was vice president for quality of health care management of the 400,000-member Harvard Community Health Plan. "It was a very interesting experience. I walked out at the end of a second day, got on a plane and flew home." So different from what he knew about management, Deming's message filled him with anxiety. "I was very, very uncomfortable." By the next morning, however, he had decided, "I think this guy knows something. I got back on the plane and flew back."

Very often organizations acquire mentors. FPL first had Kansai Electric, then the counselors from the Union of Japanese Scientists and Engineers. FPL was then able to mentor its sister company, Colonial Penn. Tri-Cities companies and agencies have looked to both Tennessee Eastman and the Quality First office for guidance. Americans at the LaVergne tire plant had a flock of Japanese advisers. The Quality Resource Group at HCA mentors participating hospitals. Mentors do not tell their charges what to do. They support, suggest, prod and offer feedback.

Someone will need to head the effort—a quality director, coach, chief facilitator. It may not be the person currently in charge of "quality."

It can be a mistake to act with haste in this appointment. Wait for the champions to emerge. "Watch for the cream to rise," Chip Caldwell said at West Paces Ferry Hospital.

This person needs what Dr. Deming calls "a system of profound knowledge," embracing statistical methods, particularly as they describe variation, as well as psychology, a theory of knowledge, an understanding of how people learn.

Stage Three: Planning and Promotion

Armed with knowledge of what is involved in the transformation, and a quality director to help, management develops a plan for introducing it to the organization, then promotes that plan in a visible way over a period of time. There is almost certain to be resistance among employees, who believe they are seeing "just another program." Symbols can be important. (A union president said he believed a penny-pinching management was serious when it spent money to hold off-site training sessions with labor leaders. It is not a bad idea for managers to give up their private dining rooms and parking places and put in the occasional appearance in the company cafeteria.

Employees may be understandably cynical. A young engineer at S. D. Warren described a company where he once worked that had this sign: PEOPLE ARE OUR NUMBER-ONE RESOURCE. "The summer I hired on," he said, "they laid off 1,700 people, including two veteran engineers in my department. You shouldn't need a sign to say 'PEOPLE ARE OUR MOST IMPORTANT RESOURCE.' They should just feel it."

Stage Four: Education

Management from top to bottom acquires a basic understanding of process improvement and team skills before asking others to serve on teams and work on processes. They will need training in both. Managers must become leaders.

In the words of W. Edwards Deming: "The aim of leadership should be to improve the performance of man and machine, to improve quality, to increase output, and simultaneously to bring pride of workmanship to people. Put in a negative way, the aim of leadership is not merely to find and record failures of men, but to remove the causes of failure: to help people to do a better job with less effort."

Along with top managers, the quality director and the initial group of facilitators or advisers who will guide teams are the first to be educated. The education begins at the top and is deployed down through the ranks. Like all education, it works best when there is a practical application. Colonial Penn required managers to lead teams, then fed them "just-in-time" training. The HCA model called on hospital CEOs to teach segments of the Quality 101 course to hospital staff.

The teams' first process improvements are part of the education and are selected with three features in mind:

—They are small enough that people don't become frustrated.
—They are likely to succeed.
—They are processes that are aligned with company objectives.

Trainers or facilitators must guard against the tendency of fledgling teams to want "to solve world hunger." If not that, they often are merely content "to move the water cooler." The water cooler mission is not to be dismissed, however, because it teaches process improvement.

The education is pushed down through the organization to the frontline workers. Each department will need to go through the same incubation process as the top management, defining its mission, vision, goals. ("Someone around here is always writing a mission statement," was a comment at Bridgestone.)

Stage Five: Neverending Improvement

Teams at all levels are working on quality issues consonant with the corporate goals. Sometimes these are short-lived task teams that disband after finishing their assignment. Others are ongoing teams in the workplace, which move from one improvement in their work area to another.

Where in the beginning, quality was the mission of a "shadow" organization, composed of a top management quality council and a quality director with a staff of trainers and facilitators, now quality is part of everybody's job. Facilitators have been supplanted by supervisors, who have learned how to facilitate teams ("supertators" they called them at FPL). An executive committee manages as a team, not an assemblage of private fiefdoms. The annual "quality plan" and the "business plan" are the same document.

Fed information from all its divisions, the executive committee drafts its annual policy, setting forth long-term goals, mid-term objectives and short-term action plans. Each division, department and office has its own similar mini-policy. Thus all systems are integrated.

Daily processes are monitored for trends and special causes that signal opportunities for improvement. Continuous improvement is simply the way the company does business.

Every company is different. Sometimes, management will not believe the new way works until its own people have carried out a money-saving process improvement. The Quality First people in Kingsport found this was almost universally true of small companies, where owners or managers were reluctant to free up people and resources until they had proof of its value.

Sometimes people have to learn from mistakes. Perhaps the most common is the widespread introduction of Statistical Process Control with no practical application, confounding and alienating workers. Another is to bypass middle management to form teams among frontline employees. As a result, the middle managers are threatened and hostile and the employees don't get the support they need. A third mistake has proven to be team projects that are too complicated and require too many resources.

Perhaps the hardest lesson of all is that there is no such thing as "getting it right"—least of all with the promulgation of quality. That too must change. When HCA revised its quality training, consolidating three courses into one with two sections and rewriting the syllabus, hospital executives who had been through the earlier version were upset. But even the quality "experts" were learning better ways.

W. Edwards Deming is continually remodeling his four-day seminar. Of course it changes, he says. "May I not learn?"

INDEX

Ordering is easy and convenient. Just call 1-800-631-8571 or send your order to:

The Putnam Publishing Group
390 Murray Hill Parkway, Dept. B
East Rutherford, NJ 07073

Also available at your local bookstore or wherever books are sold.

			PRICE	
			U.S.	CANADA
_____	Deming Management Method (hardcover)	399-55001	$19.95	25.95
_____	Deming Management Method (paperback)	399-55000	10.95	14.50
_____	Deming Management at Work (hardcover)	399-13557	21.95	28.95
_____	Deming Management at Work (paperback)	399-51685	10.95	14.50
_____	Managing the One-Person Business	399-51613	10.95	14.50
_____	*Income Opportunities*® 35 of the Best Businesses for the '90s *(coming in November 1991)*	399-52682	10.95	14.50
_____	*Income Opportunities*® Home Business Handbook	399-51611	9.95	12.95
_____	*Income Opportunities*® Guide to Successful Selling	399-51612	9.95	12.95
_____	Relationship Selling	399-51644	9.95	12.95
_____	Financially Managing the One-Person Business	399-51633	12.95	16.95

Subtotal $ _____

*Postage & handling $ _____

Sales Tax $ _____
(CA, NJ, NY, PA)

Total Amount Due $ _____
Payable in U.S. Funds
(No cash orders accepted)

*Postage & handling: $2.00 for 1 book, 50¢ for each additional book
up to a maximum of $4.00

Please send me the titles I've checked above.
Enclosed is my ☐ check ☐ money order
Please charge my ☐ Visa ☐ MasterCard ☐ American Express
Card # _____ Expiration date _____

Signature as on charge card _____

Name _____

Address _____

City _____ State _____ Zip _____

Please allow six weeks for delivery. Prices subject to change without notice.